To all the victims of the Great War 1914 – 1918

THE OTHER
TRENCH

The WW1 Diary & Photos of a German Officer

Lt. ALEXANDER PFEIFER
&
PHILIPP CROSS

True Perspective
PRESS

THE OTHER TRENCH

First published and printed in 2024

Paperback ISBN: 9781068609800

Cover Design: Philipp Cross & Rob Williams (Fiverr)
Photo Colourisations: Florian Wein (WEINconcepts)
Photo Restorations: Florian Wein & Claudia D'Souza
Cover Stock Image: Kjpargeter on Freepik

Translations: Philipp Cross
Editing: Philipp Cross
Formatting: Philipp Cross

Published by: True Perspective Press

Website: www.theothertrench.com

True Perspective

PRESS

Contents

PREFACE

TORN BETWEEN TWO WORLDS

I have never written anything about myself before, but I would like to share with you a story that has always seemed so normal to me, but may probably be seen as unique or somewhat strange to you — My name is Philipp Cross, aged 24 when I started this book, and I am the son of a German mother and a former English Army soldier. Although my family history begins centuries ago, my personal story commences in 1995 in a small German town named Hameln. This beautiful and historical little town is where my father met my mother while stationed there, and where I was born and lived for one year after their marriage. I am therefore a typical 'Soldatenkind' (soldier's child), which is what people in Germany often call people like me who were brought to this world under the same circumstances. Whereas similar families continued their lives in Germany, I moved with my parents to Greater Manchester in England, where my little brother was born when I was three.

Growing up was almost like living two different lives, as my mother consistently spoke only German to us children from the day we were born. Many of her friends and family at first didn't believe she would maintain this for us to be able to converse with our German family later in life. Well, now being in my twenties, I wish I could go back in time and tell the sceptics how wrong they were. When I was perhaps two years old, I would for example turn to my mother and say: "Mama, wo ist der Ball?", and would soon after turn to my father and say the same in English: "Daddy, where is the ball?". It showed that with extensive and consistent implementation, a small child can learn to speak and understand two languages efficiently.

I also spent a lot of time in Germany during the holidays, sometimes over a month at a time, meaning I was regularly surrounded by the German language and culture. I always looked forward to spending time with my grandmother after she returned from work, or the times when my grandfather would take me and my brother on trips for the day. I even spent a lot of Christmases over there where they have their big celebration on Christmas Eve, rather than on the 25th of December like in England. Having experienced and still enjoying both traditions, people have always asked me: "Do you not prefer waking up to presents on Christmas Day?", to which I always explained that both traditions are unique in their own ways — The anticipation of waking up and waiting all day for the 'Weihnachtsmann' to arrive at the tree in the evening, which is surrounded by the dim and cosy candle lights in the dark with the sounds of heartwarming Christmas music in the background — or the excitement of going to bed knowing full well that 'Father Christmas' will bring the long-anticipated bicycle, but only after he first ate the mince pie that was left for him along with the carrot for the hungry reindeers. These times have created many memories which I will always cherish for the rest of my life.

At home here in England, we even had German television that I would exclusively watch such as all the popular kids' shows at the time, and even English-speaking shows dubbed in German, having then made the original English versions seem strange to me. My mother would also often make us German foods, and my grandmother would send over parcels with lovely German chocolates or items which you could not get here. When guests would visit my house, it was often like stepping into a miniature Germany for them. This was evident as soon as they saw the 'Willkommen' (Welcome) sign in the hallway when they heard the sounds of a German television show coming from the next room, or heard my conversations in German with my mother.

From left to right: My mother's father, my mother, my brother Alex, and me – Weida, 2001.

When I was in school, all these factors made me feel somewhat different since I couldn't relate to certain things that my friends would often talk about. This included 'the funny programme that was shown last night' or the 'fun summer holidays' here in England because I was often in Germany visiting my grandparents. I was often known as 'The German Kid' up until the end of high school, despite only being half of what they claimed. Looking back makes me sometimes chuckle when I think of the times when I was asked: "Whose side would you have been on in the war?"; "Why is your name spelt funny?", or "Do you feel more English or German?". I would always come up with a joke of an answer for the first two questions; but for the third? — "I do not know". Even to this day, I cannot give you a clear answer to this question since it's as though I have always lived in two different worlds, which others cannot understand unless they are in a similar situation.

Fast forward to the present time that I am writing this — I still visit Germany as much as I can and speak to my family there in German. I also still embrace the cultures and traditions of both countries. I at times believe that I feel more English because I grew up here in England and speak, live, and behave like a typical person from the English North. However, when I visit my birthplace for two weeks, my German improves significantly and I understand their humour, their customs, I know and love their food, and I feel at home just as much as I do in England. I then return home and sometimes have to temporarily concentrate more when speaking English considering I haven't spoken it in a while. I then again ask myself the third question that I have asked myself since I was a child. As expected, I haven't been known as 'The German Kid' in a long time since reaching adulthood, and I don't usually mention my strong German roots unless the topic comes up. However, I do sometimes find it amusing when my mother unexpectedly telephones me when I am currently with friends or acquaintances, who then try to follow a conversation in fluent German and look at me in surprise as if I have turned into a different person; and I then have to tell them the long story that I have just told you. I am very thankful for the way I was raised, and I do enjoy telling my story to the unexpecting listeners.

However, my personal story is not the sole reason why I have published this book — it is only just a small puzzle piece of a special tale that I am about to share with you, which, without it, I and many others would not be here today or would at least be leading a very different life.

A FAMILY'S LEGACY

Now that you know my story, it may have come to your mind that the life I am familiar with is a life that a lot of people with two parents of different nationalities may similarly lead — perhaps a friend, somebody you know, or perhaps even you. But it may be a surprise to you that I am writing here in the house I grew up in, inside the living room while sitting on the 120-year-old furniture set belonging to a battle-hardened German lieutenant of the Great War; drinking a coffee that is resting on his old silver coaster with the portraits of 200-year-old ancestors hanging on the wall behind me; the photograph of this German lieutenant proudly displayed on the wall to the right of me in which he shows off his Iron Cross First Class; and below it, the portrait of his child daughter (my great-grandmother) as well as a landscape photo of their extravagant family garden; all while occasionally getting a glimpse of old books by the wall ahead of me, which are inside a 19th-century cabinet that belonged to those ancestors on the wall, who witnessed the Napoleonic Wars and the Great German Unification of 1871. On the wall before me also hangs an old picture of Karl August, Grand Duke of Saxe-Weimar-Eisenach, whose daughter's early 19th-century dress lies in the cupboard upstairs. This is all part of history — My family history.

My maternal father's side of the family really did treasure and preserve almost everything over the years. This side of the living room, which has been transformed into somewhat of a museum of my family's past, is just a small portion of what has been passed down through generations as a way to maintain the legacy of my ancestors' lives. I couldn't possibly give you the details of each ancestor hanging on the wall, and I couldn't tell you the story of each item that I know exists. However, I would like to introduce you to my great-great-grandparents from Weida, Thuringia — Alexander and Johanna Pfeifer — the son of one of three successful brothers in the textile industry who owned a large textile business in Weida, as well as the impressive 18th-century mansion directly beside it — and the daughter of an upper-class family named 'Filler' that produced vicars and talented musicians, tracing its roots back to the illegitimate daughter of a German royal duke with ties to prominent monarchies across Europe.

Our ancestor – Karl August, Grand Duke of Saxe-Weimar-Eisenach (1757-1828) – Great-great-grandson of King George I of Great Britain.

The room within the house I grew up in.

Considering these rather prestigious backgrounds, they bought themselves furniture pieces, heirlooms, portraits, and even the first car in the town. When I at times visited the old family home in Weida as a child, I would be amazed by the huge courtyard once I entered through the arched entrance where my mother's father would play as a child. I would then go up the old stone stairs ascending to the residence, down which a drunk Napoleonic French soldier tumbled and lost his life over 200 years ago; then, through the old wooden door just before I would catch a glimpse of the long hallway that seemed to have no end, where to the left and right of it were numerous doors leading to various rooms with incredibly high ceilings. I would pass these with sounds of creaking from the old 18th-century floorboards beneath me. I would walk by old paintings, mirrors, and antiques, followed by some other ancient-looking items straight afterwards. I would then enter the lounge area on the far end of the corridor and sit on part of a furniture set just like the one I am sitting on now, almost expecting somebody dressed like Mozart to greet me at any moment. I would also visit the huge family garden from where I would have a perfect view of the beautiful 'Osterburg' medieval castle of Weida. What I have just described to you is only a small part of the old family home known as 'Das Pfeifersche Haus' (The House of The Pfeifers).

When my great-grandmother moved close to my grandparents in Hameln, she brought many of her parents' items along with her from the home including furniture, paintings, mirrors, pots and pans, cutlery, books, and anything else that you can think of. Up until she died when I was 21, I would visit her home and instantly catch the sense of an old antique smell that I had never smelt elsewhere, and I would immediately see the many items in each room which once stood proudly within the family home. It was in the truest sense of the world like entering a time machine into the 19th century, with her living room being filled with items which you could not possibly imagine someone to still possess — a gigantic 18th-century painting, a gold-trimmed glass cabinet with the first golden locks and teeth of her father within, and the 250-year-old black cabinet that once belonged to a long-deceased ancestor who was a lawyer. She would always tell stories about the items and people of the past, to the point where you would not listen anymore because they were told many times before. She would sometimes even show an old book entailing the old family tree that she and her father Alexander created, with the help of extensive research and by exploring old church records and archives. This family tree goes all the way back to the 15th century, including details of the individuals' origin, cause of death, and occupation; ranging from German army generals, maids, peasants, and vicars; dying of natural causes or even in one case being murdered through a blow to the head.

Although I understand that my family wanted to pass down items like it is common in many other families, I still don't understand why they were so fixated on researching and preserving their family history so extensively as they did. Was it solely because they enjoyed doing so? A way so that they will never be forgotten? Or perhaps to treasure these items in the hope that their stories and memories will one day be shared with the world? — It will always remain a mystery to me. One day, I decided to explore some more personal artefacts, photos, and documents hidden in the drawers of an old wooden cabinet that I had never looked inside. I was simply in awe during the two hours I spent looking. I found at least two dozen photo albums of my family, ranging from the 19th century to the 1960s. I also found a large iron, square-shaped box that was completely stuffed with more photos from people from the 19th century onwards — literally the ultimate memory box. Near this was also an old leather folder with various birth, marriage, and death certificates, signed documents from the 18th century, important company contracts, and diplomas. I also found items which highlight significant milestones in my ancestors' lives such as school report cards, drawings, wedding programmes, and more.

Alexander's daughter would always mention how her parents' items would one day be passed down to us the way they were passed down to her, and now, after her death, a lot of these items are here in England like she had always imagined. With the old smell of the furniture long gone, I sometimes forget how strange and unique it is to have such a family history with all this physical 'evidence' to hand. It is all just as much a part of me and my life now as it was for my ancestors — to always be remembered.

The 'Pfeifersche Haus' (built in 1720) photographed around 1900.

The town of Weida with a view of the 'Osterburg' castle, and part of the family garden at the bottom.

From a 1908 receipt: The logo of the family-run textile company, showing the factory and family home.

From left to right: Alexander, Dieter, Gudrun and Johanna.

Alexander's close family (pre-war) – From left to right: mother-in-law Anna, son Dieter, sister Line, daughter Gudrun, sister Hilde, and wife Johanna.

ALEXANDER'S STORY

Although my family history includes several interesting characters, this book is focused on the extraordinary life of Alexander Pfeifer, my great-great-grandfather who left behind a tale that involves far more than just the inherited furniture or the portraits on the living room wall. His story begins on the day of his birth on the 4th of January 1880. As you may already have imagined,

Alexander had a childhood unlike most German children at the time, living in a gigantic home with his family, having personal maid service, exceptional education, and of course, having access to a park-sized garden where he would play, which was directly next to the factory where the many textile workers were active all week. Evidence of his childhood still exists today. We namely still have his first lock of blonde hair and his baby teeth which were kept by his mother, as well as drawings he made when he was 12.

Alexander pictured in a school photo as a child.

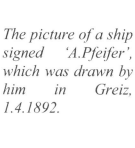

The picture of a ship signed 'A.Pfeifer', which was drawn by him in Greiz, 1.4.1892.

As a young man, he always desired to use his knowledge and education to become a paediatrician, which was not possible considering his destined future role as the director of the family-owned business. He therefore joined the Royal Saxon Jäger-Batalion no.12 in 1900 at the age of 20, soon moving up the ranks to a sergeant in 1903. This was an elite battalion of units based in Freiberg, Germany. The Jägers (translated as 'Hunters') were separate from the infantry and consisted mainly of the upper class, traditionally specialising in skirmishing tactics and being known for their loyalty and skill.

Alexander (second from right) during his service in Freiberg, 1902.

Alexander (far right) with others at an unknown celebration during his service in Freiberg.

In 1905, he married his sweetheart, Johanna; an event that we still remember through the found wedding programme, entailing amusing and patriotic songs, poems, names, and even the aged, dried splatter of wine on a corner of multiple pages which is a reminder of just how fun this day was at the time. They had their first child, daughter Gudrun, in 1909, and a few years later their son, Dieter. This led to many beautiful memories, including the day of Gudrun's christening shown below.

Alexander and Johanna (right) with friends and family, 1909.

Alexander's wife Johanna with their first-born child, Gudrun.

After Alexander's lengthy service in the army, he transferred to the Prussian Kurhessian Jäger-Battalion no.11, where he acted as an experienced army reserve while simultaneously carrying out his duties within the textile industry. However, in August of 1914, his plans and overall future outlook of the world would transform as he was called up for honourable service for his Fatherland — a service for a cause that would forever shape the world, and an opportunity for Alexander to document a significant chapter of his own life always to be remembered.

THE DIARY

According to the well-known story that was passed on to me, Alexander told his wife Johanna of his plan to consistently write a diary. He would regularly send the notes home and instructed her to keep these safe until he returned from the war. This was to become an authentic account of his wartime experiences, which he would insist on typing up and preserving once the war was over. It was not foreseeable that these notes would not only document a specific period of the war, but literally the four-year journey of this single man, from sergeant to a commanding officer within a highly regarded, elite battalion — through some of the most significant and bloody battles in 3 major theatres of the war; the actions which led to him being awarded 9 medals in total; the most detailed descriptions of day-to-day life and procedures; his relationship between friend and foe or food and nature; or even the many times he stared death directly in the face and saw one man after the other succumb to one of mankind's greatest cruelties — War.

Alexander did survive the war unscathed, which is certainly true if you don't include the scars of horror which were branded into his conscience until the day he died. When he returned after over 4 years, he commenced what he intended to do since the day he departed, and typed out the many pages he had written in the most varied conditions and places. He then combined these into a single book for the family to read. Alongside this were also numerous maps, photos that he took, postcards, and items from fallen enemy soldiers; all to coincide with his incredible story. This diary has been read by most within my family in Germany, as well as family friends and a handful of other people who took an interest in it. To all those who picked it up, it will always be remembered as being something unique. After Alexander's death, this diary was given to my grandfather, Gunter, due to their very close relationship, who treasured this and the many other items above anything else that belonged to him. After my mother's father Gunter passed away when I was 11, all of Alexander's former possessions belonged to me, my brother, and my mother.

When I was younger, I would occasionally admire the many items without having much knowledge of the Great War. I always knew that the diary existed while sometimes only reading a couple of pages and then placing it back where it was to further collect dust. It wasn't until 2020 when I one day suddenly decided to research the fallen English soldiers to whom some old postcards belonged, and once again, with this time more understanding and maturity, I decided to open up the inherited diary to gradually read it from the start which I had never done before. However, in one day, one page soon turned to five which then turned to a dozen as I was simply hooked and continuously tempted to turn to the next aged, yellow-tinted, typewriter-written page. It was like I was by his side the entire time, with each day of his being just as a surprise to me as it would have been to him, and I during this moment felt the shame of never having given it much consideration, once recognising how extraordinary it all is. I then also went and discovered documents, newspaper articles, and letters that he collected and wrote on, to explain their relevance to his war journey. I also found 6 photo albums from the war, and many envelopes stuffed with photos that he captured. Most of them entail vivid descriptions and dates on the back to explain what is depicted, all coinciding with his experiences written about in his diary. The material to hand and the extent of his documentation are genuinely so immense, which makes you think it was all a vast project or a way for him to reflect in depth, and to somehow relive these events.

I was always aware that he was "An officer who had a top presence", as was often mentioned to me, but I nevertheless discovered that he was someone who commanded men and areas in some of the most notorious battles and combat zones. He constantly survived whilst most others that he knew fell. In one instance, he even held off an entire battalion of 3000 Russians with only 250 of his men, which granted him the Iron Cross 1st Class as well as an award given to only 365 others. While reading it, I was simply fascinated by the level of consistency that he maintained throughout, regardless of what he had just gone through, with entries sometimes being written in real-time to then transform into somewhat of a detailed report. Many parts were so specific, making me believe I was reading a novel. I would then read an entry at the end of all this, which would again remind me that this really is just a diary. I was fascinated and finally understood why this was one of the most treasured pieces within the family collection, and why he was admired by all so long after his death.

I soon realised that this was not just family history, but something that truly shines a light on a side of the war that is often overlooked — The German perspective. My first idea was to make this readable for non-German-speaking people that I knew. My good friend, Matthew Webb, always knew that I had this diary, but didn't know what exactly it entailed. He most likely thought it to be a few notes scribbled into a scrapbook. He was nevertheless fascinated when I showed a book of typed notes which he then began to read from the start once I started to translate the pages into English. This translation, which he encouraged me to continue, transformed into my dedicated project over the years, with me spending many hours per page to accurately translate the diary word for word and sentence for sentence as precise and true to the original as possible. The aim was to finally provide the English-speaking world with a truthful insight into the life of a man who wreaked havoc on their ancestors who served in the war, just like theirs did on him. I then gathered the many hundred photographs. I scanned each one and included them alongside the corresponding entries with his written explanations, which allows us to consistently visualise his words, unlike any other WW1 diary.

Furthermore, I researched the fallen men he mentions and crossed paths with, which was achievable due to his precise and consistent detailing; and the fact that he collected so many items from the battlefields. I also conducted further research into people, places, and affairs which are still connected to people and the world we live in today. I also liaised with local historians and other individuals to help find and meet families whose relatives were directly involved in Alexander's journey. I even obtained my own rare copy of his battalion's diary printed 90 years ago, to provide you with maps and details to offer further understanding of significant events. I have even visited graves and old battlefields, and have delved deeper into the perspectives of his enemies during significant battles. I have acquired further photos and relevant documents regarding his experiences, and have given narrations and explanations throughout — all to provide you with one of the most authentic, informative, brutal, and visual accounts of the Great War to date. This book fully brings to life the WW1 perspective of a German (Alexander Pfeifer), fully presented by his great-great-grandson, a half-English and half-German who lives in England, and whose ancestors were once enemies. This book also aims to remember all those who served in the war, and to perhaps one day make myself be remembered by my future grandchildren and great-grandchildren, just as much as I remember Alexander and my many other ancestors and their tales. This is my family history — This is our story.

Alexander Pfeifer

Philipp Cross

MY WAR EXPERIENCES

This diary is not just a recollection of experiences written after the war, but literally the experiences I wrote down every day. They are therefore a genuine reflection of the heavy fighting against the enemy and nature that the Kurhessian Jäger Battalion (Marburg), and especially my company and I, had to endure. Particularly at the beginning, there are a lot of things that I might not have written or at least later expressed differently as an experienced fighter of the Front. However, I have intentionally changed nothing, as these reports are intended to reflect my true feelings at the time.

Alexander Pfeifer.

Lieutenant of the Landwehr, and Company Commander within the 11th Kurhessian Jäger Battalion (Marburg).

On The Western Front
(1914 – 1916)

1

4.8.1914   Today, on the third day of mobilisation, I have to travel to Weimar according to my mobilisation order. On the way there, there were huge crowds at the train stations everywhere, especially in Jena. The "Hurrah!" calling and waving is indescribable. In Weimar, many hundred reservists were gathered in the yard of the barracks, who were sorted into their troop units and told where they would be sent. I am going to the Landwehr Jäger Battalion in Marburg, and I am very happy that I will be back with my old elite group and not with the infantry. I will also meet my sister Line there who wants to register as a nurse in the field.

Note: The term 'Landwehr' (translated: 'Defence of The Country') is used to describe the organised national armed forces that have completed a required amount of training, and who are called up only in the time of war.

I spent the evening with Quensels *(a friend)*. I spent the night sleeping in mass quarters on straw, in a hall directly opposite the barracks. I slept very poorly due to the constant coming and going.

5.8.1914   Half past 5 departure in the morning — 8:45 evening arrival in Marburg. There are at least ten men on my transport from Weida alone, including Triller from Seifersdorf. I should really be sleeping in the barracks, but I quartered myself in the Imperial Court without asking for permission first.

7.8.1914   The active battalion has already left a few days ago. There are rumours of them heading to Belgium. A reserve battalion is currently being assembled from the rest of the reserves and most of the Landwehr, which will move out on Saturday. Two combat-ready companies have been formed from the rest of the Landwehr today, which will remain here as a reserve for the time being. For how long will depend on the losses to come. It could be for eight days, but it could also be for a very long time.

I am having my washing sent from home, as well as my Saxon sergeants' sabre considering the lack of sabres here. I am in the first replacement company and have three oberjägers and 30 men under my command. For now, we constantly stand around the yard of the barracks for hours on end and have a lot of free time. I checked into citizen quarters today, in a proper student hovel. We will probably have more duties after the reserve battalion has moved out.

Note: A Jäger and an Oberjäger, being separate from the infantry, are the equivalents of a 'Private' and a 'Corporal'. The word 'Jäger' literally means 'Hunter' in German.

8.8.1914 It is dead boring here. We report twice a day and then just stand around for hours. Today is the first time that I am wearing my uniform again, but just the old peacetime uniform for the time being. There will be a little training march tomorrow. There is a great stream of volunteers here. The feeling of immense confidence is clear everywhere.

9.8.1914 Our only activity today consisted of a two-hour walk. In the mornings, I drink coffee in the canteen (15 Pfennigs with a bread bun). Lunch is free in the oberjäger mess hall — very nice and fulfilling. Yesterday, we had soup, fried eggs with spinach and potatoes; and today, lentils with bratwurst. For dinner, we will go to some place in town at our own expense.

12.8.1914 We hope that we will soon be deployed to the communication zone at least; perhaps to Liège, as it is becoming far too boring here and I don't want to stay here for the entire campaign.

14.8.1914 We now march out in the open at 6 o'clock every morning, where we do some exercises and get back home at 10 o'clock. We receive our orders and our post at 5 o'clock in the evening which takes about an hour, and then we are done. Nobody from the major to the last jäger thereby has any idea about the new training regulations because everyone here is a reserve. Our commander is Major von Nauendorf, whose civilian occupation is the owner of the Manor of Pölzig in Ronneburg. The captain is a head forester, and then there are a few reserve lieutenants including a Prince Reuss, which you only rarely ever see though.

We are 500 Landwehr soldiers sectioned into two companies. Each company falls into three platoons which are led by previous-serving sergeants. Each platoon has two half-platoons. I have the second half-platoon of the first platoon. A large part of our people are only fit for garrison duties. We were physically examined today, and I am of course fit for field service. There is nevertheless no guarantee that we will all be sent to the battlefield. People even speak of a large part of us being released because there are far too many than needed. 2000 volunteers have already enlisted here, with many being students. Some connections have been closed. Only 500 have been picked though, who have been training firmly for several days.

Our reserve battalion departed the night before last (our neighbour Wieduwilt is with us). However, where it will end up is not known since everything generally seems to be kept secret. You have no idea what kind of military transports pass by here — a long train every quarter of an hour. You would think that there would be no room at the border for so many people. We also notice that a lot of troops from Saxony and Silesia are being sent to the West. The Russians are seemingly not held in very high regard, and one wants to defeat the French with one big blow first. England's declaration of war made no particular impression. The declaration of war by Serbia and Montenegro actually caused the greatest amusement.

During the month, I am to receive the generous wage of 33.60 Mark. I will be very well off on this wage considering the free accommodation and food. 1.10 Mark is more than enough a day for beer, coffee, and so forth. We have a huge number of vice sergeants here, so there is little hope of being promoted, especially if we don't end up in combat. Almost a third of our people are former Saxon jägers, with several having in fact served with me in Freiberg.

18.8.1914　　The Landwehr arrived today and will take over the internal security and guarding of the place. This will free us up and we will probably go to Belgium where our two battalions are. A few of their sick came back here from Aachen in the last few days. Because there is an abundance of us, we sergeants have apparently received the same wage as an oberjäger up to now, receiving 11.20 Mark every ten days. But this was just trickery from the paymaster. We have since complained and are now receiving full wages (19 Mark every 10 days), which will improve my finances significantly.

On Sunday, I spoke to a soldier at the train station who transported some French prisoners. These have said to him: "The German chest is not visible. Red trousers, great losses." The French still have their old uniforms that are highly visible from a distance, whereas our troops are hard to spot even from close. This is an advantage that cannot be overestimated though, because it means that we only have at least a quarter fewer losses than if we still had the old colourful uniforms. We are only to be dressed in the new field-green uniforms shortly before we move out.

19.8.1914　　Today I shot for the first time, and actually quite well, hitting a 10, 9 and a 12 from 200 metres away while lying down. The shooting has made things not so boring anymore.

23.8.1914　　I currently have train station guard duty again. There are now trains coming through non-stop with Landsturm *(militia)* troops; a load of people from Gera, Greiz and so forth. A large train is also standing idle carrying the pieces of two gigantic siege guns, the barrels of which I could squeeze myself through with ease. We are to be dressed in field-green tomorrow, but thereby only the fighting-able. We will probably still stay here for some time though. Maybe I will become a deputy officer in the near future, and then I would receive 150 Mark per month and a 150 Mark clothing allowance.

14.9.1914   We will be moving out to the active battalion ahead of Paris in the next few days. 60 jägers and the corresponding batches have been selected today. The captain thereby took me aside and asked me if I expected a promotion and wanted to volunteer to go with them. I immediately said yes, of course. I would have reported to go anyway. The rest of our companies will probably go to the reserve battalion next week, which is said to have suffered heavy losses near Paris.

16.9.1914   We are now properly dressed. I am luckily allowed to bring my officers' suitcase with me.

17.9.1914   Forward march to the train station along with music at 11 o'clock in the morning — 2 officers (Lieutenants von Boxberger and Prince Reuss), 3 vice sergeants, 6 oberjägers and 60 jägers. Huge masses of crowds. We are engulfed with flowers, cigars, and other loving gifts. I am going in a second-class compartment together with the Vice-Sergeants Radecke and Oppermann; and the Oberjägers Triller, Zwietze and Gottschneider. The journey goes via Lollar and Wetzlar towards Koblenz where we stay for several hours.

We passed the Rhine at 10 o'clock in the evening while singing 'The Watch on The Rhine'. The Rhine Bridge is manned with guns.

18.9.1914   We journey along through Andernach and straight through the Eifel Mountain Range towards Mayen (coffee break) and Daun (bread and eggs, coffee and cocoa) until Gerolstein. We have our lunch here, consisting of potato soup and sausage. It is so awfully cold here in the Eifel.

Onwards to Prüm and Saint Vith, where the last schnitzel will probably be consumed for a long time.

We continue to Montenau in the evening. We are staying in this miserable nest for 24 hours. There are only candles to light the carriages. The six of us are lying next to each other on the pulled-out pillows like sprats. You soon get used to this too.

19.9.1914   Coffee and milk in the morning for 5 Pfennigs, followed by a feast of freshly slaughtered boiled belly pork. Coffee with plums and wreath cake in the afternoon, baked by Jäger Görlich. We have had heavy rain, storms, and very cold weather since we left. In the evening, wonderful singing performances (solo and quartet) by our jägers and artillerymen who are accompanied with 15cm artillery shells on our train.

Further through Rötgen in the evening, where we have pea soup. We are in an extremely cheerful mood.

20.9.1914   We have fortunately overcome the third night in the carriage. Arrival in Aachen at 6 o'clock in the morning. It is continuing to pour down with rain — nasty cold. Onwards to the Herbesthal border station — bean soup on our dinner break. The main road forms the border that we will later cross with cheers of "Hurrah!". I am having my hair clipped to three millimetres as a result of the increasing dirtiness; a previously unexpected blessing. There are transports of troops as well as captured French prisoners and Zouaves *(a class of French light infantry)*, such as French Landwehr men in civilian clothing who were captured at the control point.

The returning soldiers look absolutely awful, and I prefer not to speak about the wounded. Even the unwounded people look in a terrible state — marched out seven weeks ago in brand new uniforms, and now they are scruffy tramps — no trace of their original brown deployment colours. They all have sunken cheeks and look withered away as though they have only just managed to stand after a severe illness. These people must have suffered terribly. We will not look much different in four weeks' time.

We slowly continue through Verviers in the evening.

21.9.1914   We wake up at Henne Station in the morning, seven kilometres from Liège. The shot-up Fort Chaudfontaine lies high up on the steep mountain to our right. The first burned-out houses are becoming visible. White flags hang out of many of the houses as a sign of peaceful attitudes. The Bavarian Landwehr is on guard everywhere. Liège is generally a dirty industrialised city — we passed here without a long delay. The surrounding area is very nice. On the heights behind Liège, there are German troops busy digging trenches and assembling wired obstacles.

Onwards towards Tirlemont via Waremme and Landen. We receive news here that 6000 English, broken out from Antwerp, are apparently marching our way — great enthusiasm. We wait ready for battle inside the train. This was unfortunately just a false alarm.

Behind Tirlemont are many burned-out houses and castles, especially along the country road. Most of the villages seem to be unscathed though, and the village folk are working on the fields.

12 o'clock at noon in Leuven — a terrifying sight. The housing district around the train station is completely burned out, and entire streets have been destroyed. The tower and roof of the old cathedral are missing. The magnificent town hall is undamaged.

Lunch in Schaerbeek, an eastern suburb of Brussels — bread, coffee, and miserable sausage. We continue around Brussels via Laeken. There is a 'Rumpler Taube' *(a pre-war monoplane aircraft)* circling above Brussels — wonderful Palace of Justice. We also see a 'Panzerzug', an armoured locomotive with its carriages protected by sandbags, with one carriage supporting an armoured turret. There are many sailors and marine infantrymen on guard duty here in Brussels. What is particularly striking in this area are the large, green cattle pastures.

Now further to Tubize where chocolate, fruit, and especially nice grapes are bought. Good bottled beer.

22.9.1914 We stop for the night in the village of Hennuyères, where in the morning I buy coffee and sugar and borrow a coffee grinder with Captain Clasen, who has since joined us. We brewed some excellent coffee. We are staying here for an unknown amount of time due to a standstill. The weather has luckily improved since yesterday. I bought myself a veal with a voucher, butchered it and cooked a vegetable soup with veal — impeccable food. We are living the proper gypsy life. I am fortunately not very demanding due to my previous tours.

We continue to Mons (Bergen) in the afternoon, via Braine-le-Comte and Soignies. In front of Mons, foxholes are still visible from a battle between our 84s and the English — two large mass graves.

At Mons in the evening, we are fetched out due to the threat of revolt from the population, and we march to the town hall while singing with loaded rifles and mounted bayonets. We spend the night very cramped and cold on mattresses that we brought from the cavalry barracks. We caused a great stir and were mistaken for Austrians due to our shakos *(a tall cylindrical helmet worn by the jägers)*.

We continue in the morning — change of route towards Charleroi.

23.9.1914 Since the sun is shining, we are sitting on the floor in cattle carriages and dangling our feet out of the door openings. The journey continuously takes us past large coal mines and factories. There are nine captured English trucks on our train.

Evening in Charleroi — a thin rice broth as our first warm meal of the day. Things seem to be getting lazier with our food the further we go. Surely our prisoners are getting better food. There are captured French artillery pieces in front of the train station.

I stayed the night in the third-class waiting room. The night was nice and warm, but your sleep was constantly disturbed because the straw was being pulled out from under you every moment for the wounded people coming through. We gladly handed it to them though because the poor guys looked absolutely horrible and smelled even more dire. Here, we are receiving a small foretaste of the terrible misery of the war. I am by no means going to the Front with illusions, but I believe that the reality is a hundred times worse. Both of our battalions must have suffered dreadful losses. Of the reserve battalion (1100 jägers), only about 280 are said to be capable of field service.

There are Catholic clergy monks as well as Samaritans by the train station. I finally drank German beer and ate Frankfurter sausages again. For our provisions for the next two days, we have gathered 70 pieces of bread and one quintal of bacon. I am probably still learning how to eat bacon. We continue in cattle carriages in the afternoon, through a nice valley towards Chimay via Thuin.

We journeyed to Robechies through the night. I have never experienced such a horrible night. Despite a jumper, gloves, felt shoes and a captured English coat, I froze like a young pup and didn't sleep for one minute.

25.9.1914 We lit a large fire outside and warmed some coffee at 6 o'clock in the morning. We cooked a pea soup for lunch, cut some bacon and shared it between us. I have to arrange and retrieve it all because I am acting as company sergeant. We drank an awful lot of cognac in the village pub, played the orchestrion, danced, and sang songs. The French have behaved very badly here in the land of their ally. They broke into the pub cash register and stole or destroyed everything. We as the enemy, on the other hand, have behaved very decently.

We are making very slow progress due to the constant hour-long waits. We have travelled for eight days now and still haven't once gotten out of our clothes.

We continue to Momignies via Chimay. We were let out here and ate nicely in a monks' monastery. We were put into march because two railway bridges were blown up. We crossed the border two kilometres from here, and after a further five kilometres, we ended up in a factory in Anor and slept the night on straw.

26.9.1914 At 6 o'clock in the morning, we continue marching through Hirson (at the top there is an old fort) towards Origny, 13 kilometres. Half of our old and fat Landwehr men are footsore, but I am not, of course. The first thundering of cannons can be heard off in the distance. Along the way are endless transport columns — many cars and trucks. At Origny train station, we lie in the sun on a stubble field from early to late in the evening and wait for a train. I prepared my own dinner — pea soup and meatballs.

We continue through Laon towards Guignicourt, west of Neufchâtel.

To The Front

Germany's mobilisation commenced on the 1st of August 1914, following the tremendous tension due to the threat of war which put the country on edge throughout the July of 1914. This reached its high point on the 31st of July. Germany mustered its combat-capable men for the defence against the enemy, whose numbers were not yet certain, but which were steadily increasing. Enthusiasm and the willingness to serve spread among all citizens throughout the country, with the thought of their numerical superiority giving them a feeling of great confidence. Marburg seemed to still lie in a state of peace as the reservists flooded in to fill up the active 11th Jäger Battalion, while also forming an 11th Reserve Jäger Battalion. The mobilisation, thought out to every detail, began immediately. On the battalion's first day of deployment on the 2nd of August, the long-unused rifles were summoned and polished, and the uniforms and equipment were rapidly distributed, followed by a battalion celebration on the evening of that day. The next day saw the arrival of the horses. The field vehicles were loaded, and the horses were harnessed followed by a test drive. In the meantime, the awaited reservists were inspected, clothed, and assigned within the active battalion, forming a prepared 1300-strong battalion that was fully convinced of bringing glory to the homeland. However, with just under two months now having passed and the realities of the war already sinking in, how long will this enthusiasm last?

On the 4th of August, the day of Alexander's journey to Marburg, the active battalion was one day before boarding two trains to transport them to Belgium as part of the 'Schlieffen Plan'. This was a deployment plan to easily take out France through the Netherlands and Belgium, rather than the common border, and to defeat France in a matter of weeks. This caused Britain to declare war on Germany because of the attack on neutral Belgium. As part of this strategy, the 11th Jägers took part in continuous clashes near Dinant, Mariembourg, Rocroi, and various other locations, leading up to the 'First Battle of The Marne' in early September. The result was the failure of the Schlieffen Plan and the initiation of positional warfare. The battalion lost a considerable amount of its men due to the unexpected overall resistance. They pulled back towards the region of Aisne as a result, where Alexander has arrived to help to replace the heavy losses — Now, his first experience of combat begins.

Before Departure — Alexander in pre-war uniform, August 1914.

2

27.9.1914 Unloaded in pitch darkness at 5 o'clock in the morning. Using wood from a garden fence, we made a fire in the train station courtyard and heated up our coffee. The cannon thunder could now already be clearly heard. We marched four kilometres to the village of Variscourt where our battalion lies. We lodged inside a manor. The hope for a comfy bed had unfortunately been deceitful because when we started to make ourselves comfortable and finally washed ourselves thoroughly for the first time in many days, we suddenly received the order to move into marching position. There are very few people in this village — everyone lies seven kilometres further ahead in the trenches.

After two kilometres, we hold behind a railway dam since we can only reach the foremost positions safely at night. On the dam, there are metre-deep holes left by shells from the heavy English naval guns which are positioned about 12 kilometres ahead of us. The rails are completely bent, and there are long and jagged pieces of shrapnel everywhere. A secured balloon, which observes our artillery hits, rises up behind us. 150 metres next to us lies a battery of heavy 15cm howitzers — incredibly loud shots. The shells whiz through the air along with loud hissing and screeching sounds. Three planes are above us, one seeming to be French. You can clearly hear the enemy shells hissing over us, but most of them sink into the soft ground far in front of us with a dull thud without exploding.

At 8 o'clock in the evening, we march off in very small sections, 100 metres apart to weaken the effect of the artillery fire, because now things are getting serious — a wounded and whimpering French soldier is carried past.

We reach the foremost frontline after around 45 minutes. Half of the battalion lies in reserve in dugouts on the edge of a pine forest, and the other half lies 50 metres further forward in deep trenches. I found a hole where I can stretch out to some extent. It is very narrow and low, but it is better than nothing. You descend two metres through a hole in the ground whereupon a low, underground passage branches off, on one side of which there are niche-like bulges in the sand and sandstone. These are our living quarters. Considering that the floors are topped with straw and the openings can be covered with straw mats, it is fairly warm and dry too in these holes. I am the only one assigned to the replacement sector of the 1st Company.

28.9.1914 A sudden alarm at 5 o'clock in the morning. Through narrow zigzag-shaped trenches, we move to reinforce the foremost trench. The French do not come, however. From the trench, a wide plain descends to a deep shipping canal about 1000 to 1200 metres away and towards the French trenches. There are tonnes of dead French people lying everywhere in the fields from a breakthrough attempt that was repulsed a few days ago. A few metres in front of me lies a dead black colonial soldier.

The artillery thunders day and night without interruption, and the shells screech over our heads back and forth. Just from the sounds in the sky, you can already tell whether it is a shell from field or heavy siege artillery. It is truly astonishing to watch the shells explode in the enemy position — a flash of lightning and a smoke cloud. Only after a few seconds does the hissing in the air stop, and you then hear the sound of the explosion. It is a similar sound to that of firework rockets that whiz into the air to then burst with a bang. The explosions here are just significantly louder, especially with those heavy calibres that produce a frightening racket. However, after a short while, you stop listening because you quickly get used to everything. Gunfire is very rarely heard.

We are unable to cross the canal because the heights on the other side are too heavily fortified and manned by the heaviest English naval artillery. The French artillery is said to be very superior to ours in finding hidden positions. On the other hand, the French infantry is supposedly not very good at all, and they do not shoot well. Most of the damage is caused by the English guns that shoot enormously far. We are apparently only here to act defensively and to prevent breakthrough attempts until the French are bypassed and completely surrounded.

Just now came the news that Lieutenant von Boxberger, who only recently joined our transport, accidentally shot himself while trying to load his pistol. It is a real shame for the extremely nice person.

A shrapnel shell just exploded opposite us in the forest. We are therefore creeping back into our dugouts.

I have received news that I have been promoted to deputy officer, but unfortunately only with the wages of a sergeant. We were replaced by the infantry at 8 o'clock in the evening, marched back for over an hour and spent a miserable night in the Guignicourt sugar factory.

29.9.1914   I loitered around doing nothing all day. Only three-quarters of an hour were occupied with drills. I had a nice lunch and drank half a bottle of French red wine. I also had my first shave again since the 20th of September. The infantry that replaced us yesterday was hit by artillery a few hours after we left, losing 20 men with many more casualties because the people were so incredibly careless as to light fires. We were a lot more careful and therefore didn't have a single casualty in 48 hours.

30.9.1914   I slept reasonably better last night — as good as it gets in a machine house where the roof and windows are completely perforated from shells and shrapnel. Sugar sacks are used as blankets. It keeps getting colder.

A sudden alarm at 10 o'clock in the morning. We march up until the next village of Condé where we stay put. We then march back at 4 o'clock in the afternoon since the attack (colonial troops and Zouaves) was held back without our support.

I stayed overnight at the sugar factory again. There was a concert by our band in the factory yard in the evening.

1.10.1914   Miserably cold, foggy weather. Later, however, a very nice and sunny day. We march off at 8:15 in the morning. We camp in a small meadow in the forest after 2 and a quarter hours. A French plane circles above us and is shot at by infantry all around us, then all of a sudden, a loud bang nearby — the guy drops a bomb, but seemingly without causing any damage. Aeroplanes can be seen here every day.

During lunchtime, we move into quarters in the village of Amenancourt (13 kilometres). We are army reserves, so are now far from the gunfire. Our battalion is most likely to be somewhat conserved after the previous heavy losses. It is a very sad sight in the villages. There is nothing available. Water is rare and can only be consumed after being boiled. The residents have either fled or, as in Variscourt, are held captive in the church to prevent them from giving off signals. Only a few starving women and children hang around and beg us for bread.

2.10.1914   I have slept properly again for the first time after many days without freezing. A suspension of the postal service has been imposed to conceal the movements of the army. I carried out some duties early today, instructions and exercises, and then had a nap. I am now eating with the officers, which is a bit annoying because of the social obligations, but it is also an advantage since you get something good to eat and drink; mostly poultry shot in the village, red wine and sparkling wine. Only the accommodation is miserable.

I have received the pleasant news that from now on I will receive the salary of an officer, so 150 Mark in mobilisation funds and 205 Mark in wages. Two enemy planes caused a lot of damage yesterday by dropping bombs in Guignicourt, where we were lying a few days ago. Furthermore, our musical instruments, which were loaded onto the baggage wagon, were damaged by shrapnel.

3.10.1914   The usual exercises in the morning, and later in the afternoon a religious field service outdoors (jägers, infantry, artillerymen, Uhlans and Braunschweiger Hussars).

In the evening, we suddenly march forward into the line of fire and spend the night back in the dugouts. The forest ahead of us is terribly shot to pieces, with thick pine trees snapped in half by shells like matchsticks. There are many unburied Frenchmen in the fields in front of us.

4.10.1914   Everything is calm in our line, with only the occasional cannon thunder in the distance. Towards the evening, to our right, there was heavy artillery fire for an hour. We were relieved by infantry in the evening and marched back to Bertricourt. I slept the night very moderately on straw. Everyone has severe diarrhoea due to the irregular diet and the seasonal flu.

5.10.1914   A French plane is unsuccessfully being shot at with shrapnel shells.

6.10.1914   We are woken up at 3 o'clock in the morning and march off to Guignicourt at half past 4. We depart with the train at 8:30 and arrive in Laon at 10:30. The large cathedral lies nicely upon the hill.

In La Fère at 2:45 in the afternoon. There are many cattle pastures like in Belgium, and large vegetable gardens with wonderful vegetables. This is an unusual sight for us, as we have come from the awful Champagne where there are almost only sugar beet fields. Some of the factories were at least operational in Belgium, but everything seems dead here in France.

In St. Quentin at 5:45. Another miserably cold night in the carriage — no sleep.

7.10.1914   Towards Cambrai at 4 o'clock in the morning. At 6 o'clock in the morning, we continue marching 16 kilometres to Arleux where we stay. We four company officers are at the doctor's.

It is a completely different life here than in awful Champagne. The land is rich with lots of vegetables and wine. I ate very well. Our host is happily donating four bottles of very good Bordeaux wine. In the afternoon, we sit in the garden under the vine trellises with a cigarette and sunbathe — thundering of cannons off in the distance.

In addition to Monsieur le Docteur's bottles, there is also a box of found sparkling wine.

Unfortunately, I can't make use of my room or bed, because at 6 o'clock in the evening, contrary to expectations, we suddenly go 10 kilometres further to Vitry where we force out the occupants at 10 o'clock and accommodate ourselves there. Although unmade, I slept in a bed for the first time in three weeks.

8.10.1914   But the pleasure was only very short-lived since we are woken up at 3 o'clock in the morning. At 4 o'clock, we set off towards Arras through a number of shot-up and burned villages. The thunder of our heavy guns shelling the Arras fortress continues with intermittent rolling gunfire. For hours, we march north behind our battle line, apparently towards a bypass. It is brilliant, beautiful weather. Aeroplanes are constantly above us, and one drops a number of bombs. We seek shelter from the shells inside and behind the houses in the village of Souchez.

Midday advance into the firing line against the enemy. We occupy a height from which we have a great view of the battle taking place in the valley to the right. The advance of our riflemen and the bursting of the shells and shrapnel can be clearly seen. We do not intervene for the time being; only now and then a stray bullet whistles over us. Orders are given in the afternoon to attack a forest in the valley occupied by French Alpine jägers — First, I leap with my platoon behind a hay bale to orientate myself, and then I continue through insane infantry fire until I reach a small earth mound that offers some cover.

The bullets virtually whiz around us in an almost eerie manner or hit around us with a piercing bang. The war volunteer, Kellerman, receives a shot through the hand next to me. As soon as the firing subsides, we carefully crawl on our stomachs down the slope and into a hollow where we regroup again. We then rapidly run forward across a completely flat field to a field of clover, where we are pressed flat against the ground and helplessly have to endure the terrible hail of bullets, as there is no sign of the enemy. It is now fortunately a little dark. We dig deep foxholes through the night. Straw is brought in, and like so we lie reasonably warm through the night. The enemy is 200 metres opposite us on the edge of the forest, probably dug in deeply.

9.10.1914   As soon as it gets light, the firing resumes and the losses increase. The infantry joins us at a running pace. Someone who tries to lie down next to me is shot through the upper arm and crashes over me. We stay like this until the afternoon. Then comes the insane command: "Platoon Wachsmuth is to advance with Platoon Pfeifer to the infantry line (the hollow path by the forest). Attack ordered by the battalion without regard to losses." — With five men (no more would follow the order), I run 50 metres ahead to a deep gully where the infantry machine guns lie. The people who were watching us later told us that the bullets had struck around us like hail. We are very lucky because we get to cover unharmed. On the other hand, the ten men who ran across later were shot down without exception, which we had to watch helplessly from a distance of 50 metres. It is a shame for those good people. The order therefore comes that further attacks by the jägers should be stopped because they are pointless. When darkness falls, I crawl back into my old position with my few men.

This day has cost us 46 dead and wounded, so a third part of the company. We are replaced by infantry and occupy a new position to the rear upon the height. We hastily dig ourselves into new deep foxholes all night long.

10.10.1914   Early in the morning, to our greatest joy, our artillery shells the forest that caused us so much trouble yesterday. In return, we are bombarded with shells for an hour, which explode very close by; one of them only 2 metres in front of my hole which is covered with chunks of earth. The explosions are so powerful that the entire ground shakes every time. We have no losses though.

11.10.1914   We dug our foxholes deeper during the night. It is such hard work on this tough ground riddled with fist-sized lumps of flint. The remaining half of the night was spent waiting for an enemy attack, but this didn't happen. I haven't washed in days. You get completely dirty in these holes. You get to drink a field flask of tea or coffee every night. There is otherwise nothing throughout the day. Our foxholes are located high up on the mountain, and to the north within the forest is the enemy. To the east, there is a wide valley stretching from south to north into which our infantry is advancing. Beyond the valley, even further east, are a number of large mining villages such as Lens, which are being shelled, and some of them are burning.

Early in the morning and in the evening, we again received heavy shell fire for some time, but without any casualties for my company. A shell went through the cover of a jäger and into his foxhole, but luckily without killing or injuring him. We were replaced by infantry during the night, and I spent the night on a mattress in the village of Givenchy-en-Gohelle. I finally washed again — a soothing rest.

12.10.1914   Two planes are being shot at by Bavarian anti-aircraft guns. It is a wonderful sight. The plane is in the blue sky, and suddenly the round white shrapnel clouds appear around it like cotton balls. Yesterday, one of the planes, which had pelted us with bombs a few days before, was brought down in this way.

13.10.1914   We stayed the night in Givenchy again and I have never slept so well. We were on standby all day for the planned combined night attack, but this never happened. The 14th Division is arriving, so there is now an entire army corps here.
   A huge shootout can be heard in the night.

14.10.1914   Rest day — ate and slept. French shells land barely 100 metres next to my house but without exploding. Yet you are already so used to it that you hardly even look anymore.

15.10.1914   We are army reserves, which is always a precursor to a huge mess. We commence marching east at 5 o'clock in the morning, via the large mining town of Lens to the town of Carvin, where we arrive at half past 9. We have found tonnes of lovely pears and a lot of wine in the abandoned house of a leather manufacturer.
   We march another three kilometres north to Annoeullin, where we lodge inside a brewery. The owner, J. Lecieux-Thibaut, Brasseur *(brewer)*, is a lovely old gentleman who wants to hear from me after the war ends. The food was touching, and I slept undressed for the first time since the 17th of September.

16.10.1914   I conducted some morning duties and then had a nice breakfast, consisting of buttered bread with bacon and sweet wine.

18.10.1914   We now have a few very nice days of rest and are preparing ourselves for the upcoming struggles. For example, we four officers from the 1st Company were invited to the following banquet of the 3rd Company — A fresh French rabbit soup, boiled ham with asparagus, potatoes and melted butter, fried chicken with fried potatoes, canned fruits, chocolate dessert, fruit, coffee, old Malaga, red wine and fruit wine. We four officers of the 1st Company usually eat together, and we have established a cash register from which we make purchases and that can't be requisitioned for free. We also bring a large box along with us on the field kitchen where all our supplies are stored. In Arleux, we captured a box of 50 bottles of sparkling wine in an abandoned house. There is plenty of red wine everywhere. Added to this are also the many generous gifts.

We often receive comical gifts. For instance, our first lieutenant received a small bottle of cognac from his wife yesterday, yet this stuff is available here in large quantities.

Yesterday evening gave me a big surprise. 11 large sacks of post had arrived, including a number of parcels and letters for me which had only been in transit for seven days. It is always a joyous celebration when the post arrives. I am well-equipped, and I have plenty of clothes. The excessive amounts cannot be carried, and I have just seen my suitcase here for the first time again in eight days. The processing of promotions is very slow. The deputy officer, Totzek, was promoted to officer at the beginning of September, and the recognition from the Kaiser has still not arrived today. It will not take long for me to get the Iron Cross, as my actions at Notre Dame de Lorette made a great impression. I should have it in four weeks' time at most if I don't get wounded in the near future. All the officers now have it with the exception of Prince Reuss, who came to the battalion with me.

When we march, I carry on my knapsack that I named Badger — a coat, a canvas and cooking tools. Inside as reserve: 1 spare shirt, 1 pair of underwear, 6 pairs of socks, 1 woolly undercoat, 1 cummerbund, wristlets, pulse warmers, 1 towel, felt shoes, a field cap, washing and shaving stuff, a map with writing tools and tinned rations consisting of 2 double portions. Also, 3 small tin cans with cocoa and one with salt; often even vegetables and 1 bottle of red wine too. Hanging on my belt: Sabre, pistol, ammunition bag with bullets, cigarettes, mints, sugar cubes and matches. My bread bag holds letters, a first aid kit, cutlery; and a load of small things like bread and bacon and so on. I also have a field flask, a cup, mittens, and binoculars around my neck. The burden is therefore quite large. I also have a load of spare clothes and one pair of laced shoes in my suitcase. Our attendants wash all our clothes on our rest days. We live wonderfully and happily here in Arleux, but we always have to be ready to leave within 10 minutes.

An alarm was expected tonight, but fortunately, nothing came of it. We are more or less on the far-right flank here. It is the purest maritime climate here; almost always damp and foggy but not cold. You can thereby survive in the trenches as long as it doesn't rain. It is in itself warmer below ground, and then there is also plenty of straw everywhere. The French don't have barns like we do at home, but all their grain stands all over the place in countless straw bales. You see hundreds of them at a glance. Wherever you build a trench, the next straw bale is immediately behind it. The common diarrhoea is nasty, especially in the trenches where you are immediately shot at if you stick your head out a little. As hard as it is, you just need to wait until the night to go.

Right near us lies Courrières where the big mining disaster occurred a few years ago.

Note: The Courrières mining disaster occurred on the 10th of March 1906, killing 1099 miners, and it is still Europe's worst mining disaster.

The Battalion Diary

It did surprise me when I discovered that Alexander's battalion produced its own diary; documenting every event that the battalion was involved in, and revealing further facts about its activities. I instantly obtained a copy for myself — printed in 1931 in the outdated German 'Fraktur' typeface, entailing numerous maps, reports, and detailed information. It also includes some photographs of the battalion's officer corps such as the one shown below, taken in the October of 1914. We are now able to put a face to some of the many names often mentioned by Alexander. As you will discover, this diary will unlock the answers to some of your likely questions or thoughts as this book progresses.

From Left Standing: *Lt. Pira, Lt. Wobeser, Lt. Prince Reuss, 1.Lt. von Apell, Lt. Swart, Lt. Mohr, Lt. Wachsmuth, Dr. Eppenstein, Lt. Brünig.*

From Left Sitting: *Lt. Prince Lippe, Lt. Berger, Captain von Graeffendorff, Major Count von Soden, Captain von Ascheberg, 1.Lt. Beutin.*

3

20.10.1914   Morning 4:30 advance northwest to the village of Salomé near La Bassée — combined attack by the 7th Corps from the south against the English. Our battalion storms the village of Les-Trois-Maisons. The 3rd and 4th Companies suffer heavy losses. Lieutenant Prince Reuss from the Silesian lineage (18 years old) falls from shrapnel, and more officers are additionally wounded. With my platoon and the company commander, First-Lieutenant Beutin, I advance further to the right together with infantry; leaping or crawling on my stomach towards the village of Lorgies, which is on the right behind Les-Trois-Maisons. We receive very heavy shrapnel fire by the large highway. Beutin's attendant, who lies between me and Beutin, receives a piece of shrapnel in the forehead and dies instantly. The terrain is favourable due to the many longitudinal and transverse trenches (almost every field here is surrounded by a trench). This is why, despite heavy rifle and shrapnel fire, I only have one dead and two wounded in my platoon. The English prefer shrapnel, whereas the French, standard shells.

In the course of the day, we come within a short distance of Lorgies, but it is impossible to get in. We spend most of the afternoon lying in the rain in a wet trench that we are not allowed to stick our noses out of. Almost more unpleasant than the bullets whistling over us is the cold wetness in which we have to lie for hours. Come dark, we regroup with our company in the captured village of Les-Trois-Maisons which is completely shot to pieces. We then provide a farm with shooting slits and set it up for the defence against a possible night attack.

Villages are burning all around, including straw bales — a horribly beautiful sight.

21.10.1914   We occupy the village outskirts in the morning and dig trenches. I dig myself into an open field with my men under enemy gunfire. We later crawl on our stomachs through wet fields of furrows and into an abandoned English trench. I unfortunately lose my sabre due to this crawling. I therefore take my rifle and shoot firmly towards the village of Lorgies opposite, which is also set alight by our artillery — the church tower collapses. We ourselves receive the occasional heavy shrapnel and rifle fire but have no heavy losses since we are in good cover. In the night, we go 20 metres further up on the high ground due to the better line of sight and dig ourselves in here.

22.10.1914   I lay there all day long, shooting and getting shot at. It rains every now and then — unpleasant wind. I froze very much. The enemy clears Lorgies during the night and heads west, causing us also to head in this new direction and dig ourselves in once again through the night. I am spending the night nearby in a small house with my platoon as a reserve.

Compared to the filthy French, you can scavenge quite a lot from the English, who are impeccably well-equipped. We found quintals-worth of provisions in the abandoned trenches — 5-kilo cans of Liebig *(tinned meat manufacturer)* corned beef, beef and vegetables, marmalade, an awful lot of cigarettes, tobacco, biscuits; and a lot of equipment such as rubber tent canvases, spades, and so on. Thousands of ammunition rounds. I have never seen dum-dum bullets though. They don't seem to be using them anymore. Their bullets look just like ours.

23.10.1914   The English disappeared in the morning. We are after them in the line of fire, and we need to run for a long time before we catch up with them again by La Quinque Rue. Opposite this street, which is occupied by a few houses, they have taken up a previously prepared position that is heavily fortified and secured with barbed wire, in which they offer the most stubborn resistance. They seemingly want to keep us away from Calais and the sea at all costs. We occupy a farmstead and dig ourselves into the left of it. It is a cold night. The comet is very clearly visible.

During our advancement today, an English plane, shot at by us, landed just 100 metres in front of us. We thought he had been shot down. But as it then turned out, he had informed the enemy artillery of our unexpectedly quick approach, whereupon they fled in full flight and had to abandon all their ammunition. My company captured several 100 shells and shrapnel in this way.

24.10.1914   At dawn, I and my men occupy another trench 150 metres further ahead where we dig ourselves in again. We really have become proper earth workers. In the afternoon, we individually crawl on our stomachs in a furrow for over 100 metres, to a trench that is only 100 metres away from the enemy trench. We can clearly see the English working there, but we few men need to remain calm due to their superior numbers.

In the evening, we return to the company in the recently mentioned farmstead, 400 to 500 metres from the enemy, which will form our base for the next few days. In front of this, we dig ourselves in, 200 metres away from the English.

25.10.1914   Finally a warm, sunny day again. You can't stick your head out of your dugout because tremendous banging will start as a result.

In pouring rain, we again dig ourselves 50 metres closer throughout the night.

26.10.1914   We shot vigorously this morning to make it easier for the 4th Company and the infantry to proceed. But we can't get through since the English are too heavily entrenched and have created wired obstacles. There is nothing we can do without artillery pre-bombardment. Our line consists just of one row of individual foxholes which lie several metres apart. Because of this, the only way to communicate with one another is by throwing notes in empty bullet casings at each other. By doing that, our dear company commander, First-Lieutenant Beutin, received a shot through the arm. Three men from my platoon, which is already down to 15 men, are wounded. The entire battalion, which deployed with 1200 men and was later provided with 200 men, is now only 200 strong.

The English-occupied village opposite us is called Richebourg-l'Avoué. Senseless shooting from the English during the night — probably because they are scared of an attack. The banging just never stops all day and night, but as soon as the English hear any unusual sounds or imagine anything else, insane firing initiates which usually lasts for half an hour. Either they are nervous, or they want to scare us away from attacking. We then simply go into our holes and rejoice at this irrational waste of ammunition.

27.10.1914   At dawn, half of the company went back to the farm to rest, where it was very uncomfortable because the English were constantly shooting at the doors and windows. This cost us several dead and wounded until our people finally got wise. The heavy shells are constantly whizzing over us. Our walls even shake when our 21cm mortars strike over in Richebourg. The explosions cause black clouds as high as a house and occasionally cause roof tiles to clatter down on us when a shot blows through our roof.

We are hunting chickens at the farmstead this morning. In the middle of the gunfire, Vice-Sergeant Schöbitz skilfully killed a young rooster with a pitchfork. We are cooking this in a Maggi soup, providing us with a sumptuous meal. In the afternoon, I in return kindly donate my coffee received from home.

News arrives in the evening that I have been transferred to the 4th Company.

28.10.1914   I spent the night in the trench — the usual gunfire.

29.10.1914   Back to the farmstead in the morning. During the day, we stay behind haybales because it is getting increasingly dangerous on the farm. My former apprentice, Kaiser, receives a shot in the leg at the farm and is awarded the Iron Cross in the evening.

We replace the 2nd Company during the night, which leaves us with very bad trenches.

30.10.1914   We have landed in a very bad area. The English are 600 metres away from us, but every moment, a wild shootout breaks out which doesn't seem to bother us anymore. It rained terribly last night — horrible mud everywhere. We are literally covered in clay.

31.10.1914   At night, we headed 15 minutes back to a shot-up farmstead where the staff lies. I was surprised on the way there by an insane hail of bullets, which I had to endure while crouching behind a thick tree for half an hour.

I rested in a barn while lying on straw during the day.

1.11.1914   We replaced the 3rd Company at 4 o'clock in the morning, and I got hold of a nice dugout protected from the rain and shrapnel. The weather is slightly sunny during the day, and not cold. Our heavy artillery fires at the enemy positions during the afternoon for several hours.

A very cold and rainy night. My looted English rubber tent canvas is working excellently.

2.11.1914   We were replaced by the infantry at 4 o'clock in the morning and moved into quarters at Les-Trois-Maisons, which we stormed several days ago. Here, we finally have two days of rest after having continuously been in battle for 13 days and nights. But we are also at the end of our strength. It is too much for the nerves — the constant shooting, day and night — no rest. One fellow falls after the other, and we are constantly soaked, dirty, and covered in mud in the process. I now know the true meaning of war, and I have an awful anger towards the English who have brought all this upon us.

We are holding a one-kilometre line with only 200 jägers. If the English knew of this, we would all be lost. Prisoners have said that a medal is being promised for every captured Bavarian or jäger. My current company commander is Captain Clasen who is a very bad bully. It was recently no longer bearable in our reserve farmstead, as there was a shot cow in the barn that we couldn't fit through the doors because it was so bloated. We therefore temporarily sealed the doors. I am just surprised that I haven't gotten my usual tonsillitis yet, even though we are suffering terribly from the cold and wet weather. I wouldn't have thought it possible that one could endure such a life.

In Les-Trois-Maisons, I am visiting the places where we fought from the 20th to the 23rd of October, as well as the graves of our men. Next to the house where I live is the open field where I entrenched myself in the hail of bullets on the morning of the 21st of October. The hole is still perfectly preserved. I also have my sabre back, but just the sheath is missing.

3.11.1914   Rest day. Both days are used for a thorough clean and to rest from the struggles of the last 13 days.

4.11.1914   We marched off in the morning and replaced the infantry in the old positions. It rained very heavily throughout the afternoon and the entire night — a very uncomfortable night — terrible mud in the trenches.

5.11.1914   We now have Indians against us. They are small, stocky guys with shaved heads except for small pigtails, who, according to prisoners, are suffering terribly from the cold and wetness. I hope the entire lot will die soon. We are often bombarded with shrapnel but have had no casualties.

6.11.1914   Replaced by the 2nd Company at 4 o'clock in the morning. We are staying in reserve at a farmstead throughout the day, 20 minutes behind the trenches.

7.11.1914 We replaced the 3rd Company during the evening. I froze very much in the night. Some sun during the day — a heavy shell strikes close in front of me.

I led the company to La Bassée at 9 o'clock in the evening, a town of 5000 inhabitants that is miserably shot up. There is hardly a house without a shell impact, and most of them are completely destroyed.

8.11.1914 I spent the night sharing a bed space with Sergeant Miesch. There are a lot of loving gifts here. We cooked, ate, drank, and slept all day.

We are receiving 80 war volunteers — In the evening we march to the trenches where we spend the 9th and 10th of November in the usual way. I have overall supervision and responsibility for the entire company, meaning a lot of work and less sleep.

Back into the farmstead as a reserve in the evening, where the captain has his quarters.

12.11.1914 We are back in La Bassée for a day today, supposedly as a rest day. But in reality, there is more to do than usual, especially now that we have so many volunteers who are still outright civilians and still miraculously believe they are above all, simply because they volunteered. They did pull beautiful faces though when they saw our trenches and got to know the harsh tone of war.

15.11.1914 I am back with the 1st Company as of today.

18.11.1914 We are going back to La Bassée for two days again tomorrow night. We are still waging the previous trench warfare here. I saw my name on the suggestion list for the Iron Cross today. The weather has been awfully miserable for the past few days, with continued pouring rain. The mud crust on us is becoming as thick as a finger. Strangely, I still haven't gotten the common tonsillitis though. You can clearly see how toughened we are by looking at the newly arrived volunteers who freeze terribly, whereas we still find it warm.

20.11.1914 Back in La Bassée. One day goes by like the other now — a few days in the trenches, two days in a nearby farmstead as a reserve, and two days of recovery in La Bassée where we are today and tomorrow. Today was an especially nice day for me, as I received no less than seven parcels from home. My 1st Company now has the following officers — one young lieutenant. The 2nd Company has two young lieutenants; the 3rd Company has one reserve lieutenant; and the 4th, one captain and one young lieutenant. This is all that is left.

Loving gifts from home are now being sent to us in quantities. It is also evident that our jägers are higher-class people who get a lot sent from home. There is now an abundance of cigars, whilst a couple of weeks ago they went for 1 to 3 Mark per piece. There is now plenty of food as well as complete mountains of clothing. What we were lacking a few weeks ago, we now have too much of. The last time we were in La Bassée, you could still buy cognac for 1 Mark a litre whilst wine was no longer available. There isn't any cognac anymore today. There is nothing left to be had in this completely destroyed nest. I live here in a very nice house and have a room for myself, although with very primitive furnishings — an uncovered mattress. The windows are not broken though in return, which is a great rarity here. The much-maligned field post isn't all that bad, as I have received all my letters and parcels mostly within eight to ten days up to now. You really can't ask for more. Today, I already read the Kasseler newspaper from the 15th of November.

I heard yesterday that over 180 Englishmen were buried after our storming of Les-Trois-Maisons. That is a huge amount when you consider that only this many jägers at most had attacked. Our main activity now is not marching and shooting, as you would have thought, but strenuous digging in the trenches, day and night. Several of our volunteers, who just arrived, had to go back due to another recurring breakthrough. You can generally see how toughened we experienced warriors already are just by looking at the recruits. When we sit in the trenches without a hat, a hood, or a jacket, and with only a short-sleeved shirt, the new ones walk around wrapped up like the riders of the North Pole and still freeze. They thereby have completely new uniforms which are much warmer than our old, worn and torn clothes.

It has been snowing since yesterday and everything is white. It must have been several degrees of cold tonight because the road is frozen hard. Nevertheless, I am still sitting here writing in an unheated room without a coat, and I am not freezing. Much worse than the cold, which you cannot protect yourself against, was the recent rainy weather, where we almost suffocated in the mud. I have not caught a cold though, despite not having removed the completely soaked boots from my feet for several days. Our active officers are very unpleasant with very few exceptions. I haven't yet noticed a hint of the camaraderie between officers and men that is always talked about in the newspapers. On the contrary, there is an indescribably rude tone. An exception is my current company commander, Lieutenant Müller, who is very kind and doesn't see you as just a subordinate. I live perfectly with him.

The reserve officers are also very nice people, of whom unfortunately there is only one left. I send all my money, namely 205 Mark in wages, home. I also received 45 Mark in contribution funds for 15 days. It is already more than enough when I have 5 Mark because you can no longer get rid of one Pfennig here. It is no longer possible to write home every day as expected by the family, because aside from the wetness, which often makes writing impossible, there are no letter boxes in the trenches. You occasionally have to hand the post over to a command messenger, medic, or similar folk, but this doesn't work every day. Anyway, I write as often as I can.

My torchlight no longer works because the replacement battery was also used up. The volunteers from Marburg luckily brought a full box of batteries along with them. It was the same case for me with matches, which have almost become the greatest object of value in the trenches. I was by chance now able to get two full boxes again. The things you don't notice at home have the greatest value here. For example, I now always carry a large potato sack around with me. The straw goes into it when in the trench, and then it makes the most beautiful warm footmuff, and you thereby keep the straw in the trenches clean too. You can never have enough gloves to change. I am on the suggestion list for the Iron Cross along with eight others from my company, and will receive it soon. This medal is not highly regarded by anyone here anymore due to paymasters, baggage carriers and other folk receiving them, who have never heard a bullet whistle. It is a shame for the lovely medal.

I didn't get my sabre sheath back, which is why I now always walk around without a sabre. This is much more comfortable in the trench. I have always taken and shot a rifle in battle. Things are looking very lazy with the promotions. Totzek is still waiting to be promoted. He is a Candidate of Theology, which you wouldn't suspect given his often very un-Christian expression and behaviour.

I spent a cosy evening with the gentlemen from the Bicycle Company today.

Note: In Germanic countries, a Candidate of Theology is a person with an academic degree in religious studies.

The Battle of La Bassée

As part of the 'Race to The Sea', the struggle of both sides to reach the coasts of the North Sea, was the 'Battle of La Bassée' from the 10th of October to the 2nd of November 1914. This was one of many battles where the opposing armies repeatedly tried to surround the northern flank of their enemy. With the Germans being the first to capture the city of Lille to the east of La Bassée, they attacked the exposed British flank further north towards Ypres in Belgium. The British have now been driven back, and the Germans occupy La Bassée and Neuve Chapelle, which the British have attempted to capture. With Alexander as part of the supporting German reinforcements pursuing the enemy, the British Lahore Division, on the other hand, has arrived to help repulse the German attacks. Both sides have therefore come to a stalemate after resources are focused on the 'First Battle of Ypres'. Trenches are dug each day and night, throughout the worst conditions and under constant fire — Positional trench warfare has now begun.

During these recent engagements, we get the first true taste of how devastating these events are. We also come to realise that the terrors do not discriminate against any age, class, or the plans and dreams of each person involved. This book will consistently remind you of this, and will always put matters into perspective. However, one victim who stands out to me the most is Prince Heinrich XLVI zu Reuss, who was one of the few German princes to fall in the war. At 18 years old, he had only just become a man and would still be considered a boy by many — What was his life like? What did he plan to do after the war? Where did he see himself in years to come with his future wife and children? — All this he would have thought and asked himself at times. But none of this matters anymore, as his existence has been extinguished by a little piece of shrapnel.

Prince Heinrich XLVI zu Reuss

The Attack From 20 - 23.10.1914

Drawn by Alexander, this perfectly preserved map details the battalion's advance towards the English positions north of La Bassée. Commencing from Annoeullin, the battalion initiated a three-day push in pursuit of the withdrawing English. They finally ended up near the English position at the Heckenhof *(English: Orchard)* which was heavily fortified and defended.

1 = The Heckenhof
2 = The Jägerhof
3 = The Apfelhof
4 = The Standby Farmstead

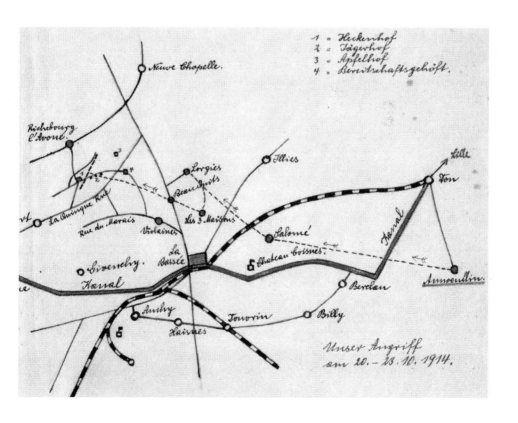

4

21.11.1914   After the recent torrential rain, which left the trenches in a terrible condition, severe frost has now set. The windows are now thickly frozen over.

24.11.1914   The joy was unfortunately short-lived — it is raining again.

26.11.1914   We were just in the trenches again for four days. La Bassée is now occupied by other troops. We are in reserve in a farmstead in the village of Violaines today and tomorrow, roughly 800 metres behind the Front. We are then going to Salomé for two days to recover; the village from which we stormed Les-Trois-Maisons one month ago. An attack on the English position was planned last week, and we had already worked our way up to 50 metres by continuously digging further at night so that we were able to throw hand grenades over. The attack was fortunately given up since the English were said to have placed mines under their entire line, and we would therefore have helplessly been blown up into the air during the assault. We then received the order to set ourselves up in the trenches for the winter.

We got to work immediately. We have expanded our officers' shelter so that you can now lie in it and stand upright. We nailed laths onto the walls and covered them with grey lining as wallpaper. A large toe board, mirror, and thermometer are hung up. A table, chairs, as well as a potbelly stove with charcoal firing (no revealing smoke) are present. Furthermore, we have two cutlery baskets, food boxes, a petroleum lamp, and an alarm clock. There are curtains on the door and there is straw on the ground. It is now really cosy inside, and most importantly, it is warm, and we can always cook. Although not as luxuriously equipped, we built similar large shelters with cooking stoves for each of the three platoons as warming and coffee rooms. Of course, every jäger also has their own hole to sleep in. The previous individual foxholes have long since been connected to one another, creating a continuous trench. Our activity now only consists of guard and entrenchment duties. Two platoons keep watch in the front trench at night, and the third platoon sleeps in the back. They then alternate during the day. An officer has to keep watch at the front every night, which we do in turns. So, in the four days that we are always at the front, I get one turn. You can endure that.

It was recently deadly cold for a few days, but now we have this miserable, wet, cold and dirty weather again. We are thereby all the more pleased about our lovely structures. We cook and eat all day long. We mostly have cocoa in the morning, which we had yesterday while eating the wonderful cake sent by Auntie Anna. The three of us, namely Lieutenant Müller, Deputy-Officer Totzek and I live out of a shared food box. What one gets, the others eat too. This way we always have variety because we come from very different areas, each with its own specialities. Solid breakfast is served for lunch; in the last few days mostly raw and cooked ham and Swiss cheese, as well as red wine. We have coffee in the afternoon, and field-kitchen soup; and in the evening, the same as for breakfast. Everything imaginable sent to everyone is eaten in between. We are thus not suffering now. We often cook bouillon from stock cubes. Yesterday, we made a very strong grog from arrack until we got tired enough for bed. I finally had a bed available again in Violaines, and I slept wonderfully.

We have now provided the trenches with signposts and have chosen the names based on Marburg. It sounded too funny when Vice-Sergeant Schöbitz recently announced: "Reporting to the lieutenant that I have moved to the corner of University Road and Haspel Road." We are just making it as fun as possible. The accordion is being played with enthusiasm all while the bullets whistle over our heads, which rarely cause any damage unless you are not careful, as our trenches have gradually been built so deep that you can stand upright in them. Little by little, we are demolishing all the farms in the immediate vicinity and are using the wood to build the shelters. Entire barn doors are dragged forward at night. The owners of the fields will later have to work for months to get the huge number of installed and battered-in beams out of the ground again. In particularly wet places, we have installed large wine barrels in which our guards can now stand dry.

We now have to choose another farmstead as a replacement, as the previous one has been too heavily shot at with heavy shells in the last few days. There are duds (unexploded shells) measuring 40 to 50 centimetres long and 15 centimetres in diameter. A shell of this calibre is enough to completely shatter a farmhouse. Four women and one child still live in our current homestead, despite the fact that shells and shrapnel burst and the infantry bullets hit all around us every day. My language skills have improved greatly, by the way. We communicate with the French without any difficulty. They get mad when you tell them that the English are their friends, as they are deadly hateful towards them since they wreaked havoc here like the Russians. I have been told quite a lot that they prefer the Germans ten times more than their allies. But we do also give the people some of our food and the children get chocolate and so on. In return, they are much more willing and eager to serve than if we treated them badly.

On many houses in La Bassée and various other places, signs written by our soldiers, state: "Good people, please preserve." Where there are no longer occupants, everything that we can use is of course taken to our trenches. The town of La Bassée is more or less cleared out in this way. For example, our ovens and other equipment come from there, and it was a huge job to bring all of this forward during the night and in the face of enemy fire, as the distance to us is about the same as if we transported ovens, tables, chairs and so forth from Weida to Wünschendorf or Hohenölsen. Our trenches are lined with arched protective defences every few steps to limit artillery fire to a small area.

29.11.1914   We are not the 'Freezing & Hungry Warriors' anymore, but now often live better than at home. Our people get sent far too much. We have received complete sacks full of loving gifts, especially pieces of clothing which we had to take onto the delivery trucks because everyone had the same of everything twice or more. It has even gotten so far that people just throw their clothes away instead of washing them. It is often a shame about the beautiful, expensive things that are sent out. Of course, you wouldn't want to believe this at home.

We have now discovered the device to produce dum-dum bullets for the English rifles, with which the bullet tips can be broken off. It seems to be rarely used, however, as the wounds I have seen so far were not abnormal. Projectiles that we picked up from the ground also showed no change.

We are here with all kinds of troops — Bavarians, people from Baden, Westphalia, the Rhineland, and so forth; nobody from our area because they are probably all in Russia. We now belong to a new brigade again. We are currently resting in Salomé, and I am living in a small house with Totzek and three attendants. The owner is away with his family. We are using Madame's red silk, lace-trimmed ball gown as a tablecloth.

The Indians attacked last night but were repelled. We heard the heavy gun and rifle fire here in Salomé. Since another attempt to break through was feared that night, we had to be ready to move out within 5 minutes. But everything stayed calm, and I slept great. We now eat jacket potatoes with butter every evening, which we haven't done in a long time. It was recently a special day because the four of us drank a bottle of German beer. Yesterday, we even had a bottle of sparkling wine to celebrate the impending attack. We are again heading back into the trenches for four days tonight.

1.12.1914   I have just completed a 14-hour night watch. We fought with the English all night long, especially when the flares lit up the area as bright as day. I am now free from guard duty again for eight days and have next to nothing to do. The war volunteers are a terrible nuisance. There is no trace of the feeling of the military, and they are so clumsy in every respect that you have to show them how to chop wood clearly and start a fire. They are also a weak bunch that can't stand anything. Half have already called in sick in the last eight days, with four today alone. We have nothing but trouble with the guys.

4.12.1914   We have now bettered ourselves again and have built a new shelter that is as big as the previous one. It is a proper living room with a door, window, folded floorboards, an oven, a large round table with an oilcloth, four chairs, and so forth. We will be applying wallpaper tomorrow. Mattresses and quilts will also be coming, as well as a large hanging petroleum lamp. Everything is driven up close to the trench during the night in our company wagon, which is of course commandeered free of charge, and then brought inside. When we ask our attendants how much the items cost in La Bassée, they always reply: "Nothing. There was no salesman in the shop." We took some wonderful porcelain out of a deserted shop, for instance. The French language of our people is also fine. My attendant went to fetch a coffee grinder, which he executed using the following words: "Madame, le Grinder". He still delivered it though.

Today, we tried the cocoa received from home. With this, we also had black bread, bread rolls, tongue, brawn, and raw ham. We are having a big dinner tonight, to which we have invited the artillery-observation officer. The sparkling wine has already arrived. You can bear it here with the current nice weather; if only it weren't for the constant shooting and danger to your life. The English watch out like hawks. The bullets whistle around your head as soon as you stick your head out. There are casualties almost every day, usually instantly fatal headshots. No wonder given the short distance. We are only 50 metres apart in the foremost line. At least we have it ten times better than if we had to attack. I am spending the next evening in the reserve farmstead with the lieutenant, where I can finally wash myself after five days. That is the biggest problem in the trench, that you can't wash yourself, because the water can only be brought in at night from the farms behind you and is therefore far too valuable for washing.

Now back to Salomé we go for two days.

5.12.1914   While arriving in Salomé, I just found out that I had been awarded the Iron Cross. They will probably be prouder of it at home than I am. I received the Iron Cross, especially for leading my platoon during the attacks on Souchez-Loretto and Lorgies. I will send it home because here you now only wear the ribbon through the buttonhole.

Note: The Iron Cross is the medal awarded for outstanding bravery. The Iron Cross 2nd Class is held by a ribbon, whereas the 1st Class is pinned to the uniform and awarded more rarely, holding a greater level of prestige.

We will be vaccinated for typhus for the second time tonight. I have had such a stream of parcels in the last few days that I don't even know where to put everything. I just said to the lieutenant that I would probably get sent a fruit loaf, and then there it was a few hours later. I was particularly happy about the included fir branch because there are no fir trees here. A single large coniferous tree stands between the English and us, but it has been torn in half by a shell and the crown is hanging down. Nothing has occurred here in recent days, apart from the usual shooting. However, we did almost end up in a bad way yesterday due to our own artillery. I was simply walking down the main road of Salomé, and over me circled an enemy plane that was being shot at by our defensive guns. We were then happy that the shrapnel exploded so close to him, when several pieces of explosives suddenly came whizzing down with an eerie whirring sound, with one hitting the middle of the street right next to us.

I now have food supplies for four weeks. A large part of it will be going in the suitcase so that I am not tempted to eat it all at once. The weather is currently bad again; warm, but terrible rain and storms. I am already dreading tonight when I will have to go back to the Front for six days, even though I have had to get used to so many things. Just how often have I now spent doing 14-hour guard watches in the pouring rain, without a minute of sleep, always in the foremost line outdoors while always in danger of being shot?

8.12.1914   It is very warm, but it is raining almost every day in return. I have never seen so much mud in my entire life as I did last night. We are all covered high above our knees in a thick crust of mud. When we relieved the other company, we waded in the mud with it up to our knees.

9.12.1914   Contrary to expectations, we haven't yet suffocated in the current unbelievable filth. There are rumours here today of a great victory over the Russians. Hopefully, it is true.

It is fairly calm here apart from the usual shooting. I used my pistol for the first time the day before yesterday; not against the enemy, but on a chicken hunt. There were still several half-feral chickens in the farmstead behind the trench. Two of them we managed to catch, but the others then got too wild, and I had to shoot the third with my pistol. We then cooked it with a stock cube of 'rice with tomatoes' and had a very good lunch.

10.12.1914   It is only with horror that you go out of the beautiful shelter into the bottomless mud.

12.12.1914   We are already looking forward to tomorrow evening again, when after six days of mud we will be back in La Bassée for two days to dry. Of all days, my company will be on the Front again on Christmas and New Year's Eve.

13.12.1914   We are back in La Bassée. The six days in the trench were awful. It rained every night, and therefore knee-deep mud in the narrow trenches. It then also, just like a stalactite cave, started to drip through the ceiling of our shelter during the final days. The dirt was so terrible that we no longer got angry about it but rather laughed it off. It was the greatest level of gallows humour. We are now only 30 metres away from the English, at the point where they have converted a living hedgerow and a completely destroyed farmstead (the so-called Heckenhof) into a small fortress. You can clearly hear them coughing over there.

They are constantly throwing hand grenades at us, which explode with a loud bang, but are otherwise pretty harmless because you can see them coming as if someone was throwing a hand-sized stone high in an arc. You then just have to pay attention to the direction of the throw and then quickly disappear around the next traverse *(a trench dug perpendicular to a trench line)*. At least 100 of them have already been thrown into our front trench without anyone being hit so far. Much more dangerous are the rifle shots. As soon as someone shows themselves in the slightest over here or there, the bullets whistle. You are at least safe from that here in La Bassée, but the poor town gets bombarded daily with heavy shells in return. There is now nothing left to buy in this pile of rubble because everything has been shot to pieces. Today we are making mulled wine from the arrack that has been sent. Compared to the past, when we only had dry bread and bacon aside from field-kitchen soup for days, we now lead the purest gourmet life. Cigars sent as loving gifts are now available in such abundance that we don't know what to do with them.

Through His Eyes

The way Alexander describes the series of events still gives me the same shivers down my spine as on the first day I read them — the sheer brutality, the appalling conditions, and the unthinkable imageries. A part of me wishes I could get a true glimpse of what it was like in order to truly understand, even though the reality would be terrifying. It is also not only the brutal fighting and living conditions that grip me, which are some of the most discussed topics of the Great War, but also the comradeship, day-to-day experiences, and the individual people involved with lives that are now mostly forgotten. Just like you, I use my imagination and form images in my mind when reading any sort of story or description of events, with each person's depiction being different from the next. Just what did he see and feel? What did his friends and fellow soldiers look like? What was it like at that exact moment which he describes so vividly?

The vast majority of historical documents and diaries leave this aspect to the reader's imagination, or at the very least, provide some imagery that has not been captured by the writer. What if I told you that the same quality and detail of writing in this chapter will soon be consistently accompanied by hundreds of self-made photographs; which, together with the diary, portray the war like never before? Of course, it is still 1914. Alexander could never have anticipated how long this war would last, and bringing a camera into this mess is currently the last thing on his mind. However, as the war soon progresses, this is exactly what he does. He also collects postcards, documents, and other material for us to see over 100 years later. All combined, this gives us a perspective of the Great War that has rarely been publicised so far.

The shot-up town of La Bassée.

5

15.12.1914   I have received a family photo with the children from home. For this, I crafted a fine picture frame using a mirror with yellow celluloid edging that I found to stand it up, as everything somehow gets put to use here in the war. Things still seem lazy when it comes to our promotions. So far, no one has become an officer.

We are heading back into the trench tonight. The weather keeps getting worse — constant storms and rain. The cold will hopefully come soon so that the paths will become more passable.

17.12.1914   It is getting more and more unpleasant due to it constantly dripping through the ceiling; not to mention the conditions of the trenches.

We were relieved this evening and I had to remain on standby with my platoon for another two days in a farmstead, a few 100 metres behind the Front. We should then have gone back to La Bassée. Unfortunately, things turned out completely differently — During the day, we amuse ourselves with chicken hunting, and I once again kill one of the last chickens in this area with my Browning pistol. A lot of letters and parcels for me come along with the field kitchen in the evening, and everything seems fine. There is however a strange restlessness in me, as if I could suspect what the next few hours would bring us. Completely against my usual habits, I pack up all the loving gifts and get everything ready for an immediate departure. The windows are shot up, and it blows inside in the everlasting storm.

At about half past 4 in the morning, I wake up to insane artillery and infantry fire, which initially doesn't bother me since the English often get these sorts of shooting tantrums. But then all of a sudden, the door rips open and a wounded oberjäger from the machine-gun company collapses in, who is mad with fear. I understand from his confused speech that the enemy has attacked our 2nd Company, destroyed a large part of it, and also took machine guns. The Indians had supposedly cut out everyone's throats with their crooked knives and stabbed everyone. I immediately alert my men who sleep next door in shelters. Then, under the fiercest fire, we occupy a trench in front of the farm that had already been dug as a reception position, so that if our people were pushed back, we could take them on here and offer resistance again. Kellerman, who was once already wounded next to me in the Loretto Heights and had just returned recovered, gets shot next to me through the foot. Wounded people come past and also tell horror stories, but no precise information is available. However, we later hear that no Indians were involved in this attack.

After approximately one hour, I receive the order from the Front to go forward into the trenches to offer support. This is easier said than done because the road is impassable, as it was literally showered with artillery and rifle fire. It is well known that the artillery fires mainly at the rear area during such attacks, in order to prevent reinforcements from arriving. The communication trenches dug towards the Front are completely full of water though. After all, it is better to be wet than shot dead, so into the mud broth — it was a blast — over one kilometre ahead in water and mud. The bullets continue to whistle over our heads either with a loud hissing sound or, if they come from further away, with a quiet singing tone. Every now and then, a ricochet buzzes past like a cockchafer gone wild. It is thereby a pitch-black night that is lit up like lightning every few seconds; then, immediately afterwards, there is a terrible crash and shrapnel balls rain down around us. Bullets from rifles strike around us uninterrupted accompanied by a piercing, unpleasant tone, similar to the sound of a whip.

Note: Communication trenches are built to serve as a protected way through to the rear and frontlines, dug at an angle to those opposite the enemy. These help transport men, supplies, and food.

We finally arrive at the Front safe and sound except for a few lightly wounded people, where the company commander of the 2nd Company, Prince Lippe, welcomes us with a sigh of relief. There is indescribable confusion here. It is still dark, and no one really knows what has happened and who is friend or foe, because the English, who harass us so much anyway, have put on the shakos of our dead jägers and are therefore not so easy to recognise as enemies in the semi-dark. Patrols are consequently sent forward from the communication trenches, where we finally discover that the English had not been so fortunate with their raid as they had hoped. Only half of the foremost trench ahead of the 2nd Company is in their possession — two machine guns too, unfortunately — an entire platoon is also missing. Anyone who didn't fall was captured.

We can see the English working feverishly from just 30 metres away. With the sandbags they had brought with them, they quickly built shooting slits facing us, and now the most beautiful shootout is already in progress. It is no child's play given the short distance. I repeatedly urge my people to be extremely careful. I just call a volunteer standing two steps next to me who holds his head out for too long after the shot. At that moment, his head jolts, the familiar and terrible dull sound of the bullet's impact sounds, and the man slowly collapses. The bullet penetrated the forehead and tore off half the skullcap behind. Still mid-fall, he claws his hands into the wound and smears himself over and over with his own brain. It was a terrible sight. I have seen this wound in particular very often though, because in the trenches there are almost only headshots which have an explosive effect at such a short distance.

Recapturing the trench with an assault does not seem advisable considering the expected large losses. We therefore decide to advance into the communication trenches with hand grenades to try and get the English out this way. But first, the pioneers *(engineers)* are to work on them with mortars. However, most of the day passes when everything is ready, and the mortars first begin their task late in the afternoon. These are small mortars that hurl powerful explosive charges fitted with fuses through the air at short distances. We soon see the mortar shells swaying in the air. The explosion occurs shortly afterwards with an incredible bang — clouds of black smoke rise as high as a house. The English fire at us in the same way, only their mortars are a lot smaller and not as effective as ours. Besides this, they were poorly aimed on this day.

Our grenade throwers now also advance — Two pioneers in the trench ahead continue to throw hand grenades in front of them. As soon as one explodes, they immediately jump forward into the smoke and throw the next one. A platoon of jägers follows afterwards with fixed bayonets. The rest of us subject the enemy to heavy rifle and machine-gun fire in the meantime. The attacking column occasionally holds up a hat on a stick so that we know how far they have pushed ahead. We then adjust our fire accordingly. We slowly advance this way, and we gain back half of the lost positions in the evening. We of course spend the night in tense vigilance, as it is not impossible for us to be attacked again. Everything stays calm though, and we begin cleaning up the trench as soon as it gets light. This kind of approach must have become a bit scary for the English, as we regained our old positions in a very short time and without any casualties.

We receive our revenge the next day. We blow up an earth mine in front of the English so-called 'Heckenhof' that they had developed into a small fortress. We then storm the Heckenhof and several rows of trenches before the English can even recover from their bewilderment, capturing a whole number of Englishmen and Indians (Gurkhas). The night after next, the English, who have now brought in two new regiments as reinforcements, attack us again. We set the hay bales opposite us alight with flares, so that when we see them arrive, we would greet them with heavy fire. Many of our rifles unfortunately fail as a result of the horrific dirt, and we therefore take English rifles instead which are seemingly less sensitive. That night alone, I fired an entire ammunition belt of 200 rounds from an English rifle. We have to give way to their superior forces after heavy fighting, but the retreat to our old position takes place in perfect order and on command. I am the last of the whole battalion to leave the English position with my platoon. It was about time because we would have been completely surrounded and captured five minutes later. The very next morning, we attacked again and conquered even more than the day before. The English regiments got completely shot apart, but even my battalion had 300 dead and wounded in these battles.

I saw gruesome images — two heavy shells struck in the middle of my company. Once the poisonous yellow-green smoke disappeared, the ground was covered with dead and wounded. Only the head and an arm were left of two jägers. But even our artillery and hand grenades had a terrible effect. Torn Englishmen and Indians lie around in masses. Nevertheless, you are so dulled that you no longer get upset about anything. We don't need guns much in these trench battles. We do everything with hand grenades that each of us now knows how to use. We captured huge amounts of loot — Indian sickle-shaped throwing knives, wonderful furs made from long-haired goatskin, tobacco, cigarettes, jam, biscuits, canned food, knitwear, and so forth. We have been living at the expense of England for days. You have to give the English credit because they are impeccably and, above all, extremely practically equipped. The war is costing England a lot of money.

While I was supervising the foremost trench yesterday, I crept one trench forward with a jäger, which leads to the English trenches and is filled with dead Englishmen. In one hand the pistol, in the other two hand grenades — Like so, we snuck ahead and looted marvellous stuff from their knapsacks such as socks, breast warmers, Scottish scarves, tissues, woolly hats, and so on. On this occasion, I also stole a brand-new, silver-haired goatskin kilt that the most distinguished lady would envy. Almost everything that we now wear, eat, drink, or otherwise use, comes from the English. All of our people are walking around in nice, warm, and waterproof goatskins. They look like Eskimos. Unfortunately, my company commander, Lieutenant Müller, the only officer in the entire company, was shot by an Indian while storming the Heckenhof. We haven't had any joy out of the Christmas festivities. I sat in the captured Indian trench and froze terribly. The heavy shells continued to strike a few metres in front of and behind me in the meantime. When it later became dark, we all sang Christmas songs along the entire trench line, but this must have really annoyed the English because they graced us with shrapnel fire in return.

Moonlit night. The dead are scattered all over the fields in front of us — this was an image that I will never forget. We achieved extraordinary things and endured terrible suffering these past few days. Our worst enemy of all was the knee-deep, tough mud that required great effort to get your feet out of. Our feet swelled and became sore, and every step was terrible agony. We dragged ourselves laboriously through the trenches while groaning. I was stuck in my completely muddy and dripping clothes for 14 days, I only slept properly for two hours in four days, and today I washed myself for the first time in 14 days. We are physically and mentally completely broken down, and I am not ashamed to say that we sometimes cried in despair. The only consolation is that things are no different for the English. Death narrowly missed me twice again yesterday. Two shrapnel shells burst so close next to me that I was nearly deaf all day. The splinters just whizzed around my head. Half of my uniform has turned yellow-green from the poisonous fumes of the English heavy shells. Our lovely shelters have been shot in by the enemy artillery.

27.12.1914   We are finally back in La Bassée for two days. I am still stunned by the horrors of the last few days. I would never have believed that a human being could endure such hardships. At home, you couldn't possibly imagine how terrible it is here. I saw people who went insane in the middle of battle. This is why my reports are also going slightly topsy-turvy and muddled up now. These days will become a special chapter of glory in the history of our battalion.

It was awful — everywhere wetness, the groundwater constantly rising from the bottom, the perpetual rain dripping through the ceiling of our shelters; and in between, that cursed and tough Flemish mud — always wet up to the stomach for days — no way to change the socks because you wouldn't have been able to put the boots back on your feet, which had become swollen, sore lumps of ice — the hands full of bloody cracks that almost go down to the bone. No sleep — almost always in combat or in anticipation of a night attack. Hopefully, we will go into reserve next time, as we cannot stand this life much longer. In addition to Lieutenant Müller, Lieutenant von Seebach also fell. Captain Clasen is seriously wounded. He went forward to the Front with me on one of the last nights to mark the line for a new trench to be dug. He received a direct hit in the abdomen next to me in the process.

Tonight, we are going back into the trenches for several days.

The Story of Percy Walsh

Among the possessions preserved by Alexander, there exists a compilation of postcards that were once carried by his British enemies on the day they died. My mother tells me that her father kept these in a cabinet with many of Alexander's other old belongings, and that she remembers taking them out and looking at them as a child. She never really knew the significance of the photos at the time. Below is one of these postcards that I would like to draw your attention to:

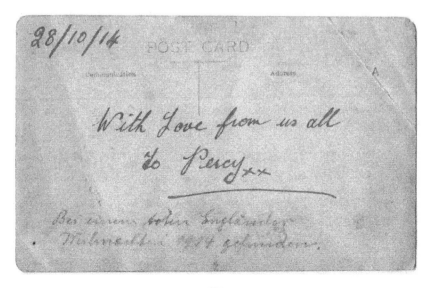

"With love from us all – to Percy xx" — This is a message on a postcard that was found on Percy Walsh, aged 22 from Blackburn, Lancashire. He was killed on 22.12.1914 when the Germans recaptured the trench they had lost. Below this, Alexander wrote: "Found on a dead Englishman, Christmas 1914". From this simple message along with Alexander's description, most would at first probably think this is not enough information to identify the owner of this postcard. However, after searching for 'Percy' while using the Commonwealth War Graves Database, I found only one soldier with this name who died just before Christmas. He was the only one who could have crossed paths with Alexander. This soldier is buried at the Le Touret Memorial, less than a mile from the Heckenhof and beside the same road where this fighting took place. To confirm my discovery, I then researched Percy's battalion (The Loyal North Lancashire Regiment) and found that this regiment was in an engagement in this exact area. They were the ones pushed back out of the trenches directly within Alexander's sector — This postcard belonged to this man.

As you can imagine, I was excited and somewhat overwhelmed once I finally had a positive match. After all, this postcard has always been part of my family for over a century, and I now had information that would unlock so many more answers to where it all began. I did this by using further archives, and I discovered that Percy Walsh originally lived in Blackburn, which lies only a 30-minute drive away from where I grew up. He was also 22 years of age, married for one year, and had a young 6-month-old son at the time. I also found out that he was a weaver, and I even discovered his address and the names of his direct family members. All this eventually led me to information on a website organised by Blackburn Central Library, dedicated to the history of Blackburn. As I was searching through this website, I found details of Percy's battalion and its activities — and then there it was — a picture of Percy along with his information that I had previously uncovered. I immediately got in touch with the library to find out more.

My Visit to Blackburn

Along with my brother, I visited Mary Painter and Philip Crompton (local historian) at Blackburn Central Library On 20.08.2022. They showed their strong interest by offering me their help, as they also wanted to learn more about the diary and Percy's life. With the postcard, Alexander's pictures, and copies of his diary extracts in my hands, I explained my family history and how all these items landed in my possession. This was all extremely interesting to them as well as moving, considering the fact that this postcard belonged to a man who lived not far from the library where we were sitting. This visit also granted me access to his regiment's roll of honour and soldiers' photographs, which included a picture of Percy from a newspaper article enquiring about his whereabouts since he was missing. As we know, Percy was already dead when this was published. After this, I went and visited the place where he worked, the Jubilee Mill on Gate Street, built in 1887. Although this site is of no significance to most people, being hidden in a backstreet that you would have no reason to explore, it was extremely fascinating to me. This was where he went almost every day and spent most of his time during the week. It was a place where he would have made friends, formed good and bad memories, and where he spoke and interacted with people on a day-to-day basis. His home sadly doesn't exist anymore, but I did visit a nearby war memorial at St. Jude's Church that has his name marked on it. These visits allowed me to get a firsthand impression of what his life may have been like, and what type of environment he grew up in. As I was thinking of this, I then realised the uncanny similarity between Alexander and Percy — Alexander, from a family that owned a large textile company and employed weavers; and Percy, who also came from a family of Weavers:

Private Percy Walsh (1866, Loyal North-Lancashire Regiment, 1st Battalion) - B. 1893 - D. 22.12.1914 (near Lorgies) – *Remembered at the Le Touret Memorial, Richebourg (Panel 27 and 28).*

MISSING AFTER BATTLE

Private P. Walsh, of the 3rd Battalion *(in reality the 1st)* Loyal North Lancashires, has been posted as missing after an engagement on December 22.

Private Walsh, whose wife resides at 4 Black Diamond Street, was a weaver at Jubilee Mill. He has only been married a little over a year.

When visiting the library, Philip Crompton also provided me with information about Percy's battalion which was directly opposite Alexander at the time. It also included reports on the battalion's perspective during the battle:

22.12.1914 *"The line was held throughout the night. We suffered some casualties from bombs that were thrown from a German trench running obliquely to our right flank. At 3.00 a.m., the Northampton's, less one company, were withdrawn owing to the trenches being overcrowded. Shortly after daybreak, a very strong German attack developed from the direction of La Quinque Rue, and by 10.00 a.m., the line became untenable chiefly owing to the enfilade fire from our right flank which was heavily exposed. After suffering heavy losses and putting up a very stubborn defence, the retirement commenced from the left and about 300 men succeeded in reaching Rue de Boise. The battalion was collected and reformed on the Rue de L'Epinette. The machine-gun detachment, co-operating with the Northampton's, went up in support and a line was held by them roughly on the line where the attack was started on the night before. At about 3 p.m., the Battalion was withdrawn and went into billets at Lacouture."*

"Our losses were: Captain Smart, Captain Graham — Killed; Captain D. (unknown); Lt. Batty-Smith, 2nd-Lt. Gillibrand — Missing; Captain Hay — Slightly Wounded. 408 other ranks were killed, wounded, or missing. 85 Loyal North Lancashire soldiers killed in action — all on 22.12.1914 and commemorated at the Le Touret Memorial".

Finding The Walsh Family

With Percy Walsh identified, I researched his family tree with the help of Philip Crompton. I found that Percy's wife, Alice Walsh, later remarried, but there was little to no information available about what happened to his son. I began to think there was little hope in finding any living relatives, but I soon came across Percy's brother Frank Walsh, who did raise a family. Frank was part of the public family tree of a man named Francis. Frank was listed as his grandfather, and Percy his great-uncle. I immediately got a rush of excitement, as you would expect. I instantly got in touch with Francis for him to confirm these relations, and I explained the story of Percy, the postcard, the life of Alexander, and the events that led to his great uncle's death. This was welcomed with great interest not only by Francis but by numerous cousins of his who also descend from Frank. It was also interesting to hear that they all come from the same Blackburn area where this journey first took me. After liaising with Francis, and with Mary and Philip, who I previously met at the library, I arranged something that I never really imagined doing or even thought possible when I first started this book.

On Saturday the 22nd of October 2022, I drove half an hour from my hometown to Blackburn Central Library to meet the Walsh family. I had been very excited about this day ever since we made the arrangement. As I was driving to Blackburn with Alexander's diary, his photos from the war, and Percy's postcard by my side on the passenger seat, these feelings of excitement and anticipation grew even more — At this point, I was completely immersed in Alexander's diary and story for over two years. I just kept thinking about this entire concept of meeting the people related to this once-unknown soldier, who was always somewhat part of my family history, and whose legacy has been passed down to each generation. Having read and studied the diary so much, you could say it had become my favourite book, and it was like I was about to completely bring it all to life with me being part of the story too. Not only this, but I would finally be able to do it all so close to where I grew up in England. With all the items in my hands, I was greeted by Mary at 10 o'clock in the morning, who led me to the large table where we first met. Here, I was greeted by Philip Crompton and six members of the Walsh family.

There were nine of us sitting around the table with the postcard, war photo albums, relevant pictures, and the diary all spread out on the table for everyone to examine. I explained the story of Alexander and how everything has now ended up in the North-West of England. We shared stories, and I learned that they don't know much about their ancestors on the Walsh side; not even about their grandfather, Frank Walsh, due to his untimely death. But they do recall details such as the fact that he had one leg missing, which could potentially have been lost during the Great War. They took a look at Percy's picture, and it was surprisingly the first ever time that they saw what he looked like. Before this meeting, Philip Crompton conducted some research and traced Percy's life and military activities up until the time of his death. It was found that four of the soldiers pictured in the postcard, based on their cap badges, were from the 'Duke of Cornwall's Light Infantry Regiment'. The day may have been special since they were all visited by their wives and partners.

Percy was on sick leave in England, away from his battalion. He had to make his own way back to France via ship from Southampton, where the mentioned regiment was partly stationed at the time. He thus spent time with the people in the photograph until his embarkment, meaning that one of the two soldiers on the right, not from this regiment, was Percy. I was almost certain that it was the soldier lying on the floor, considering the similarity to the picture of Percy in the newspaper. When a member of the Walsh family looked at this man in the postcard lying on the floor, he immediately saw his own father — the smile, the eyes, the overall facial structure and appearance. He showed me a picture of him, and there really was a similarity. But of course, this story wouldn't be complete without me giving Percy's postcard back to his living relatives, so this is exactly what I did.

The postcard now belongs to the Walsh family again after 108 years. It first started its journey as soon as the camera captured that special moment in Southampton, later making its way into Percy's pocket. It then travelled with him to the war-torn fields and villages around Richebourg in France and was present when Percy was part of the attack against the Germans. Alexander and his men retook what was lost, resulting in the death of Percy who was left in the recaptured trenches. Alexander then spent Christmas near Percy's dead body, when he discovered and kept the postcard. Like so, it made its way to Germany. After 100 years, it was then passed on to me and my immediate family before making its way back to the region in England where Percy originated from. After all this, it is now back in his family and the town he called home. This day truly felt like closure to this story, and it is certainly a memory that I will never forget. Despite the unfortunate situations so long ago which linked Alexander and me to the Walsh family, it is these events that brought us all together in a different lifetime under very different circumstances. I do wonder what Alexander would think of all this if he were still alive, and a part of me likes to believe he was there by my side when our two families came together. This is left to my imagination, but one thing is certain — he would be very proud of me.

Me (left) with the Walsh Family

42

The Welsh Fusilier

Alexander found another postcard, but unfortunately without any information to identify the original owner. But based on the fact that the soldiers in the photo are Welsh Fusiliers, we can assume that the soldier belonged to this regiment.

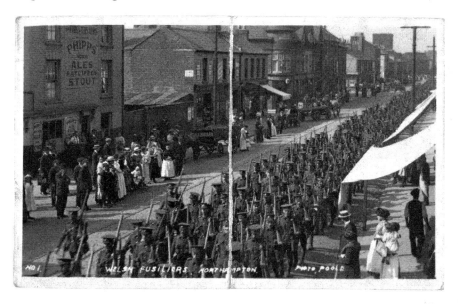

Written by Alexander: "This is the regiment against which we fought – Christmas, 1914."

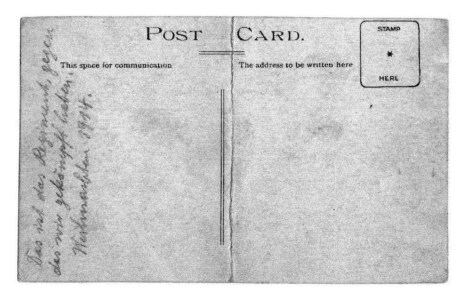

6

1.1.1915   It is terrible up here. Our new position is not an improvement, as we are already encountering groundwater after just half a metre in some of the newly dug trenches. Our old and nice shelters are mostly shot up and flooded. New ones can barely be created in the mud. It keeps raining all the time too, and you can't get dry at all. Everyone is sick — no wonder given these circumstances. I slept on New Year's Eve but was woken up at midnight by terrible firing across the entire line which lasted for a quarter of an hour. This was our New Year's greeting to the English.

4.1.1915   Today, on my birthday, we are back in La Bassée for one day where I found a lot of letters and packages. I don't even know where to put everything anymore. We have another five terrible days behind us. It is just like in Ypres here. They feel sorry for us at home because of the cold, yet we want nothing more than the cold so that the wetness and dreadful mud are finally put to an end. You can protect yourself against the cold. A nice big load of straw is thereby put into the shelters, and you then no longer think about freezing. On the other hand, there is no protection against the groundwater that keeps rising. It is a real shame that we didn't have two fresh regiments behind us at Christmas, as we would have wreaked havoc right up to the sea. It started so nicely, but we couple of 100 jägers couldn't advance any further. We otherwise would have been in danger of being cut off.

6.1.1915   The small spirit stove I received from home is serving me well. There is enough fuel because there is a large fuel factory in La Bassée whose supplies were confiscated.

8.1.1915   I am back in La Bassée again and now have at least a week of rest. The day before yesterday, I got caught on barbed wire in the pitch black and fell headfirst into an old English trench, twisting my right knee. It isn't severe, but I can only limp with difficulty. I am not at all angry about this accident, because now I can dry myself properly and rest and don't have to worry about sudden alarms for a few nights.

The weather is always terrible. It rained through our shelter like a sieve last night. I can now calmly send the thank you cards for the many packages.

9.1.1915   I have just come out of the sickbay where they painted my leg with iodine. I am supposed to rest like this for two days, and then the massaging will begin. It continues to rain all day and night. People who haven't really gotten dry for weeks now are reporting themselves sick every day, and this is supposed to be the praised land of France. Along with this also comes the continual artillery fire. We recently counted 85 rounds in three hours in my small company section alone, and yet this was just a normal day. When the guys get jumpy, you can no longer distinguish between the individual explosions. We then have to endure this without any sort of safety at all. These days of Christmas, which I still haven't lost the chills over, were among the worst I have experienced in the entire war. I still think about it with horror today. We had imagined the Christmas festivities to be completely different. After the death of Lieutenant Müller, Captain von Appell, previously the battalion adjutant, is now our company commander. He is a very capable and energetic man with whom the company is in good hands. However, like with Lieutenant Müller, the comfortable co-existence with him does not exist anymore now.

I haven't really had many duties lately, because Totzek and I took turns supervising the foremost trench during the night; so, one of us guarded from 8:30 in the evening until 2 o'clock in the night, and then the other until about 8 o'clock in the morning. We then swapped the next day — in total just six hours, but even that can be torture if you are constantly standing in water and rain. When you then get into the shelter, you lie on wet straw and cover yourself with wet blankets, and let the rain drip down on you through the roof. We have hung empty cans up on the ceiling in the worst spots. When you then bang into them in the dark, the whole load falls down on you at once. We don't have any vermin because only water fleas at most could thrive here.

12.1.1915   I now sit in my warm room in La Bassée and eat all day. I had roasted wild duck meat and asparagus yesterday. Perhaps it doesn't really go together, but it tasted great. Now you can also get beer here; a large bottle of Löwenbräu, Hofbräu, or Mathäser for 40 Pfennigs. We have now received a lot of replacements again. As a result, the companies are only at the frontline for two days and then always have two days of rest. The sun finally shone again for two days after weeks of rain.

But on *13.1.1915,* the weather is terrible again in return.

15.1.1915   The weather does not want to improve, and the groundwater keeps rising. It was just discussed that a jäger from the 3rd Company drowned in the trenches last night. We had trenches where we put up a sign: "For Swimmers Only." This gives you an idea of how things look here. Maybe I will get a promotion on the Kaiser's birthday. In this regard, you should not compare the conditions here with those in the infantry, as we are an ancient battalion with a large number of officers and reserve officers. On the other hand, this element is of course missing in the many newly established reserve and Landwehr regiments, and they are therefore dependent on rapid promotions. This coercion is only now taking place with us here after a large number of the old officers have either fallen or have been wounded. I would have been a lieutenant a long time ago in the infantry.

20.1.1915 I found many letters with Indian writing at the Heckenhof. The Oriental Seminar in Berlin has determined that it is a rare Gurkha dialect from Nepal, entailing mostly prayers, lists of names, and company orders in which people are exhorted to do their duty. We also handed in many English letters to the battalion. In an unsent letter, an Englishman wrote to his wife that they had a 48-hour rest in Hazebrouck. There, the news had come that the Germans wanted to break through to Calais and they were transported here, to the worst place he had seen since he landed. They were unable to get to the drinking water for two days due to our firing, so they caught and drank the rain from the tent canvases. He hoped that this miserable war would end soon — Well, the war was certainly over for the writer of this letter, as he lay there with a shattered skull with many others in the trench where I looted my goats' fur.

Note: Both armies would regularly collect and read the letters of their enemies to gather potentially useful information. Alexander is fluent in English and French and therefore plays a part in this process.

After I have the Iron Cross, I will also be receiving the 'Falcon Order of Weimar'. One of our oberjägers, who hails from Weimar and knows the leaders of the local warrior association there, wrote to them that we had probably been forgotten since we belong to a different army corps. The governments of Lippe and Oldenburg have already asked the battalion whether any countrymen have the Iron Cross and whether anyone else has been suggested for an award. After all, I couldn't care less because the main thing is that you get home safely from this mess.

The Fallen Gurkha

During the Winter Operations of 1914-1915, the Germans were frequently up against the Indian Corps (Lahore Division) of the British army; namely, the Nepalese Gurkhas. In the same trench where Alexander discovered Percy's postcard, he also found a written report on a fallen Gurkha sergeant, which is written in a rare Gurkha dialect. He additionally found a corresponding list of names as well as a Kukri knife. All these items have been preserved for over a century, still existing to this day for me to show you. My mother has vivid memories of the Kukri knife, a machete originating from the Indian Subcontinent and closely linked to the Nepalese Gurkhas. It was a constant presence throughout her childhood. She says that she used to look at it as a child, and how it seemed so normal for her family to have. However, it would always cause visitors to be amazed when they heard about its fascinating yet rather brutal story. This 17-inch weapon — still sharp and suitable for combat — to this day still has visible impact marks on its edges from being used by the original owner. Just imagine what this would have seen in the fields and trenches around La Bassée. Was this perhaps used against Germans during the battles in December?

The following is what fascinates me the most about Alexander, which will become more evident as his diary progresses — The fact that, no matter what is happening around him, he often comes across as more of a reporter than a soldier, occupying himself with learning about every detail of what and who he is up against. On the next page is the list of names of the fallen Gurkhas found on the deceased sergeant. Having recently been verified by a translator, he somehow managed to decipher these names himself:

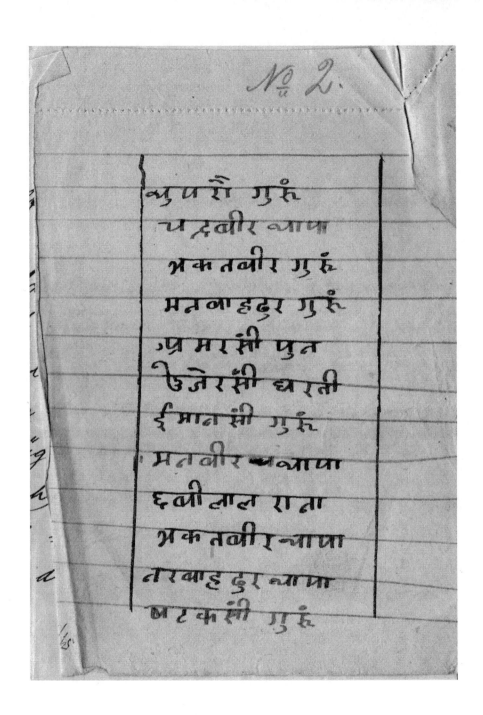

Top to Bottom: "Thuparau Gurung; Chandrasing Thapa; Bhakatbir Gurung; Manbahadur Gurung; Amarsing Pun; Ujarsing Gharti; Imansing Ghurung; Manbir Thapa; Chhabilal Rana; Bhakatbir Thapa; Narbahadur Thapa; Khataksing Gurung."

To be able to fully understand this next handwritten note from the same Gurkha sergeant, I had to do my own research — After reaching out to journalists and research groups in Nepal, the notes were presented to Lt-Col. John P Cross OBE (British WW2 veteran and Gurkha historian fluent in Nepali), and Buddhiman Gurung, a Nepalese cultural expert. After analysing the text, they discovered that it was written in a rare Gurkha dialect that was difficult to decipher. Nevertheless, after 20 minutes, they were more or less able to understand its meaning:

"In his prime, the unfortunate Captain (20) spent his years fighting. All are killed at the hands of the enemy. Although within the regiment, his love remained with Nepal. He died and his spirit went to Kailash. Towards Gandal-Sikkim were Captain Bimsing Bhandari (21); Harke Thapa; Jataraj Dharma Khatri; Commander-Adjutant, Nainasing Khatri; and Sarup Kumar — Partiman Thapa."

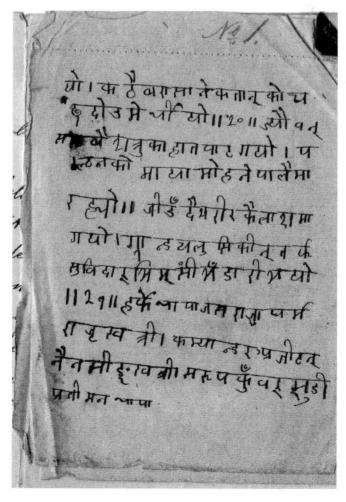

My Visit to The Western Front

In 2024, I set out to do what I had intended for a long time, and I visited the WW1 battlefields and war cemeteries of France & Belgium. This opportunity allowed me to see firsthand where many of the events in this diary took place and enabled me to see other major battlefields, memorials, and the graves of people connected to Alexander. However, with the areas now seeming so ordinary and peaceful, and with the people here so casually getting on with their daily lives, it is even more difficult to comprehend that all this that you have read so far actually happened here around La Bassée — The main roads leading to Festubert and Richebourg are busy with cars, the farmers work the surrounding fields, and residential houses now stand around and over the spots where the Heckenhof position and battle trenches once would have been. The only obvious evidence of the war here is the many military cemeteries scattered across the region. In between the areas of the recent fighting around the Heckenhof now lie the Commonwealth Le Touret and Indian Neuve Chapelle memorials. I visited these and also found Percy Walsh among the many thousand mentioned names.

Below and Right: *At the Le Touret War Memorial – visiting Percy Walsh*

Right: *The Neuve Chapelle Indian Memorial*

7

22.1.1915   We constantly receive loads of parcels with loving gifts. We have already written home that they shouldn't send us so much anymore.

24.1.1915   The division has just asked me whether I was 'Landwehr I or II'. So now things seem to be getting serious regarding the promotion.

26.1.1915   A major English attack is expected tomorrow on the Kaiser's birthday — a proper reception is ensured. I am still not fit for service again. The doctor is said to have told my captain that it could take another 14 days. This is fine by me. Large troop transports just came through here. It has been quiet here lately, meaning what you call quiet on the Front. The shooting never really stops.

27.1.1915   I have been sent smoked eel from home. I am using this to make myself a gourmet breakfast for the Kaiser's birthday today. We have a little better weather now because it has gotten slightly colder and, as unbelievable as it sounds, it hasn't rained for eight days. You don't get any leave here. You at most get a few days of recovery time in the recreation home in Don near Lille.

The wheat is so rare at home, yet we are lying in the trenches on unthreshed wheat straw and are shooting the enemy's straw stacks on fire — there go thousands of Mark lost. But in the beginning, just how many shot-dead cows and pigs were lying around that no one cared about?

30.1.1915   A new vice sergeant, Assessor Rosenthal, joined us several days ago. He is namely a baptised Jew and he plays the piano beautifully, including many of the classical stuff that we play at home. Ever since the war volunteer, Kirpeit, who was also a musician, fell at the 'Jägerhof' at the end of October, I finally heard some nice playing again today. This was a special treat. We are now organising musical evenings within the closest circle. Hopefully, the war will end soon. We are thoroughly fed up with it.

1.2.1915   Yesterday, I had my sergeant secretly ask the captain whether it would be acceptable to be transferred to the infantry because there was apparently no possibility of progression in the battalion. To this, the captain told him that I had already been put forward and that the confirmation from the Kaiser could arrive any day. Nothing else of importance has happened here, just the English have become very nervous. Their planes circle above us every day and the artillery fire doesn't stop anymore. All around, the sounds of infantry fire continue all night. On the morning of the Kaiser's birthday, there was a religious field service in the goods shed of the train station because the church was completely shot up. Then there was a promenade concert.

If I have forgotten to thank someone for a parcel, the excuse for this is due to our exciting lives. You get old and jittery very quickly in war. The nerves no longer work as well as they did at the start.

5.2.1915   Today was a wonderful sunny day. Spring apparently arrives here in this lousy country too.

6.2.1915   There was just a so-called bad atmosphere here in La Bassée, as the English bombarded the town with heavy artillery. The shells struck all around my house, and three from the heaviest calibre struck a house barely 50 metres from me. It looked wonderful how the clouds of smoke and the timbers rose 50 metres into the air.

9.2.1915   The weather here is different every day. It is sometimes the most beautiful spring weather, and immediately afterwards when the wind comes from the sea, which is usually the case, it rains and storms like mad. When you hear people say they are disappointed in France, it is because the inhabitants are just as filthy as the country. Water pipes and sewage systems probably only exist in the largest cities. It is a hundred times nicer at home.

During the bombardment here in La Bassée on the 6th of February, a shell struck the stable of our machine-gun company and killed ten horses — a very great loss for us. In our officers' mess, where someone's birthday was being celebrated, an explosion cleared the entire coffee table. But only one officer was injured in the head by a splinter of glass. On the street in question, all the remaining windowpanes were shattered due to the air pressure, which is particularly painful because there is no replacement for them.

Totzek has now finally become a lieutenant on the Kaiser's birthday.

I have now arranged a room all for myself with an oven, bed, cupboard, chest, mirror, wall clock, pictures, and a large fan palm. On the wall hang English rifles, bayonets, ammunition belts, pistols, and so forth. It is very cosy. We will hopefully stay here for a while longer.

11.2.1915   I became a lieutenant last night. The assistant doctor was just with me, and he was very much in favour of me going to a real hospital for a few weeks instead of sitting here, where there is no real care. It isn't anything serious with the knee, but it isn't enough for the service in the trenches and for running over the shell-torn roads and fields. I am thus going to the sick-collection point in Don, either tomorrow or the day after, and will most likely end up in Douai. But if it is somehow possible, I will try to get to Lille where Line is. I will probably stay in the hospital for two to three weeks.

13.2.1915   I took the train from La Bassée to Don yesterday, where I spent the night and was invited to dinner and lunch with the chief medical officer and a dozen other doctors and pharmacists. I was examined this morning. The outcome is: "Lieutenant Pfeifer suffers from a strain in the collateral ligaments of his right knee combined with muscular atrophy (i.e. weakening of the muscles due to lack of movement). In order to restore fitness for field service, a mechanotherapy massage and bath treatment lasting several weeks is necessary".

I travelled further towards Douai today, where I am staying overnight in the field hospital.

14.2.1915 I slept in a made bed again for the first time since my advance into the field, and I have spoken to German nurses. Since there are no suitable apparatuses here, I am going further to Valenciennes today, where I will most likely be staying. I will of course try to get to Germany.

I just had a look at Douai and had a morning drink.

15.2.1915 I am in the Valenciennes stage hospital, which is located in a huge, brand-new school and is immaculately furnished. I am living with a deputy officer in a nice room with central heating, an electric light, and a paradise bed — service by Catholic nurses — very good food. Last night I had sirloin beef steak; and this morning, coffee, bread, and butter; bouillon at 10 o'clock; at 12 o'clock, soup, German beef steak, fried potatoes, cabbage, compote, and one bottle of red wine; at 2 o'clock, coffee. All is very good and plentiful. You can therefore endure it here, but it is just extremely boring. After months of agitation, this peace, order, and cleanliness seem very eerie, and you can't sleep because the usual shooting is missing. You generally feel like you are in another world here — no destroyed houses anymore — elegantly dressed, pretty French women on the street — finally the opportunity to speak to German girls again. Only then do you realise how terribly feral you have become.

My knee was photographed with X-rays this morning. The result will determine whether I will stay here or will be moved even further back. I will be sending 500 Mark home today, and I am keeping 150 Mark here since I need to buy various things such as epaulettes and so forth. I will also receive my contribution funds of 70 Mark in the next few days. I now receive a 310-Mark salary. Of course, I get everything for free here. I will be taking a look at the town this afternoon, assuming that I can get out of the hospital.

16.2.1915 I took a look at Valenciennes yesterday afternoon. It is a large and dirty industrial town. The only nice things are the old town hall and one church. You cannot see any traces of the war here. All the shops are open, and the electric tram is running. But all the women, at least the better ones, go dressed in black, and many are deeply veiled. I drank coffee in a pastry shop, a celebratory event for me. The other knee was also X-rayed as a checkup this morning. I then bathed in a proper bath, which was a very special treat.

The weather is wonderful today. I will be going for another walk in the afternoon. No one even asks whether it is allowed, of course, because the answer is definitely "No". I want to buy apples and oranges in a delicatessen that I discovered yesterday. Tomorrow, it will be decided whether I will stay here or go to Germany, which I don't think I will though, because people have been very strict about it lately.

17.2.1915   There was a lot of life here today. The capture of the 50,000 Russians was celebrated with a market concert and bell ringing. The faces of the French were worth seeing when many 100 soldiers started singing 'Hail to Thee in The Victor's Crown' and 'We Want to Beat France Victoriously'. I then had a morning pint of German pilsner — one half for 40 Centimes.

The doctors seemingly still haven't figured out what is actually wrong with my knee. The three of them stand around it and shake their heads. I can still walk quite well though, as I go for walks in the town every day. I just can't fully straighten my leg or bend it completely, and it twinges inside with every movement. The doctor said today that he wanted to observe me for a few more days. He seems to believe a nerve is damaged.

19.2.1915   I am feeling very good — no wonder considering the flawless food. We get one bottle of red or white wine every lunchtime. I recently visited the hospital inspector, and the outcome was: 2 bottles of red wine, 1 bottle of white wine, and 1 bottle of sparkling wine. You learn to rob in the war. They are all pleasant people here. All the doctors and officials are people from Bavaria or Württemberg. There are now three of us in my room — a deputy officer from Schleswig with the Iron Cross 1st Class, a reserve lieutenant from Baden, and me from Thuringia. I am being massaged daily.

22.2.1915   The doctors have unfortunately put me in bed for a couple of days. Rest and fomentation treatment is now to be attempted.

24.2.1915   There was a big surprise this morning. The door opened and my brother Friedrich and my sister Line came in. We talked all morning and then had lunch in my room.

26-27.2.1915   The first post in 14 days has arrived along with a whole lot of letters and parcels. People seem to have a strange understanding of our lives at home, but this is only because of these cursed war reporters who write such lovely articles without ever having been on the Front. In any case, I have never seen one during the entire war and neither have any of the gentlemen I asked. At home, you get upset because you have to restrict yourself slightly and eat potato bread. I grant these people just one single day in our water trenches. They would be forever healed.

Here in the hospital, I was once again able to notice that those who were actually under fire on the Front, are usually very quiet and not very talkative. On the other hand, the ones who behave dangerously and tell the biggest cock-and-bull stories are the automobile guys, postal workers, the luggage guys and so forth. There are many characters like that here. When you see guys like this walking around proudly with the Iron Cross, you don't want to wear it anymore.

Lieutenant Caroli is travelling to Germany with the field-hospital train today. I am now all alone in my section. Next door lies only a chief of the communication zone, who fell off his horse and roughly has the same as me.

4.3.1915   I have been able to go out again since yesterday.

9.3.1915   Everything has been overcrowded here in the last few days. A lot of wounded arrived here following the assault on the Loretto Heights. There was much to tell, as I partook in my first battle on the same height at the beginning of October. In the small valley where we made the unfortunate attack, jägers are said to still be lying unburied because no one could get to them. I would be there too now if I hadn't been so lucky back then. There are conditions on the Front that you cannot even imagine at home. The pioneer lying next door to me also attacked the Heckenhof at Christmas. As I have now found out, the mine that we blew up had an explosive weight of four quintals. If you consider that just a single small stick of dynamite in the Loitscher Quarry is heard in Weida when it explodes, you can get an idea of how the earth shook when four quintals exploded barely 200 metres away from us.

The doctor was just here again. I am supposed to do a lot of walking so that my knee becomes flexible again. I don't know how much longer I will stay here. I shudder when I think about La Bassée; not because of the shooting, as this leaves me completely cold, but because of the miserable, filthy life and the hour-long night watches in mud and water.

13.3.1915   My poor battalion was almost fully annihilated on the 10th of March. As a reward for withstanding the water trenches near Richebourg, we were moved slightly more east to dryer trenches with very nice shelters on the 3rd of March. Three days later, the English apparently opened up horrifying fire on the position from 64 artillery pieces. Except for a few people, the 1st and 3rd Companies were shattered and buried by the heavy shells. Two English and one Indian regiment then broke through and occupied the village of Neuve Chapelle, approximately 800 metres behind them. The 2nd and 3rd Companies moved forward with a couple of machine guns and attacked despairingly, but even they suffered very heavy losses from the artillery fire. Pioneers, Bavarians, and whatever else was in the surrounding places came to help, and they managed to push the English back somewhat.

800 to 1000 Englishmen supposedly lie dead just in front of the village alone. We are said to have only had four guns on our side, which soon fired their few shells and only received new ammunition after a long time. So far, I know that one officer of ours is dead and that five are wounded. I couldn't find anything out about the many others. Perhaps they have been captured or lie buried in the trenches. Three-quarters of the battalion are probably dead. A great number of wounded jägers have arrived here and they are telling horror stories, but of course, they don't know anything about the final outcome. It is a pity. As if we haven't had enough losses already.

It has gotten better with my knee. The tendon only starts to hurt again when I walk for a long time. I am otherwise fine, and we are having as much fun as we can in this dirty place. My knee injury probably saved my life, because out of my company of 200, only 7 men are said to be alive.

19.3.1915   Yesterday, I told the medical officer that I wanted to go back to the battalion since we had almost no officers. But he said I should stay here only for a few more days. It isn't easy to come away from the Front, but it is seemingly even harder to go back again.

A new division is being assembled here. The people are equipped with Russian rifles.

On *21.3.1915*, I received the following letter from my Company Sergeant, Dinter:

"Things have been rough here in the last few days. On the 6th of March, we advanced to a new position in Halpegarbe. The 1st and 3rd Companies moved into position on the evening of the 9th. Ridiculous artillery fire began the next morning. One shell after the other struck our position so that there was soon no cover left. They showered the premises behind the trench with shells and shrapnel so that reinforcements could only be brought forward with heavy casualties. The English then assaulted in dense columns, broke into the trench of the 3rd Company, and then attacked the 1st from the rear. The little remnant that was left was taken prisoner. It was terrible. In the four days, the 1st Company lost 1 officer (Ziegler), 2 vice sergeants, 8 oberjägers, 13 lance corporals, and 110 jägers. You can get a general idea from this. Lieutenant von Baumbach fell; Lieutenant Wachsmuth and Küsten are heavily wounded; and Prince Solms and Swart are lightly wounded".

The Battle of Neuve Chapelle

While Alexander was recovering from his knee injury, his battalion was involved in what is known as 'The Battle of Neuve Chapelle', which lasted from the 10th to 13th of March 1915. It is today marked as a significant chapter of the war, having been the first planned British offensive. The result of this was a breakthrough in the German lines which resulted in the capture of the village of Neuve Chapelle. The British tried to take advantage of this to take Aubers Ridge further east, and potentially Lille, but this failed to materialise due to the lack of communication and resources. Casualty estimates for the British are said to be around 12,500, and 10,000 for the Germans. This offensive came as a surprise to the Germans, who were ill-prepared and outgunned. With Alexander not there as a witness, he has to rely only on the information from others to tell us what happened. However, subsequent post-battle reports help give us a greater insight into both perspectives.

The British Lincolnshire Regiment (2nd Battalion) was involved during the first infantry attack, following the long bombardment of the German positions. Lt-Col. George McAndrew, commanding the regiment, was unfortunately killed. His regiment's war diary describes this like so:

"At 8:05 a.m., the guns lifted their sights and infantry attacked. The Colonel was with the assaulting companies. The battalion all rose simultaneously and rushed the first trench after cutting the barbed wire in an incredibly short time, losing only about 20 men. The blocking parties then proceeded down the trenches, chasing all before with their grenades. Captain Peake did good work. He was soon afterwards shot in the head... Lt-Col. GB McAndrew was killed between the first and second German trenches. His right leg was blown to pieces by one of our own shells. He died asking after his regiment, without any complaint of the pain he was suffering".

Despite being startled by the British assault and their lines having been infiltrated in many parts, the Germans did not give up as easily as many would have expected. Even though the odds were against them, and the casualties were high, Alexander's battalion was able to hold off the British for as long as possible, as is described in the battalion diary:

"The 1st Company, still half deafened from the ear-tearing sound of the bursting shells, rushes to the rubble of the sandbag wall and, together with the machine gun that remained intact, places the storming Englishmen under energetic fire — The attacker is taken aback when the resistance, which was no longer expected, flares up. Their dense ranks thin out due to the dead and wounded. They stagger — they flee back to their starting position with heavy losses".

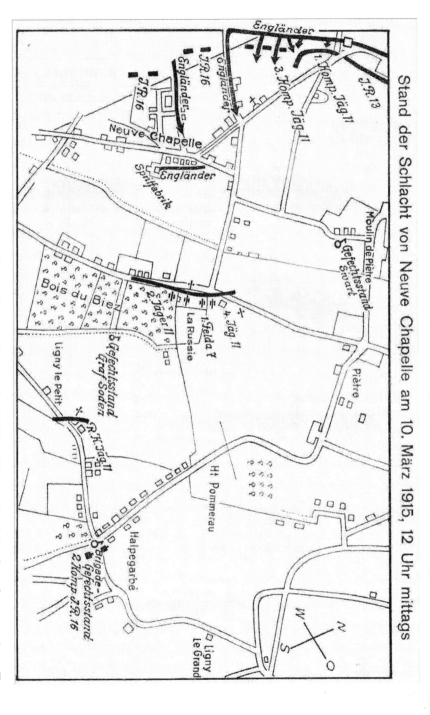

' The situation during the Battle of Neuve Chapelle on 10. March 1915 at 12 o' clock in the afternoon' – From the perspective of Alexander' s 11th Jäger Battalion - English attacking from the left.'

The Twisted Right Knee

Have you ever heard of the butterfly effect? This is something that I sometimes think about, which is a phenomenon whereby a split-second decision or change of events can significantly affect the future, often completely altering its course. This diary has many of those instances. As Alexander said following the Battle of Neuve Chapelle, which almost completely reduced his company from 200 down to 7 men, his knee injury very likely did save his life. He could very easily have decided not to take the risk of sneaking into the English trench, and would instead have spent the remainder of the time in position with his company. Also, think back to the time when Captain Clasen was shot in the abdomen directly next to Alexander, as mentioned on 27.12.1914. The English soldier could easily have aimed for Alexander first, but something made him choose otherwise.

I would like you to imagine what could very possibly have happened if Alexander had not decided to go into the English trench on that day, as well as the various events leading up to this that led to the 'lucky' fall. Considering his rank, the overall events detailed in the diary, and his future life after the war, it is clear that the fates of many individuals on both sides would have been heavily altered — People would be living today who we have never heard of — those people would influence the lives of others and further continue this butterfly effect — me and my family would not exist — everyone that I have ever come into contact with would have lived a different version of that day. With these considerations, it becomes clear that Alexander's diary would not exist, as well as my opportunity to present all this to you. Now reflect while thinking about yourself. What alternate life would you be leading right now if you were not spending your time reading this book?

Whatever it is that has come to your mind, we can both agree that your day would be different if the English soldier had not aimed for Captain Clasen, or if Alexander had not been so lucky fighting against Percy and his battalion; and especially if Alexander had not twisted his right knee.

23.3.1915   It finally seems to be spring because the sun shone for two days. A plane threw three bombs on the town yesterday morning, but only one exploded. Other than a few broken windows, no further damage was caused. The communication-zone guys here are tremendously proud that they too have heard it bang for once. They will be writing home some lovely horror stories. I dread every letter that I have to write. There is enough time for it, but you don't feel like doing anything. You can't sleep either because you are always in a state of eternal restlessness. Others feel the same way. I felt more comfortable on the Front in the trench compared to here, where you feel so useless.

26.3.1915   I have more than enough money here, although I do spend a lot since everything is very expensive: eggs — 15 Centimes; oranges — 20 Centimes; 1 half of German pilsner — 40 Centimes; 1 kilogram of apples — 1.60 Francs. Methylated spirits are no longer available in the entire town. As I have heard, Totzek is lightly wounded. He got a bullet graze on his large gob which the entire battalion is happy about. I have never come across a person as unpleasant and unpopular as he is, and yet he is a Candidate of Theology. I will be going back to the Front in the next few days. I will travel via Lille because I first have to find out where the battalion is now. I will visit Line given the opportunity.

30.3.1915   I have been dismissed from the hospital as fit for service.

31.3.1915   I am currently sitting having lunch with Line in the Hotel Royal in Lille. I will be continuing to the battalion tomorrow. It looks bad in places in Lille. Entire rows of houses are shot apart, especially at the train station. It is otherwise extremely busy.
     We were in Roubaix in the afternoon.

Line Pfeifer (Alexander's sister) – Lille, 1915

Eglise St. Martin, Roubaix.

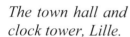

The town hall and clock tower, Lille.

1.4.1915   I drove south to Phalempin via Seclin, towards the general command of the 7th Army Corps, where I learned that my battalion lies in position south of the La Bassée-Béthune canal; and that the resting position is at the towns of Billy and Berclau, southeast of La Bassée. Since there was no connection from here to there, I drove back to Lille where I stayed the night.

2.4.1915   I am travelling to Don by train today, where I will order the car over the telephone. It has been wonderful spring weather here for a few days. It must be very nice in the trenches now if there isn't too much shooting.

We are said to have received replacements of over 800 men again.

8

3.4.1915   I am now back on the Front again and I am very comfortable with it. The hanging around behind the Front is not to my taste. So yesterday, I took the train from Lille to Bauvin-Provin via Don, where I happened to meet a replacement transport (130 jägers). There were also five new lieutenants who had only joined as volunteers a few months ago. After a few months on the Front, they completed a five-week training course in Germany and then immediately became officers. So now things are going faster than with us poor frontline pigs at the beginning. In general, the battalion is currently put together strangely, as we are now assigned 2 transport officers, 1 Uhlan *(light cavalry)* officer, and 1 artillery officer.

I have come to the 3rd Company, namely to my old company commander, Captain Beutin, under whom I was involved in Souchez, Loretto, Les-Trois-Maisons and so on; and who is healed from being badly shot in the arm. Billy is a larger village and isn't shot apart. I have a very pretty room for myself, but of course, only pretty in terms of the Front. Our position is south of the canal near the village of Auchy. The trenches are supposedly dry, two metres deep, and therefore much better than at Richebourg. French Landwehr lies 40 to 120 metres opposite us. In any case, everyone is very pleased with this position and accommodation. When the company is at rest, we eat here together with the staff in the casino, a large villa. From 8 o'clock in the morning we have coffee, bread rolls, filled pancakes and cold sliced meat; lunch from 12 to 1 o'clock, and warm dinner at half 6 in the evening. Munich beer is now available in quantities.

7.4.1915   I spent the Easter holidays in the trench. We were summoned by telephone on Saturday afternoon. I had my wagon harnessed at 7 o'clock in the evening, and I drove for one hour across Douvrin and Haisnes to the village of Auchy. You need to wait until it is dark in Haisnes, otherwise you will be immediately shot at by the artillery. Inside a house in the middle of the fully destroyed Auchy begins the communication trench, which is two metres deep and leads 45 minutes to the Front.

The weather, which was so beautiful early on, continued to deteriorate and there was the most beautiful rain in the evening and throughout the night. My new raincoat made from our waterproof canvas fabric has proven itself very well. I put waterproof underpants over my trousers, and even though I stood in the pouring rain for hours over the two days and was covered in mud from head to toe, nothing got through. On the other hand, some of the new raincoats that the officers had brought with them were already torn on the first night. Like so, I walked in the dark for three-quarters of an hour past Castle Les Briques, and through the railway embankment under the tracks to the Front, where I was greeted very kindly by Beutin. He apparently required me especially for his company because I have a lot more experience than the young rascals. The position and the routine of duties were briefly explained, and I then had the oversight from 9 until 12 o'clock at night. The leader of the 2nd platoon had their turn from 12 until 3 o'clock; the one from the 3rd, 3 until 6 o'clock, me again from 6 until 9 o'clock, and so forth; so, six hours of rest between every three-hour watch. Everything is very precisely regulated and has become much stricter ever since the misfortune at Neuve Chapelle. You always need to be in the trench during the watch. The position is simply ideal compared to our previous one — two metres deep in clay soil — no groundwater because we are on a slight elevation and the many coal mines nearby seem to be drawing in all the groundwater.

The trenches are flawlessly constructed. Every rifleman has a small niche of his own with steps leading up to it. Everything is reinforced with sandbags, and everyone stands behind a defensive shield of steel. Most people have tent canvases stretched over them so that they stand dry. Small boxes for bullet cartridges are built into the niche walls, and there are also waterproof boxes with hand grenades scattered throughout the trench. There are even special depots for trenchwork tools, ammunition and so on. Nice and deep shelters are plentiful. As a platoon leader, I have one for me and my attendant. Inside are two sleeping spots on top of each other like in a ship's cabin. I even have a mattress. Of course, there is a table, wicker chair, oven, wall shelf, coat hangers, and pictures. To heat, we use hard coal which we can conveniently get from the nearest mine. Opposite us lies the French Landwehr. Only single shots are fired during the day, whereas it gets somewhat livelier at night. We are also graced with a few shells from time to time, but they haven't caused any damage so far.

The weather was nice all day and night on the first day of the holidays, but it has been raining heavily since the morning of the second day. It is now rather filthy in the trenches as a result. We should have been replaced at 9 o'clock in the evening, but it was 1 o'clock in the night when the first replacement arrived. I then led the way through the communication trench all alone and didn't get lost despite the many diversions. The mud reached high above the ankles, but this was an outright stroll compared to the past. The trench at Richebourg would have been impassable after such tremendous rain. The carriage I had ordered over the phone was waiting for me in Auchy, and I arrived in Billy at half past 2 in the morning where I quickly made a ration (sausage with kraut) on the spirit stove. I was suddenly woken up during the deepest sleep at half past 5 in the morning — highest alert. I thus got out of bed, got dressed, packed my suitcase and loaded the wagon. Just when I was finished, it was said that everyone could lie back down because it was just a practice alarm for the entire division. I then slept the whole day in return.

There was a strong storm with rain last night. Things will look lovely in the trenches tonight. I had some duties today — rifle inspection and instructing the oberjägers. I am going back to the Front for a couple of days again this evening. Captain Beutin is now the commander of the entire combat sector, and I am the company commander during this time. This means that I no longer have to do guard duty, but there is a lot of written and telephone work.

We eat together in peace in the mess hall here, which is set up inside the manor. The price is surprisingly cheap for the good food and drink; only 30 to 40 Mark a month. Extra drinks are of course charged separately. Food and drink are also delivered forward from the mess to the trench. Our electricians have laid wires throughout the entire place so that we have electric lights everywhere. A cable has also just been laid towards the front so that we will have electricity in the shelters in the near future too. We have built shelters at the front that are four metres underground. I feel significantly more comfortable again since being back here. It is a completely different life here than in the boring hospital.

10.4.1915   I am back in the trench again for six days. We have just had a thrilling morning behind us. I had just written the required 5 o'clock report and was lying down again, when the ground suddenly started to shake like an earthquake. A dull bang then sounded, which was followed immediately by wild rifle, machine-gun and artillery fire. I went out like greased lightning, alarmed everyone and fired frantically out into the darkness. But we stopped firing very soon since no attack followed. This time, for once, our artillery also worked promptly. A patrol sent out to the right reported that the French had blown up a third part of a company from Infantry-Regiment 16 from underground, and that everyone was buried and probably dead. An attack did not follow. They lie only 40 metres opposite each other over there. The distance for underground mining is in fact very large here by us, but we are still busy pushing forward two mine tunnels.

I am doing well. I have already fully gotten used to the frontline operations again.

11.4.1915   We are now sitting dry and warm. The immaculate trenches are being swept with a broom, which would have been simply ridiculous at Richebourg. We are now expanding our position into a kind of fortress with a lot of barbed wire. I am going to the second line tonight, into the reserve trench about 50 metres behind the battle trench. I am then in Billy for two days to rest. We constantly have losses, even in our safe and relatively quiet position. Yesterday alone, we had two wounded, and one dead who fell over just when I got there. It has already been banging up high all morning — enemy planes are shot at with defensive guns. But this is now already such a familiar sight that you hardly look anymore.

12.4.1915   Yesterday, we relocated to the reserve position 30 to 100 metres to the back for two days. Shelters come in a wide variety of types, depending on the taste and skill of the builders — rather comfortable log cabins underground, or even incredible robbers' dens. For decoration, everything that was of any use was brought in from the neighbouring villages during the night. I even have a big regulator clock in my current villa.

The French were very nervous tonight. They uselessly shot an incredible amount of ammunition and also pelted our foremost position with a load of mortar shells, the effect of which was in direct contrast to the great noise they made. It was as if the French had sensed what was about to happen to them — I had just phoned the usual morning report to Les Briques at half past 4 and had just laid down again when suddenly, there was a terrible tremor with a thunderous crash — The 16th to our right took revenge and blew up part of the French position. The French responded with a wild shootout with rifles, machine guns, artillery and mortars. They probably thought we wanted to attack.

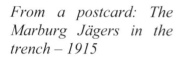

From a postcard: The Marburg Jägers in the trench – 1915

Tonight, and this morning, I have been walking around in the maze of trenches for hours to orientate myself and to be able to find every way during the night too, which isn't that easy. I also sounded the alarm tonight as a test so that every man knows where his place is, even at night. Day and night shifts otherwise involve heavy entrenching, building shelters, widening paths and much more. We have a lot to do. All the fields in Billy have been cultivated. There are signs on each field stating what has been sown. At Billy, for example, it says everywhere: "Spring wheat sown on 28.3.1915 by the M.G.C, Jäger 11." All the small fields have disappeared, and everything has been ploughed together into large plains. This will cause a lot of trouble for the farmers later when they can no longer find their boundaries.

One of my jägers has found several quintals of copper and brass in the neighbouring mine, which are now being picked up. Like so, everything that can somehow be used is taken away. Since our enemies have cut off our supply, we have to take what we need wherever we find it.

14.4.1915   I got back from the trench at 11:30 last night. In the past six days, I haven't been able to take my shoes off my feet or wash myself for one moment, because water has to be fetched half an hour from Les Briques through the narrow trenches, and can thus only be used for cooking and drinking. It therefore took an hour and a half to go to the toilet this morning — C'est La Guèrre! *(This is war!)*.

Of the men from the 3rd Company, who were captured at Neuve Chapelle, 40 men have already written that they are doing well, but just have to endure the 'Kohldampf Schieben'. This is the soldiers' term for starving. The English censor allowed this expression through because he couldn't explain it and probably thought it was some kind of game. If the guys had written the word 'Starving', the letter would certainly have been suppressed. You just have to know how to help yourself.

Note: Literally translated as 'to push coal steam', 'Kohldampf Schieben' is still used today in Germany to express hunger, with most not knowing its origin.

There are now holidays in turn; not to Germany, but only for a few days to some rest home for which various castles have been set up behind the Front.

15.4.1915   I am going to the Front for four days again tonight, and then I have another four days of rest. In the afternoon in Billy, there was a very interesting practical demonstration of throwing hand grenades. There was soon a lot of fuss when we reached the front trench in the evening. Knocking and scraping could clearly be heard under my shelter and the one next door, so we had to assume we were being tunnel-mined from below. Everyone lay on their stomachs, one ear pressed to the ground, listening. It was quiet again from midnight and I slept quite well, although the thought of being blown up at any moment is quite embarrassing. The whole matter was cleared up later though — shelters were being built about 20 metres behind us in the 2nd position, and it sounded as if the knocking was directly below us. Nevertheless, everything must now be quiet for 15 minutes every two hours each night. Everyone then lies on their stomach and listens, although we haven't heard anything again so far.

We are pushing two mine tunnels forward. I crept into one yesterday over by the 16th Regiment, which is over 30 metres long. An enemy drilling machine could seemingly be heard, but it was nothing. Crawling in such a dark tunnel, which is only one metre high, is a big challenge, but you have to experience everything. In general, things are all rather peaceful here apart from the tunnel mining. We hardly have to suffer from artillery fire at all. Just as I had moved into my new shelter, which is three metres underground, I received the message yesterday that I would have to take over the leadership of the 2nd Company until further notice, because Prince Lippe was on leave due to illness. I am now in the second line today and tomorrow, then four days in front, and then four days of rest in Billy.

We now have wonderful weather and are sitting in the sun all day. Food and drink are plentiful, the shelters are luxurious, and the enemy is sensible. The war can therefore be endured. We haven't had it this good in a long time.

An unknown soldier: *'In the trench near Auchy'.*

23.4.1915   I arrived in Billy for four days after eight days in the trenches.

27.4.1915   It is now like paradise here compared to the winter months. Everything is already green, the fruit trees are blooming, and we usually sit out in the open for coffee. It is ten times nicer here than behind the Frontlines. My four days of rest are over today, and we are going to the Front again for four days.

2.5.1915   I just fortunately survived another four days in the trench. I now have two days of rest in Billy. We get the latest newspapers much sooner from Lille than from home. You have little desire to read books, as there is no peace and quiet for it. It is nicest when you can sit outside in the trench under the sun and doze off for hours. This is the best for the nerves. There is no longer a mine hazard in our section. We have been paying close attention lately and haven't heard anything. But to the right, over by Infantry-Regiment 16, there is solid mining on both sides.

I recently chose a safe spot where you can get a good view of the area. About one kilometre to our right, you can see a large number of piles of bricks, each the size of our barn at home, which were heavily fought over in January-February. Most of it is now in our possession. As I happen to be looking over there while watching the shrapnel shells burst, a huge black cloud suddenly rises 200 metres vertically into the air, the earth shakes like an earthquake, a dull crash, and then millions of bricks explode into the sky — our miners had blown up an enemy brick pile. Whatever was not already torn apart or buried by the explosion over by the English lying there, was struck dead by the falling bricks. This is already no longer a war. Whoever concocts the greatest vulgarities is at an advantage. In Ypres, we also only made progress by using poisonous gases. We will surely do this more often from now on.

A view towards the enemy position.

Another view towards the English lines before the explosion – The long stack of bricks is to the right.

The French here have become much more nervous in the last few days and are now firing a lot of artillery, especially at the mines and villages behind us. The large village of Auchy is nothing but a heap of rubble. They fired at least 50 shells at a few houses directly behind us yesterday, where they probably thought we had guns. This was a highly interesting spectacle, but I wouldn't like to have been there. To the left of us, probably in the Loretto Heights, we have been hearing continuous artillery fire for a few days now. Nothing of significance has happened here. We got intoxicated with alcohol on the 1st of May to celebrate the day.

9

Left: 'In the trenches at Auchy near La Bassée – In the box in the wall is a hand grenade – May 1915'.

'In the trenches at Auchy – May 1915'.

Left: 'A part of a trench with high sandbag walls in the background – May 1915 at Auchy'.

9.5.1915   Today is the most beautiful Sunday weather, and all hell is breaking loose here. You could already tell that something was going on by the number of enemy planes in the last few days. At half past 4 this morning, I had just telephoned the first-morning report when I suddenly heard the familiar aeroplane 'Brum', and immediately afterwards a heavy shootout broke out in our area — I whiz out of the shelter and I see a very low French plane coming towards us, 300 to 400 metres at most from over there, which is greeted by mad firing from our 1st, 2nd, and Bicycle Companies. Something was seemingly broken on the altitude control because the machine didn't come up. It flies away over us despite the terrible hail of bullets, and we are already pulling long faces. It then suddenly turns around and comes back the same way, gliding. The engine or the propeller is seemingly hit — double rapid fire from us, of course.

We already think it is going to fall into our trench, but it still hovers until just before the enemy trench whereby we continue to fire at it. It then suddenly starts to burn, and a large brown cloud rises — the petrol has exploded. Only the iron frame was left after a few minutes, resulting in our tremendous joy and cheers of "Hurrah!". The occupants burned if they hadn't already been shot. It was the first time that I saw an aeroplane being shot down, although I have seen the shooting at aeroplanes many thousands of times. We were of course extremely proud. But now the French, after they had recovered from their shock, began to fire heavily and put various shells and shrapnel into our trench. Our artillery then started to fire in return.

I had just viewed the aeroplane frame from a pushed-forward sap *(a short trench dug ahead into no man's land)* and was on the way back to my shelter when we heard the recognisable whooshing sound in the sky — "Aha. Our Heavies!" we think — two sudden thundering strikes, barely 15 metres away from us. Black smoke rises up and fragments wail through the air. The officer candidate standing next to me receives a piece of igniter on his leg. The fragment was luckily weakened though, and bounced off the wrap puttees. As a joke, I say to this newcomer that he should keep this splinter as a souvenir, which he cluelessly does. But as soon as he touches it, he pulls his hand back from the red-hot iron with a scream and I laugh out loud. Of course, I immediately got on the phone and insulted our artillery since they were the sinners. No further damage had fortunately been done.

In response to the shock, we want to have a few cups of cocoa in our shelter when suddenly, at 6 o'clock sharp, a great cannonade starts to our right — the guns boom continuously — the individual explosions can no longer be distinguished. The main shooting is far away from us in the north, but the 16th is also being lit up badly. It looks wonderful how it tremors over there by the heap of bricks. There are round clouds of shrapnel hanging everywhere, and thick black and yellow-green clouds rise from the shells down on the ground. Rifles and machine guns fire at the same time — three aircraft buzz in the air. It was a hell of a racket. But things were about to get better because suddenly we too were under fire. One by one, the shells crash into our trench which is soon filled in in many places. Quantities of sharp shell fragments lie around everywhere. I have everyone but the most essential guards crawl into the shelters, and like so, we endure the bombardment for three hours. To set an example, I am now and then forced to walk along the entire trench with a calm step and an outwardly indifferent expression, whistling a song, so that people cannot say that the officers had slipped away. We remarkably didn't have one wounded person although at least 100 shells fell into my company section alone. On the contrary, the neighbouring company is said to have three dead and several wounded.

It is now half past 3 and we are not being shot at anymore, but it is still continuing uninterrupted in the north. We are informed that the English attacked again at Neuve Chapelle with great superior numbers, but were repelled. We were probably only lit up like this so that we would believe that we too were being attacked and, in this way, to prevent us from moving our reserves north. I have got a real headache from the hours of banging and roaring. Hopefully, this shooting doesn't put a damper on our plans, as we actually have to be relieved this evening.

13.5.1915   The idyllic peace is over. There has been heavy fighting all around here since the 9th of May, and the cannon thunder still hasn't stopped. There have been major attacks to our right and left, but these have been repelled apart from a few small successes. So, when will it be our turn?

I was relieved on the night of the 9th through to the 10th and came to Billy at 3 o'clock in the morning, where I am staying to rest until the 17th of May. I am now back with the 3rd Company and should really have gone back to the Front again the next evening, but Captain Beutin, who is very kind to me, notified the battalion that I am also to have a longer rest for once. We are constantly on high alert since we could be attacked at any moment. However, they would experience a very nasty disappointment if they wanted to get through to us. It is incidentally raining again today after days of the most wonderful sunny weather. There are temporarily no holidays for the time being, as we are stuck in such a dangerous corner here which makes it difficult to get even a day's holiday to Lille. I have no extra uniforms, but rather two squad uniforms and a squad coat that I had altered slightly by the company tailor, and which cost me nothing. All our officers do it this way.

It is now 5 o'clock in the afternoon, and the cannons have been thundering incessantly since this morning. It is an outright barbaric cannonade. The windows are shaking on our end, even though we are 8 to 10 kilometres away.

14.5.1915   I have never heard such a cannonade like tonight between 2 and 3 o'clock. Rapid fire from our heavy mortars — everything trembled and shook. I don't actually know what happened.

Prince Solms just received the Iron Cross 1st Class for Neuve Chapelle. He really did deserve it.

21.5.1915 Those were once again some unreal days, and it is still unbelievable to me that I escaped with my life because I have never experienced such artillery fire before. On the night from the 15th to the 16th of May, the 3rd Company returned after six days in the trenches. We were alerted at 5:30 in the morning. The 4th Company had already moved to La Bassée. At 6 o'clock, we likewise marched through Chateau Coisnes towards La Bassée, which was heavily bombarded with shells and bombs. Here we learned that the English had broken through to the 3rd Battalion of the 57th Infantry Regiment during the night. We were to prevent further advances until more reinforcements arrived. The position in question is in front of Richebourg, to the right of our former Heckenhof position.

I marched ahead with 16 men. The rest followed at a distance of 200 metres, on the right around La Bassée since it was too dangerous in the town. We were soon also forced to spread out because artillery shells were hitting all around us. We move forward across the very flat fields in leaps and bounds. We are struck by the first direct hits. The wounded moan — the rest of us move on as quickly as possible. Like so, we worked our way ahead for over three kilometres until we reached the rear of a shot-up farmstead on La Quinque Rue, which I recognised as the old carpentry where we often camped in December. Several of the 57th lay here, as well as a lieutenant named Brauch.

It was too dangerous here in the long run because heavy shells kept hitting us, and shrapnel was just flying over us. One after the other, we therefore crawled across the road and then into a shallow mud trench in which a shot-apart machine-gun unit lay dead. We then continued forward until we reached the communication trench leading to the 3rd Battalion. In this, I went further ahead with my few men (there were probably only 12 now) until the so-called 'Apfelhof', where the trench was so shot up that we couldn't continue. Captain Beutin followed us here with approximately 50 men. With wire cutters and spades, we made our way through the wire and wicker netting, all while being shot at by the English from both sides leaving several dead and wounded. There were gaps shot into many places of the trench walls that we had to jump past one by one. As soon as you were over, the English rifle volleys rained down behind. Like so, over the course of the day, we worked our way in constant danger to within 40 metres of the 3rd Battalion's second position, which we found to be heavily occupied by the English. We stayed here until the evening. Behind us were infantrymen from all sorts of regiments. We were supposed to attack in the night, but this did not happen. It would also have been completely hopeless.

As I was holding the foremost section during the night with 12 jägers and three bags of hand grenades, Captain Beutin entrenched himself further back to the right with the remaining jägers and infantrymen. At 5 o'clock in the morning, I received the sad news that Beutin had fallen. I couldn't believe it at first. I crawled back into the trench, and there I saw the poor man lying, dirty and bloodstained. A piece of shrapnel hit him in the chest in the night between 12 and 1 o'clock, and at the same time, Lieutenant Brauch from the 57th was hit in the forehead. Both were instantly dead. With Beutin, one of the best, most idealistic, dutiful and bravest people had gone. His death especially affected me dearly, because I was on very good terms with him and always got along well with him. I reported the death of both officers to the rear in writing.

I was now the only officer on the Frontline. I didn't receive any orders, but I did receive artillery fire that increased from hour to hour. I did finally find four Saxon officers near the Apfelhof, but I took over the command because they were shorter serving than me. I then ate Auntie Anna's can of lobster with these officers, and with this drank rainwater that we had collected in tent canvases. This was our only food in two days. The English infantry attempted to attack our trench several times, but they were always repelled.

The artillery fire became more and more intense in the afternoon. In addition to shrapnel and shells from the field guns, they now also showered us with a hail of the heaviest shells — 10, 15, 21, and even 28cm howitzers and mortars. The shells from the latter came rushing through the air as though a heavy freight train was approaching. And then the appalling bang — explosion after explosion with all kinds of sounds. The shots and fragments whistled and screamed through the air, and at the same time the moaning and lamenting of the wounded — shredded corpses or parts of them everywhere. It was just horrific, and all this we had to patiently endure. I wonder where I got the nerves from to do this. I have seen images that were so atrocious that I would rather remain silent about them. I received three shots in a short time, but they didn't do me any harm. A shell fragment tore a triangular hole in my pants above my left knee; a shrapnel ball ricocheted off my left shoulder, leaving a very painful blue bruise; and some projectile ripped the national emblem from my shako.

Towards the evening of the second day, the English systematically shot our communication trench into the ground, piece by piece, so that we were forced to retreat gradually. The bombardment finally reached such an intensity that we completely cleared the trench as soon as it got dark, and retreated across the open field towards the old standby farmstead (where we had cooked jacket potatoes so often in the winter). Infantry and some of our jägers had already dug a shooting position in front of this completely shot-up farmstead during the day. We were entrenching with them until 3 o'clock in the night while constantly being harassed by shrapnel shells. We were then replaced. Bavarian regiments had arrived, and one regiment stood behind the other as far as La Bassée. We also heard that large quantities of light and heavy artillery had come.

We arrived in La Bassée at 4 o'clock in the morning during fog and pouring rain, where I was happy to receive a cup of hot coffee from a field kitchen. The battalion had luckily sent us all the available wagons to La Bassée, and so we drove back to Billy dead tired. I was already pronounced dead here. We didn't sleep for a single minute for two nights. At noon, I had to report to our battalion commander, Count von Soden. He shook my hand at the end and said: "I express my appreciation for your conduct." This has brought me one step closer to the Iron Cross 1st Class.

The commanding general's order for the day said: "Undertaken with far greater superiority, the prepared English attempt to break through, which was done with the most powerful artillery and unusual ammunition expenditure, has failed due to the bravery of the strengthened army corps. I express my full appreciation to all command posts and the troops involved."

Although we were not able to take the captured trench back from the English, as for this we were far too weak, we can claim great credit for preventing the enemy from advancing further for two days all while in a trench that offered hardly any cover, until large numbers of troops were on the scene.

Yesterday morning, there was a funeral service for the fallen by the division priest, who gave a real revenge sermon that I would never have expected from a clergyman. The Count then gave a speech to the two involved companies. My company has 15 dead, 53 wounded and 6 missing; so almost half. Many of the returned jägers subsequently collapsed due to their nerves and became sick. I am now taking a good rest.

22.5.1915   Today we are going back to our old, quiet position again for a few days. We would all much rather be on the Front in the trenches, because there you can at least be sure that you won't be sent into such a huge mess as we just were.

23.5.1915   I will be relieved for two days tomorrow evening.

'May 1915 – To the right (wearing a coat) is Commissioned-Officer Pelz. To the left is Oberjäger Schmidt, who, in the night from the 17th to the 18th of May, was heavily wounded from a shrapnel shot to the head during the battle near La Bassée.'

The Battle of Festubert

The recent traumatic series of events experienced by Alexander is today known as 'The Battle of Festubert', fought just to the southwest of Neuve Chapelle. This was the so-called 'second phase' of the earlier failed British offensive, 'The Battle of Aubers Ridge' on the 9th of May, which he was partly involved in at the start of this chapter. As well as this, the British attack on Festubert was the contribution to the 'Second Battle of Artois', which was initiated to push past the German lines and into the Artois Region of France. With the French having planned an offensive against the German lines at Vimy to the south near Lens, the attack by Festubert aimed to lure the German reinforcements to the British, rather than the attacking French forces. This event marks the first British night attack of the war. They did achieve some minor territorial gains but failed in their overall objective. In the ten days of battle from the 15/16th to the 25th of May, they suffered an estimated 16,648 casualties, whereas the Germans, 5000.

A victim of this battle was Captain Walter Beutin, who, like Prince Reuss, stands out to me very much compared to all others mentioned to have fallen in this diary. When reading Alexander's reports, you may have already noticed that he rarely discusses his personal emotions in much depth when it comes to a person's death. He keeps his reports very professional, factual and centred around ongoing events as initially intended. You will notice this more as the diary progresses. I do find this peculiar. However, despite all that he has and is about to experience, talking about Beutin is one of the few instances in which he somewhat breaks his regular professional way of writing, and reminds us that

each experienced loss must have hurt him more than he often makes us believe. Considering this analysis, and the fact that he regularly praises the man for his good character and kindness, it becomes clear that the relationship with Beutin would have developed into a close friendship, which would have given Alexander a sense of normality in this war. Nevertheless, Beutin now exists no more, along with the thousands of others at Festubert. He is just one of the many fallen. How many of those thousands had close friends, children, wives, and family that needed to come to terms with this same outcome?

Alexander's Map

The following map was drawn by Alexander. It shows us his movements from Billy on the 16th of May, up towards the area of Richebourg and Festubert in the northwest:

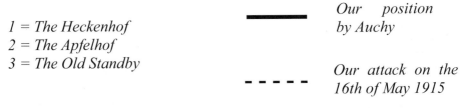

1 = The Heckenhof
2 = The Apfelhof
3 = The Old Standby

———

Our position by Auchy

- - - - -

Our attack on the 16th of May 1915

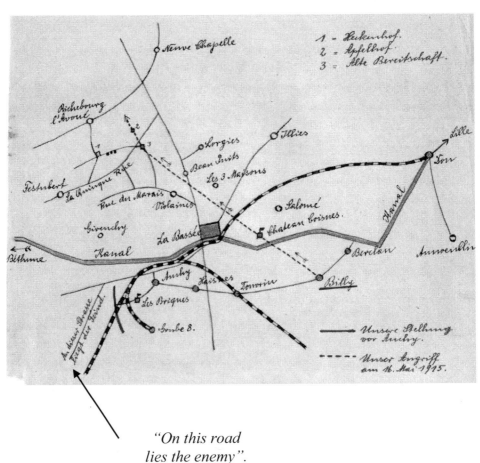

"On this road lies the enemy".

The 2 Cap Badges

From Alexander's items, now in my possession, are two cap badges from two different, presumably fallen British soldiers. After identifying the regiments to which these badges belong, I was able to confirm that they were indeed involved in the Battle of Festubert and that they most likely would have been found by Alexander during this time.

Below: The Oxfordshire and Buckinghamshire Light Infantry

Top: The Cameron Highlanders (1/4th Battalion)

When I hold these cap badges, I just imagine what they could have seen while resting on the caps of the Englishmen in their last moments before falling during battle. They would have gone through the same emotions as Alexander at this time. With the battalions identified, I discovered a written report by Major Archibald James Fergusson Eden, which gives us an idea of the British point of view. He was a commanding officer within the Oxfordshire and Buckinghamshire Light Infantry during the night attack on the 15/16th of May. At 7 o'clock in the morning:

"During the attack, Whitfield, and a party of men, by good work, succeeded in capturing a German machine gun and 3 prisoners, after killing 7 or 8 of the gun detachment; and established a strong post which marked the extreme left of our success. This point was then most ably held by Kite and a scratch party of bombers throughout the day. Shortly after I had reached the new line, I came across Beaufort and gave him some orders about the consolidation of the line. The poor fellow had not gone two paces from me when a bullet, fired by a German sniper, passed through his head and killed him stone dead on the spot."

Visiting Beutin & Brauch

During my time in France, I visited Billy-Berclau, the place of recovery for Alexander's battalion. This is also the location of the German military cemetery where many of its soldiers are buried, including Captain Walter Beutin. I visited this cemetery as well as the grave of Beutin, whose cross stands peacefully among many others on a field of grass surrounded by trees.

Billy-Berclau German Military Cemetery – Hauptmann (Captain) Walter Beutin - died 16.5.1915 – Block 3, Plot 187.

I also visited the Lens-Sallaumines German Cemetery, which is significantly larger than the one in Billy-Berclau. Here lies the body of Lieutenant Friedrich Brauch, who died alongside Beutin on the same day.

Lens-Sallaumines German Cemetery – Leutnant (Lieutenant) Friedrich Brauch - died 16.5.1915 – Block 7, Plot 103.

10

26.5.1915   Last night, I suddenly received news that I have been granted leave to the Chateau-Thumeries rest home until the 1st of June. This morning, I set off with my attendant on a butcher's wagon covered with a tarpaulin, and I arrived in 2.5 hours going via Berclau, Bauvin-Provin, Carvin and Libercourt. The rest home consists of two small chateaus belonging to a university professor in Lille, and it lies in the middle of a large deciduous forest. It is surrounded by fields, pastures, and forests; all like a single large park. There is even a mountain nearby, although only 100 metres high and the only one in the area. There are only half a dozen officers here, and you are very uninhibited. Everyone can do as they please between meals. I will be going on big walks and spend the rest of the time lying in the grass. Luckily the weather is lovely and warm. My nerves, which were quite shaken in the last battle, will recover nicely over the next six days. I will visit Line in Lille the day after tomorrow.

30.5.1915   I was in Lille with Line all day yesterday. The weather is always nice here. It is the purest summer freshness.

2.6.1915   The nice days of Thumeries are now already over again. I will be staying to rest here in Billy until the 5th of June. It is quiet in our position except for the usual shooting. I am now living in the third sector; currently in an old farmhouse 300 metres away, lonely in the field — the purest summer freshness. I have a very nice room all to myself and I am currently in the process of collecting the missing furnishings from the surrounding shot-apart villages, such as glasses, washing bowls and so on. Italy's declaration of war made little impression here. We all really wish to go to Tyrol. We are counting on it very much.

When I was in Thumeries, I once again saw how good the people in the communication zone have it. They live in the most beautiful castles, ride horses all day long, only hear the thunder of cannons from far away, and think all day and night about how they can get as many medals as possible. I am now doing what many frontline officers have done and no longer wear the Iron Cross ribbon, because everyone behind the Front has it.

5.6.1915   We are going to the Front for four days again today, where it is much nicer because you don't need to fear an alarm every day there. I would like to see if I could perhaps get 14 days of leave. If I depart Lille at 7:30 in the morning, I would already be in Weida at 8:30 the next morning.

6.6.1915   I received some very good 'Zeiss' prismatic binoculars from the battalion. I am therefore now sitting next to my shelter for hours in wonderful weather, where I can see and observe the entire area from good cover. It is currently very quiet in our sector. A shot rarely fires. Our trenches are being swept every morning and I am walking around in slippers. The brigade staff has now moved to Billy and has driven us out of our beautiful chateau. Our mess hall is now in a pretty villa with a garden; everything is much smaller, of course.

10.6.1915   I will be in the 2nd line for another two days, and then I will be going back to rest.

19.6.1915   As a result of large English attacks to our right, which completely failed with heavy losses, by the way, I will not be relieved until tomorrow evening. The day after tomorrow, I will write my holiday request in Billy. I hope to be home in 14 days.

23.6.1915   The English and French have constantly been attacking in our corner since the 9th of May, but strangely enough only to the right and left of us. They want to take La Bassée by all means. They have achieved nothing but terrible losses to our right by the canal. It is even worse to the south in the Loretto Heights, where the small victories are disproportionate to the hundreds of thousands that it cost them. You just have to wonder where they keep getting new people from.

When you compare the West with the East, we indeed have it much better here when it comes to food and accommodation. We also don't have any marches here anymore, but we are instead just nightwatchmen and earth workers. Yet this eternal waiting for an attack breaks your nerves more than manoeuvre warfare. We are not for one moment safe from the blacks that come sneaking up like snakes in the high grass, or from being blown up. We also have to suffer much more from the heavy artillery fire here, as we have ten times as much artillery in the same area as in the East. I would rather not even talk about the terrible winter in the swamps of La Bassée. I will probably receive the Falcon Order of Weimar soon. I have been put forward for this since the 7th of June.

I am going to the Front again for six days tonight.

26.6.1915   Totzek will be on leave from the 1st to the 13th of July. I am now excited to see when my turn will come — probably not until he gets back. We are to be relieved again tomorrow night. If I leave Lille at 7 o'clock in the morning, I will be in Frankfurt at 11 o'clock in the evening after travelling via Brussels, Leuven, Liège, and Cologne, and will already be in Weida at half past 8 the next morning.

29.6.1915   The old hustle and bustle is still here. Day and night, the thunder of cannons all around never stops. Our position is being worked on feverishly — nobody is getting through to us here.

We are going back to the Front for four days again tonight.

2.7.1915 It has become quieter for a few days — the great offensive between La Bassée and Arras has failed. It is now nice weather again after eight days of heavy rain. I will be relieved tomorrow evening and will go back to Billy again for four days. My holiday will now also be determined in the next few days.

'Suckling pig meal – early July 1915 – Motto: "The poor and starving men dressed in field-grey." – me 3rd from left'.

7.7.1915 Telegram to home from Herbesthal: "14 days leave — I will arrive from Gera at 8:30 tomorrow morning."

<u>HOLIDAY!</u>

Rest & Recreation

It does surprise me that Alexander has a lot of leisure time while on the Front; not constant misery in the trenches which many today would believe. These leisurely occasions are regularly offered to soldiers to boost morale and to take their minds away from the realities of the war, entailing opportunities such as sports, cinemas, sightseeing and holidays to see family. When behind the Front, Alexander often refers to the 'Communication Zone' *(German: 'Etappengebiet')* and those wretched communication-zone pigs living luxurious lives. It comes across as rather comical at times, considering you can sense his obvious anger and urge to write about them at every given opportunity. They are based in the area behind the frontlines where the soldiers go on leave, which also entails the lines of communication, supplies, and other means needed for the support of the frontline forces.

What does strike me, which you will also notice, is that Alexander never talks about his time spent at home during the war. This would be his only place that offers a true sense of comfort and safety during this period. Why could this be? — I cannot say for sure, but considering the efficient and history-loving man that he is, it shows the true professionalism and consistency he maintains to create this personal memoir and project of his; written and documented solely to tell us about events surrounding the war without what he considers unnecessary, just as originally planned in 1914.

Alexander on leave, pictured in his garden with his wife in Weida – July 1915.

20.7.1915   I have happily arrived back in Lille, and I am sitting with Line in the hospital garden. I won't leave until tomorrow, because today I won't arrive in Billy until late at night and might find my room occupied.

21.7.1915   I arrived back in Billy at noon today. Nothing has happened here while I was away. I will be joining Prince Solms in the 4th Company but will be leading the 2nd Company for six days in the meantime. I will be staying here in peace for the next few days. Due to the extreme heat, the strawberry juice that I brought from home in the suitcase had fermented out of the bottle and completely ruined the new uniform, underwear and so on. It looked lovely in the suitcase when I opened it in Lille last night. It is currently the most beautiful weather here. The body of Beutin was found by a patrol and buried here in Billy yesterday.

24.7.1915   I am off sick for four days — tonsillitis. I probably caught it from Gudrun *(daughter)* at home. It is incredibly boring to sit so alone in my den of flies. It is very quiet here now, apart from the usual artillery fire. I am safe from being tunnel-mined from below here in the section of the 4th Company, which lies south of the railway, as the distance to the enemy is too great.

27.7.1915   The tonsillitis is gradually getting better, but it will still be a few days before I can undertake duties again.

30.7.1915   I am healthy again and I am going to the mess hall again today.

1.8.1915   I am back in the trenches on the Front for six days again since last night. With Prince Solms, named 'The Good', I have it very nice and have very pleasant duties. I had barely arrived last night when the English, who now lie opposite us, orchestrated great fire magic. Whilst normally only a few shots are fired, furious rifle and machine-gun fire began all at once, which lasted 10 minutes. They probably thought we were outside working on the obstructions. There was luckily no one outside though. Everyone simply ducked their heads, and only one listening sentry was lightly wounded by a shot in the foot. Everything has been quiet again since then, especially given that our artillery immediately planted a dozen shells into the enemy trench upon request.

'The company commander shelter in the 2nd Position – In the middle is First-Lieutenant Prince Solms; to the left, Lieutenant König (Artillery); and to the right, Lieutenant Bode.

2 beds will be coming on top of each other on the left, and to the right the oven, bed of the attendant and so on. Everything is covered with red curtains, and it is all 4 times larger than this small cut-out visible through the door'.

'My shelter – Summer 1915'.

5.8.1915 I had to call in sick once more today because I have tonsillitis again. This time, I am going to give myself a thorough treatment before I take part anew.

8.8.1915 I got up again today, but I am not going back into the trench for the next eight days so that I don't have another relapse. I don't notice any rheumatism, which people ask about at home. Everything is quiet here, but a house in Billy just recently blew up in the middle of the night. A pig intruded a living room, went over a sack of hand grenades and then started to eat around it. There was unfortunately nothing left of the pig either. When the capture of Warsaw was announced a few days ago, the church bells rang and the bands played. When asked what was going on, our jägers said to the French: "Russ

Kaput", to which they shook their heads in disbelief. One woman replied: "Nix Reell." ('Nothing Fair')

My landlady, Mademoiselle Albertine, washed my uniform which had been soaked in strawberry juice. It is like new again. I get on great with my fellows in the 4th Company. I couldn't have gotten it any better. I don't need to say a word about Prince Solms 'The Good'. There are also two very young lieutenants here: Kauert, who is a forest enthusiast and the son of a schnapps manufacturer in Bielefeld — particularly characterised by his dry humour and an uncanny thirst. His regular saying is: "Why shouldn't we drink an old corn schnapps?". Then there is also Petersen, who wants to stay active — father is the commander of the 41st Infantry Regiment.

The companies that are on the Front usually invite each other to dinner. Totzek is now leading the 3rd Company. He got married when he was on leave. The plague of flies is at its worst at the moment. I have no longer been hanging up flycatchers which are available to buy in the canteen. You don't even notice the couple hundred that are caught on it. A half-hour fly hunt with a folded newspaper and with the window closed works much better.

It has now become a requirement that every officer up to and including a captain no longer carries a sabre, but rather a short bayonet.

'The church in Billy and the soldiers' graveyard – A shell has ripped out a piece of the left corner of the tower – August 1915'.

13.8.1915   I am going to the recreation home of Chateau Attiches between Seclin and Phalempin for eight days. Lieutenant Nugel is there at the moment, and I am replacing him. It is supposed to be very nice there, even nicer than in Thumeries. The Count believes that I shouldn't report myself as being healthy for a few days until the 17th.

A terrible explosion almost threw us out of bed tonight. At Marquillies, almost 5 kilometres north of here, a large cache of hand grenades exploded. The windows shattered here despite the distance. Otherwise, there is a noticeable calm on the whole Front. Apparently, they have had enough.

19.8.1915   Yesterday, I drove via Carvin and Phalempin to Attiches, where it is much nicer than at Thumeries. It is a very modern castle that is wonderfully furnished with hundreds of valuable oil paintings, a music room with a Steinway piano, a billiard room, and so forth. I have never lived so fine in my entire life

— an impeccably maintained park, garden, and greenhouses. The deceased owner was a botany professor at the University of Lille. His wife and daughter live here. They are seemingly very fine people, but they are very reserved. The three sons are in the war. There are currently very few people here: one reserve officer from Infantry-Regiment 57, and the Catholic priest of the division who is a very sociable gentleman. The weather is unfortunately very alternating — thunderstorms every day. We play billiards when it rains. Even the surrounding area is very nice — large oak forests. One week is unfortunately far too little. Here you can see once again how wonderfully the communication-zone pigs live behind the Front.

20.8.1915　　　I was in the neighbouring village of Avelin yesterday, where there is a convalescence home in a very nice, large castle, and where I visited Lieutenant Kellerman. He was wounded twice next to me, and now his car overturned with him just a couple of weeks ago. He is one unlucky person.

'The officers' recreation home – Chateau Attiches – August 1915'.

'The officers' recreation home of Chateau Attiches – a view towards the park – August 1915'.

'The officers' recreation home – Chateau Avelin (from behind) – August 1915'.

21.8.1915 I have just received the message that from tomorrow, I have been assigned to a training course for company commanders in Annoeullin for 14 days. This unfortunately means that I will miss 3 days in our beautiful rest home. I was in Lille yesterday, but I didn't meet Line. I did however come across Crown Prince Rupprecht of Bavaria on the street instead. Line visited me here today. The weather isn't very good. It is raining a lot.

22.8.1915 I am travelling to Annoeullin this afternoon. Although it will certainly be very nice there too, I don't want to leave here because it is just too beautiful.

11

24.8.1915 I have already experienced a lot in the two days here in Annoeullin. On the 22nd of August, I drove here in the division chaplain's car, where we reported over 30-man strong. There are officers from all sorts of regiments in the area. Lieutenant von Baumbach from us is still here. We were first given our quarters and received the letter with the duties for the following day. I have a pretty room with a good bed, but I couldn't find any washing facilities. My landlady, who is an old bag, said: "J'avais deux bassins, mais vos camarades les ont cassés." *("I had two basins, but your fellows broke them").* So, the next morning, I had to make do with a bucket, whereupon I went to the local headquarters and made a racket. The 'Maire' was then ordered to get what was missing. I now have one bucket made of paper-mâché, as well as some kind of small children's bathtub made of enamel sheet, a jug that holds a maximum of a quarter of a litre, and one water glass.

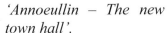
'Annoeullin – The new town hall'.

The food in our mess hall isn't exactly renowned, but it will probably get better now that we have chosen the fattest of us to be the mess-hall manager. We wanted to go to a variety show on the first evening (by soldiers, of course), but it turned out differently — Two enemy aircraft appeared, which were in a firefight high above with one of our fighter planes. They were also being heavily shot at by our defensive guns. One of the course participants next to me was just saying that he had never before seen an aeroplane being brought down. A shell then burst directly next to one of the enemy planes, and it came down at the same moment, continuously tumbling sideways. You could clearly see that a wing was missing. But now there was life on the streets. Everyone shouted "Hurrah!" as if possessed and ran towards the direction where the crash had occurred. The French pulled dumb faces and said: "Malheur, Malheur!" *("Misfortune, Misfortune!").* We were of course off and running there too. Once again, you could thereby see how you can misjudge the distance of the aircraft.

We thought we would be at the crash site in 15 minutes, but we had to run very strenuously across the country for an entire hour. There were cars, trucks, bicycles, and pedestrians from all sides, like a proper mass migration of people in manoeuvre. There were also four of our planes that landed there too. When we arrived, several generals, hundreds of officers and over 1000 soldiers were already gathered. The place was cordoned off by military police, Uhlans, and later by the infantry. Only officers were allowed into the circle — it was an English monoplane. It was completely wrecked, of course, and next to it lay the bodies of an English officer and a corporal. All the bones were obviously broken in multiple places, but the people were at least not as shattered as you would expect from such a high fall. The Englishmen had a machine gun and a camera with them. It was interesting to see our aeroplanes take off again. Our fighter plane in particular, a tiny single-seat monoplane, jumped up like a flea after a short run-up.

We were on exercise with an infantry platoon from 7 o'clock to half past 10 yesterday morning. Two sections have been formed, and I am in the one belonging to Baron von Wangenheim, a captain of the guards who seems to be very nice. In the afternoon, we shot at discs by the large mine rubble heap at Carvin. The pioneers have their training ground next door, where the people are trained in constructing trenches, shelters, and obstacles; and in destroying and overcoming the latter. We were shown a very interesting attack using smoke and gas bombs. The first produces a white, opaque fog so that the enemy is unable to see a target. The gas bombs, on the other hand, spread an invisible gas that affects the respiratory system and especially the eyes. The effect was extremely unpleasant despite only a weak filling being used. At the spot where such a bomb had exploded 5 minutes ago, we all had to cough violently even with the very strong wind, and our eyes were watering so much that we could hardly see anything.

Then came the main fun — the riding lesson. Only very few can ride properly. A lot have only ridden on some horse in their spare time, and many, including me, have never sat on top of one. The more advanced are having lessons with an Uhlan riding master, and the rest of us with a patrolman. We walked and trotted around in circles for an hour, and this also went very well and without falling off since we received the most patient Uhlan horses. Only the sitting region hurts terribly today. We had the same usual exercises again this morning, then an hour of lessons this afternoon, and now it's back to riding. We are all supposed to exercise an entire company on horseback tomorrow. How I am supposed to do this after just two riding lessons is a complete mystery to me. In any case, it will be great entertainment for the public. Our captain has already offered to write us holiday tickets to Ostend for next Sunday. I will be going there with Baumbach, of course. We also want to visit Bruges and Ghent if possible.

The 2 Fallen Pilots

On the 22nd of August, Alexander witnessed the crash of an English aeroplane brought down by anti-aircraft guns, which was a rare occurrence at the time. He also saw the bodies of the two English pilots next to a camera and machine gun. Due to the great detail of Alexander's account of what happened, and because the event has been well documented on both sides, I was able to identify the two men as well as their final resting place. The pilots were Lieutenant William Middleton Wallace (Scotland Rugby International player) and Second-Lieutenant Charles Gallie, who were flying a B.E.2c aircraft while on a photographic reconnaissance mission above the areas of Annoeullin and Sainghin. The postcard shown below depicts the German officers around the crashed aeroplane and the corpses of the two pilots.

'English aeroplane shot down on 22.8.1915 by Field-Artillery Regiment 58'.

William *'Willie'* Middleton Wallace – B. 23.9.1893 – D. 22.8.1915 – *Remembered at the Cabaret-Rouge British Cemetery – Plot XII. D. 11.*

William was the son of Robert Walker Wallace and Mary Parker Wallace, of 7 Inverleith Row, Edinburgh. Before the war, he was a rugby union fullback for Cambridge University RFC and was capped for Scotland between 1913 to 1914. He was named the best fullback in the United Kingdom between 1912 to 1914. At the start of the war, he was commissioned as a second lieutenant in the Rifle Brigade (Prince Consort's Own) while an undergraduate, possibly making him the first undergraduate to see military action. In February

1915, he was attached to the Royal Flying Corps, and shortly after became the senior observer of No. 2 Squadron.

Charles Gallie – B. 4.2.1892 – D. 22.8.1915 – *Remembered at the Cabaret-Rouge British Cemetery – Plot XII. D. 11.*

Born in Skipton, Yorkshire, Charles was the son of J.A and Louise Gallie of High Green, Worcester. Joining the Royal Flying Corps in 1912, he worked his way up from Air Mechanic to 2nd Lieutenant in June 1915.

Charles Gallie   *William Wallace*

During my time in France, I visited both William and Charles, who are buried side by side at the Cabaret-Rouge British Cemetery. As I made my way through the cemetery and stood before their graves with their faces in my mind, I saw exactly what you now see in the image above. It was astonishing yet strange, as I then thought to myself: 'Well over a century later, I now stand over the 2 fallen pilots, just like Alexander once did near Annoeullin on 22.8.1915'.

27.8.1915   We have the nicest weather for our course. The duties are rather strenuous due to the unfamiliar movements, but you also learn very much. I fell headfirst off the horse in the third riding lesson, but it didn't do me any harm other than general hilarity. I will be taking part in the field-service exercise on horseback for the first time tomorrow.

29.8.1915   I have just had a wonderful swim in the sea at Ostend. There is huge activity here along with military music. There are hundreds of officers. Entire companies are being led to swim. You get very jealous of the troops that are stationed here.

'Our   soldiers   are searching   for seashells'.

31.8.1915   Our duties in Annoeullin include exercises on horseback on the terrain from 7 to 12 o'clock in the morning; then, a change of clothes and lunch; lessons from 3 o'clock to half past 4; a riding lesson from half past 5 to half 6; get changed; dinner at half past 7, and then I go to bed extremely tired soon after. I have already made quite a bit of progress in riding. The day after tomorrow, there will be an inspection by half a dozen generals and some other bigwigs. I am then in Billy again on Friday.

4.9.1915   I arrived back in Billy at noon yesterday, and I am going into the trench for three days tonight. The course was very nice, and I have learnt a lot. We were specially trained as company commanders for manoeuvre warfare, which is something completely different from our current positional warfare. One person always acted as the battalion commander, one as his adjutant, and four as the company commanders. Tasks were then given. The battalion commander deployed his battalion, the company commanders deployed their companies, and the attack, defence or retreat was practised.

'My accommodation in Billy – September 1915'.

We were on horseback for 6 hours every day and it was very tiring. I flew off my horse headfirst two times. Someone fell off every moment on some days, especially when we went over the many trenches. We now also have riding lessons here in Billy; initially, 8 hours without stirrups, as this is the only way you can learn to ride properly. There was a large inspection of our course on the 2nd of September, for which we had an entire battalion available. Various generals, as well as our Corps-Commander General von François, and several other officers including a son of von Hindenburg *(a German field marshal),* were there. In the evening was a farewell dinner attended by Major-General von Etzel and the two apprentice captains.

The Sunday in Ostend was very nice, especially the seaside resort. It unfortunately started to rain in the afternoon. The locomotive broke down on the return journey, so we arrived in Lille three hours late and didn't catch the last train to Don. We were finally given a small special train and therefore didn't arrive in Annoeullin until 3 o'clock in the morning dead tired. We were back out at 6 o'clock in the morning and exercised until 12. The course participants were very nice for the most part. We were from nine different regiments. They were all cheerful guys, although there were a few of them who had taken part in even more than I had. Some, although still only 30 years old, had very grey hair from the English barrage fire at La Bassée. And yet no one had forgotten how to laugh, which is so horrible to imagine at home. Unfortunately, the old Mr. Lecieux-Thibaut, with whom I stayed in Annoeullin in October and whom I wanted to visit again, has died in the meantime.

9.9.1915 This morning, we had a big field-service exercise in Billy, then a vaccination against cholera, and now we have a riding lesson again. After we were last relieved, we were still entrenching at a reserve position on the Front until 2 o'clock in the morning and didn't arrive in Billy until 3 o'clock. The English have once again bombarded us heavily with shells and shrapnel in the last few days. We generally believe that the mob wants to attack us again in the next four weeks. As an old warrior, you gradually get a fine feeling for something like this. But they will certainly experience very little joy from us.

Riding without stirrups is one of the biggest problems. I feel like I am battered all over, but you also learn something this way. I have received a lot of canned goods from home that I plan on saving for eventual meagre times, as we get enough here. I haven't gotten back into the habit of smoking since my tonsillitis. The plague of flies has fortunately subsided a lot due to the wet and cool weather. The nights are already miserably cold.

11.9.1915 To make up for the days I spent completing the course, I have been granted leave to Attiches again from the 13th to the 17th of September.

'At the stage on Sunday; concert in Attiches – September 1915'.

14.9.1915 I drove to Chateau Attiches with our stagecoach yesterday morning. As well as me, Lieutenant Seemann and two infantrymen are still here. Towards the evening, we rode our bikes to the neighbouring airfield where Lieutenant von Scheffer, the brother of our fellow who fell in January, was just taking off in a fighter plane. The leader of the place, a captain, knows my cousin Leo very well. As a result of these relationships, it was not difficult to gain permission for a sightseeing flight.

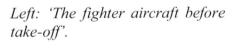

Left: 'The fighter aircraft before take-off'.

Right: 'The fighter aircraft during the moment of take-off'.

94

Seemann flew first, and then I. I was in the air for about 15 minutes, namely at an altitude of 400 to 500 metres, and it was simply wonderful. You don't notice the ascent. You suddenly see everything deep down below without any jolts, and the landscape very slowly glides away beneath you. The forests, villages, and the many castles surrounded by moats look delightful, and the roads stand out sharply — a very indescribable, beautiful sight — no trace of dizziness. You feel completely safe and travel much more smoothly than in the best car. The only unpleasant moment is when the engine is turned off for gliding. You thereby have the feeling as though you are plummeting down forwards. The ground literally flies towards you, and you are suddenly rolling on the ground again. I am very happy that I was able to experience this. I would prefer to fly every day. You thus understand why everyone is rushing to go to the aeroplanes.

In the evening, we then fought bitter billiard battles for the championship of Northern France. I think I would learn to play very well if I had more practice. It is now unfortunately dull and rainy weather again. Tomorrow or the day after, I want to go to Ostend again with Seemann. The trip doesn't cost us one pfennig. People at home got annoyed about the gourmet meals that we occasionally organise. I don't understand this, because why shouldn't we live well when we can have it? It is completely forgotten that we have often had times when there was nothing, and when a measly bottle of beer, for example, could not be found for weeks. There was only dry bread with sugar available in Guignicourt, to the point where you felt sick even when you just heard the word 'Sugar'. In October, there was only one oil sardine for four men, and just recently, I and four officers had nothing more than a small can of lobster in two days, with which we drank rainwater. We would therefore have to be dumb muttons if we wanted to live badly without necessity. Times of hunger will come again in return.

16.9.1915 We are doing a big trip through Belgium. Even the departure from Attiches was a lot of fun — seven of us in a small car that only held four people. With us were Lieutenant Seemann from our regiment, Lieutenant Rische from the neighbouring 16th Regiment, and our three attendants. Like so, we went towards Wattignies via Seclin with the car, and then with the electric railway to Lille, where we stayed overnight at the Hotel Royal. I visited Line for a few minutes.

We continued to Ostend at 8 o'clock the next morning, where we arrived after 10. During a morning drink, we then waited for our company which arrived an hour later. The whole army is in fact now going one by one to Ostend for a day to swim. Count von Soden was also there. After a lovely swim in the sea, we ate lunch together in the mess hall of the Marine Corps. While the company had to leave again immediately afterwards, we extra excursionists were able to stay until 5 o'clock and lay in the sun on the beach in our swimming trunks all afternoon. We then took the electric railway along the entire dunes to Blankenberge. On this trip, we saw torpedo boats, two submarines, and all the coastal fortifications. We then took the train to Bruges, where we had to wait over an hour for the express train from Ostend, which was delayed due to engine failure. It was unfortunately already so dark that we couldn't see much of ancient Bruges. After the endless French, we had a lot of fun with the Flemish language, which you can understand quite well if you pay close attention.

'Ostend – To the left: Lt. von Baumbach – To the right: von der Mark'.

'Ostend – September 1915'.

'Spa house in Ostend – September 1915'.

'Ostend – September 1915'.

We arrived in Brussels via Ghent at 1 o'clock in the night, where we initially found free hotel accommodation at the commandant's office. When we wanted to plunge into the nightlife, we noticed that all the local venues had been closed since midnight. However, in return for a handful of cigarettes, a Belgian policeman then revealed to us that you could now supposedly still get into the 'Merry Grill' cabaret; not through the main entrance, of course, but through a back door where you have to knock in a certain way. This worked perfectly, and we enjoyed ourselves very much. Merry Grill is a hotel where the Belgian fine world has its doss house in peacetime. There is dancing and singing in a small hall, and only ladies from the half-world are of course there; some in leotard pants or very short skirts. I saw wonderful Maxixe dancing there. A very good tap dancer also performed. There was only sparkling wine for 15 Mark a bottle. 'Chambres Séparées' *('separate chambers')* are also there, of course, so that everyone is taken care of. In any case, it was very amusing to see the activity.

The next day in Brussels, we looked at the city, the wonderful marketplace with the old gold-gilded houses, and the huge Palace of Justice that lies high above the city. Brussels is a very nice and clean city that shows no sign of war. There is bustle on the streets in the evenings like in Berlin. You get approached by 'ladies' at every step, who complain about having to walk so alone. It is pleasant that you barely see any military compared to Lille, where you have to keep your hand on your hat all the time. We then took the midday express train back to Lille, and in the evening we took the car to Attiches. We had to arrive in Billy again the next evening. It was a very nice and very cheap trip because we got the transport, accommodation, and most of the food for free.

The Unidentified Photos

While stationed around the areas of Annoeullin and Attiches, some photographs were taken by Alexander, which are unfortunately not described on the back like most others that you have seen. Below are some of these that, although we have no further information, allow us to imagine the stories and events surrounding them:

12

20.9.1915   Everything is as usual. For 24 hours, we have heard very strong artillery fire day and night from the Loretto Heights. There was just tremendous buzzing in the air. A fleet of nine English planes is heavily but unsuccessfully fired upon by our guns.

'My attendant in the entrance of a mine tunnel – September 1915'.

'Shot-up houses behind our trench – September 1915'.

23.9.1915   My intuition hasn't betrayed me. We are in a very big mess again — trouble is brewing here. Since 8:30 in the morning of the 21st, so for three days now, we have been receiving uninterrupted barrage fire day and night. Our beautiful trenches, which we were so proud of, have been completely destroyed and partially levelled. Many shelters have been shot in. Nevertheless, compared with the huge waste of ammunition of at least ten thousand shells and shrapnel per day, we have very minimal losses because we are sitting 5 to 6 metres underground in our bomb-proof mine tunnels. The English attempted an assault this afternoon, but it was already suppressed from the start. I am doing well so far, although I am just terribly tired and filthy. It is no fun to crouch in the narrow and only 1-metre-high tunnels for three days. We only have very few observation posts outside that are constantly being replaced.

Left: 'My attendant Viereck with a dud (a non-exploded English 12cm shell) – September 1915'.

Right: 'Me with a 15cm dud. Our shelters were shot up with these sorts of shells – September 1915'.

26.9.1915   Those were once again some bad days, and there is still no end in sight yet. We were horribly barraged for four days and nights, and our entire position was destroyed. Then came the most horrifying — an English gas attack yesterday morning. The entire area was covered for kilometres with a thick, white mist of gas. We would have suffocated if we hadn't had gas masks. Then came the English assault which was brilliantly repelled. This was followed by another artillery bombardment with heavy 15cm guns, and then another assault which was nevertheless repelled also. The Scottish, the 'King's Own Scottish Borderers', had a terrifying number of casualties. 400 to 500 lie dead and wounded in front of my company section alone. We captured roughly 40 Scots and looted one machine gun and one bagpipe. The Scots, who emerged in thick heaps from the gas mist in front of us, were greeted by an insane hail of bullets from rifles and machine guns.

    In response to our red flares, our artillery then released a rapid fire, and it sounded very frightening how the shells of the field guns swept in layers close over our heads and into the assaulting columns; and how the shells of our heavy artillery rushed high above us, to then explode at the back in the trenches stuffed with English reserves. What we can see ahead of us in terms of the dead is only a small part of the English losses. Just what might it look like in their assault starting positions? Our people did brilliantly. I am unwounded, but Lieutenant von Baumbach was killed early yesterday morning, meaning I am now the commander of this sector that was most heavily attacked. It is relatively calm today. The Scottish have probably had enough.

Note: The Germans during this war often refer to the British as 'English', regardless of their background.

27.9.1915   Idyllic peace this morning. There was ridiculous artillery fire again in the afternoon, which was followed by another gas attack at half past 6 in the evening. The gas was transparent but much sharper this time. I am still very sick from it. The expected English assault did not materialise though. They are probably still tired of us from the day before yesterday. On the other hand, they attacked Infantry-Regiment 16 to the right of us but were smoothly beaten back. To our left, terrible battles have been raging since yesterday. A sergeant from a Bavarian regiment, who fetched grenades from us, said that he has been involved right from the start of the war, including Ypres, but he has never seen so many dead English as he has here. Our entire Front from Neuve Chapelle up to Loos-Vermelles is being attacked by frightening numbers of English. They have lost at least 10,000 men in two days.

'A Scottish captain (lying face down) – Fallen on 25.9.1915 in our trench due to a hand grenade'.

'Me with a gasmask to protect against stink bombs and gas attacks – To the left is the way down to my shelter – September 1915'.

29.9.1915   I have now been in the trenches for 14 days, and in battle for 9 days. I received the Knight's Cross of the Falcon Order of Weimar today. I have unfortunately not received any further post for a week because our company bicyclist was torn apart by a shell, and most likely all the post with him.

30.9.1915   After we were not shaken by either 100 hours of barrage fire or two assaults, they tried it with shells yesterday that produced gases that burn the eyes and make them tear. But they only achieved great hilarity success with this. We are tremendously proud that we completely held our position and inflicted such enormous losses on the English. Things are relatively quiet here now.

2.10.1915   The worst now seems to be over, although the shooting doesn't stop all day and night. The English attack from Ypres up to our battalion has completely failed, and we haven't lost a single metre on this long stretch. On the other hand, they did break through to the 11th Infantry Regiment, which is next to us on the left, and they were almost on our backs, but they were repulsed again in extremely bloody battles lasting several days. Currently, there is still fighting with hand grenades around a small, far-advanced trench piece to the left of us, around the so-called 'Hohenzollern Redoubt'.

It looks terrible in the recaptured trenches. I took a look at them. You only walk over English corpses on 40-metre-long stretches, including an English major general over whom I have personally repeatedly climbed away from. The English suffered very terrible losses. From us have fallen — both Lieutenants von Baumbach, First-Lieutenant Swart, and Officer-Candidates von Bothmer and Brieden. Wounded — Lieutenants Pira, Werth, Jenner, and Kauert. The battalion has lost approximately a third of its other enlisted men.

4.10.1915 We have now been in the trenches for nearly three weeks straight and look like vagabonds — filthy and with wild beards.

The battalion has issued the following order: "Despite heavy shelling lasting over 90 hours, despite several gas attacks and the enemy having broken through into the adjacent section, the battalion managed to hold its position and inflicted enormous losses on the enemy. This great success, which we are proud of, could only be achieved through the unwavering perseverance and heroic bravery of every single officer, oberjäger, and jäger. This was our revenge for Neuve Chapelle! — Honour our fallen brave heroes."

Since yesterday, the English have now also been thrown out of the last small trench piece to the south of us, meaning they have achieved nothing but huge losses.

6.10.1915 It is now relatively calm here again, at least compared to the barrage fire. It is very uncertain when we will be coming out of the trenches again. There is miserable dirt in the shot-up positions due to the constant rain. Everything is filthy and full of lice, but the food is luckily excellent at least. If I didn't have so many men on the Front with me, I would surely now receive the Iron Cross 1st Class.

8.10.1915 We have the usual artillery shooting day and night here, but it no longer causes any damage. We have only had one wounded in the last eight days. We have already repaired our trenches quite a bit and have also replaced the wire obstacle that was swept away by the barrage fire. Billy also came under heavy fire during the days of the attack. We then blew up the church tower to make it more difficult for the enemy to aim. Nothing is known about our replacement yet, but it is now rather easy to hold out here again.

The Battle of Loos

With the battles of La Bassée, Neuve Chapelle, the 1914 Winter Operations, Aubers Ridge, and Festubert now long passed, which all resulted in no significant changes, Alexander has just been subject to another significant chapter in history — The Battle of Loos. The battle began to the south of La Bassée on 25.09.1915 and will continue until mid-October. The British initiated this offensive to eventually break through the German lines before the upcoming winter. However, this has failed. As of this point in the war, it is the largest British offensive so far, and also the first time that the British have used gas on the battlefield. Due to the formidable German defences and the alteration in wind direction, which caused the gas to blow back towards the British lines, the casualties of the British forces totalled 50,000, twice that suffered by the Germans. Alexander is currently positioned to the west of Auchy-les-Mines, one of the most heavily assaulted sectors. This position is named 'Mad Point' by the British and is well known to have inflicted some of the most terrible casualties among the British-Scottish troops.

Being interested in history, I did have prior knowledge of the Battle of Loos, but I was surprised to discover the extent of Alexander's involvement during this; not just being part of the sector that was one of the focal points of the battle, but indeed becoming the sole commander of 'Mad Point.' This position played a significant part in securing a German victory. Mad Point inflicted appalling British casualties at the cost of Alexander's predecessor, Hans Erich von Baumbach, and according to the battalion diary, it came like so:

"The jägers everywhere jumped up onto the embankment. In a roaring "Hurrah!," they vented their enormous tension of nerves of the last few days and shot while standing, calling out to their opponents their "Revenge for Neuve Chapelle!". On the left wing, where the artillery and gas had the biggest effect, the wave of the enemy came up to 40 steps of the trench and then threw itself down to avoid the firing — and was shot down to the very last man. Parts of the enemy advancing to the south of the battalion's sector fell into flanking fire of the jägers' machine guns. Despite this, their weaker forces penetrated the subsequent trench, and then from there into the position of the battalion. The leader of the 2nd Company, Lieutenant Hans Erich von Baumbach, threw himself towards them with his jägers and men from the 57th assigned to him. Through the attack, simultaneously led from both the open field and trenches, the English were fully wiped out. The jägers took possession of 45 prisoners and 2 machine guns, but the sacrifice for this triumph was the lives of the company commander and the Officer-Candidate, von Bothmer."

- The War Diary of The 11th Kurhessian Jäger Battalion

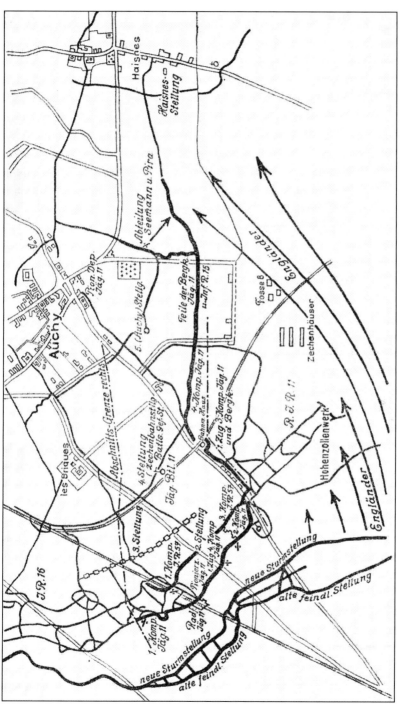

Positions of Jäger-Battalion 11 at noon on the 25th of September – Alexander in position with the 2nd Company, known to the British as 'Mad Point' which lies to the northwest of the Hohenzollern Redoubt (German: Hohenzollernwerk) – Arrows show the direction of the British attack from the left.

105

When visiting the Billy-Berclau German cemetery, I visited the graves of the battalion's officers who fell during the battle. Alexander knew these men personally:

Right: *Hubert Brieden – Block 6, Plot 19*

Left: *Ernst von Baumbach – Block 6, Plot 20*

Right: *Erich Swart & Hans von Baumbach – Block 6, Plot 21/22*

Left: *Alfred von Bothmer – Block 6, Plot 23*

The Hohenzollern Redoubt

This redoubt that Alexander mentions, known to the Germans as the 'Hohenzollernwerk', got its name from the German royal dynasty of Hohenzollern. The British thought this to be the strongest defensive work on the entire Front and so had to be taken, which was briefly partly accomplished by the 9th (Scottish) Division. But as we know, the attempt to hold this failed. Alexander personally observed the aftermath of this failed British assault when he visited the recaptured trenches on 2.10.1915. The British remain determined to take this stronghold, and will soon attempt another assault on the 13th of October to achieve this. However, with this also due to be a failure and to suffer just over 3600 casualties on this one day, the general British opinion of this attack would later be that: 'The fighting had not improved the general situation in any way, and had brought nothing but useless slaughter of infantry'.

George Thesiger & Queen Elizabeth's Uncle

When reading Alexander's diary extracts alongside other historical records written after these events, I was shocked by the severity of the aftermath. This was also clearly noticed by Alexander, who visited the recaptured trenches filled with so many dead by the redoubt. He simply describes the end result as 'terrible'. He also talks about repeatedly climbing over a fallen major general, which instantly encouraged me to find out who this was. Considering his high rank, it did not take long for me to discover that only one major general had fallen in this area on the 27th of September. He was a nephew of the Anglo-Zulu-War General, Lord Chelmsford, and he was also the grandson of a lord high chancellor of Great Britain. This individual was:

Major-General George Handcock Thesiger – Commander of the 9th (Scottish) Division – B. 06.10.1868 - D. 27.09.15 (Auchy, near La Bassée) - *Commemorated at the Loos Memorial, Panel 1.*

Two days after the battle began, the heavy casualties of Thesiger's division prompted him to visit the frontline opposite the Hohenzollern Redoubt to assess the situation. The Germans began to blast the position with artillery, with one of the first shells killing him instantly. The British withdrew from the trench not long after due to the heavy losses; and because of the chaos of the situation, they had to leave behind their fallen men including Thesiger. The fate of Thesiger's body was unknown after his death as a result, and his body was never recovered, currently being listed among the missing at the Loos Memorial along with approximately 20,000 others.

George Handcock Thesiger - husband of Frances Thesiger of 13 St. Leonard's Terrace, Chelsea, London.

I also discovered that another victim of these events was the older brother of the Queen Mother; so, the uncle of Queen Elizabeth II — Captain of the Black Watch, Fergus Bowes-Lyon (Born 18th of April 1889 - Died 27th of September 1915). He too died from the German artillery fire at the Hohenzollern Redoubt. According to reports: "He led an attack on the German lines, his leg was blown off by a barrage of German artillery and he fell back into his sergeant's arms. Bullets struck him in the chest and shoulder, and he died on the field". His death apparently affected his mother dearly, who withdrew herself from public life until the marriage of her daughter to the King of Great Britain. Up until 2011, he was among the missing but was finally given his own gravestone at Quarry Cemetery, Vermelles – (Plot A. 15). When I was in France, I visited his grave in this small cemetery that lies in a depression in the middle of an open field, right in the centre of the former Loos battlefield.

Quarry Cemetery: 'Buried near this spot – Captain The Hon. F. Bowes-Lyon – The Black Watch – 27th September 1915, Age 26'.

The Story of J.A Langford

I would now like to introduce you to another postcard and cap badge found by Alexander, which belonged to a British soldier who fell at some point during the first day of the Battle of Loos:

Front: *"Loving Greetings – Only a wish deep and tender, only a greeting that's true, straight from the heart of the sender, memory's message to you."*

Back: *'Pte. J.A Langford – 11962, 6th Batt. - K.O.S.B'.*

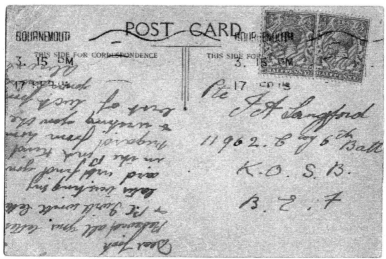

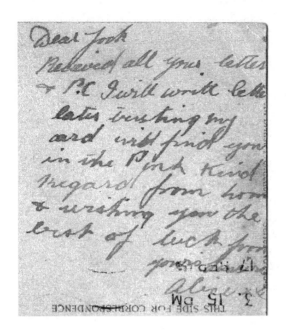

Back: *"Dear Jock — Received all your letters and P.C (postcards). I will write a letter later, trusting my card will find you in the pink. Kind regards from home & wishing you the best of luck. From your loving Alice xx"*

A cap badge of the King's Own Scottish Borderers Regiment, found by Alexander.

For over 100 years, this postcard has been a mystery to those who picked it up in Germany. However, with the amount of written information available on it, I was precisely able to identify the fallen soldier — Joseph Andrew Langford, a private within the King's Own Scottish Borderers Regiment (6th Battalion) who died on the 25th of September 1915, the first day of the Battle of Loos. Like with the discovery of Percy Walsh, I was instantly fascinated and moved once I was finally able to attach information and a story to this long-mysterious person. Using genealogy services and the Commonwealth War Grave Commission databases, it was possible to find his resting place which is close to where these battles took place in France:

Pte. Joseph Andrew Langford (11962) – B. unknown (Oldham, Lancashire) - D. 25.09.15 (Auchy, near La Bassée) – *Remembered at the Cabaret-Rouge British Cemetery, Souchez - VIII. J. 16.*

Using what I had found, I was able to reveal that he resided in Oldham in Lancashire (near where I grew up) and that he enlisted in Ashton-under-Lyne.

I also found digital copies of the original death register with his name and information, as shown below. This was a record often signed by the fallen soldier's next of kin. When I took a look at this document, I was almost lost for words — In the exact same handwriting as on the postcard, was written: "Auntie and Uncle, Alice and Richard Keating." For years thinking that Alice was Joseph's wife or girlfriend, we now know that she was in fact his auntie who was his legal guardian.

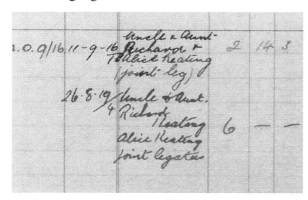

'Uncle & Aunt, Richard Keating & Alice Keating – joint legal custody'.

From here, I was then able to do some research into Alice and Richard Keating. In 1911, the United Kingdom made it mandatory for all households to take part in the national census, which gives information about all its occupants, their age, occupations, marital status, and house address. With this being publicly available, I discovered that Alice was a cotton mill worker and that Richard was a machine packer, both living with their three adult and teenage children at 7 Marple Street in Oldham, Lancashire. Both Alice and Richard were around the age of 50 when Joseph's postcard was written by Alice. There is little information available about Joseph's biological parents and background. Considering this, and the fact that he carried a different surname to Alice and Richard, it could suggest that he was perhaps adopted or fostered.

All this information did give me a sense of closure, of course, but there was something that made me feel as though I needed to do more to fully bring this story to some sort of an end. Well, this is exactly what I set out to do — After the postcard having left Joseph well over a century ago, and since then remaining in Alexander's family for all this time, I did what I thought about doing for a long time but never imagined possible…

111

In 2024, I visited the Loos battlefield and the grave of Joseph Langford. I was undeniably filled with excitement and anticipation leading up to this day, because this man, who was always just some unknown entity to me and others in my family, was now someone I could literally stand beside and meet. As I stood in the same spot where Alexander's old position was while looking towards the area where the hundreds of Scots were gunned down, the place seemed so peaceful and ordinary. It also felt eerie, knowing that so much bloody fighting took place here. When I later finally found Joseph's grave and walked closer up to it, an unexpected rush of mixed emotions shot through me; both of happiness and sadness. It was wonderful, sunny weather on this day. With the sound of the wind blowing through the trees and with the birds singing in the background, I stood looking at his grave in front of me and carefully placed the postcard next to his headstone along with a cross as a sign of respect. After the death of Joseph at the Battle of Loos in 1915, and after my great-great-grandfather having taken and treasured a part of him to be forever remembered — I can proudly say that it was me who brought closure to this story by returning the postcard to where it all began such a long time ago.

13

12.10.1915   As a reward, I have been assigned to our division's recruitment battalion for two months in Cysoing, southeast of Lille. All officers, who have been with the battalion for a long time, are given this cushy position in turn.

13.10.1915   Yesterday at noon, I took a truck to Provin, then went with the train to Lille and then took a car to Cysoing. This is a very nice little town, very untouched by the war and roughly the size of Auma *(a town in Thuringia)*. Here we still have to teach the makeshift replacements, who have been poorly trained in Germany, what only people can do who already have practical war experience; such as throwing hand grenades, building field fortifications, field exercises, lessons on the entire frontline service and so on. The commander of the battalion is supposedly very nice. This entire command is a recovery. We also have a very neat mess hall inside a chateau. I haven't had any duties yet because the replacements are still to arrive.

'Chateau Cysoing – The officers' mess hall – October 1915'.

17.10.1915   I have already made myself at home here and live alone with my attendant, Viereck (a colonial goods dealer from Dessau), in a small house that belongs to an abbot who has left. In there, I have a heated living room, two bedrooms (a very good bed), a kitchen with a gas cooker, a cellar, and a rabbit stall with three rabbits. My fellows here are very nice people for the most part. The food is superb. Today, we ate pheasants that are available here in large quantities, just like rabbits and partridges.

'My accommodation in Cysoing (the house with the sign on the door)'.

21.10.1915   It is now always cold, wet, and foggy — the proper La Bassée weather. The plenty of time spent outdoors is doing me very good though. We all looked very bad when we came out of there, and the commander said he was shocked by our appearance. The communication-zone pigs look different, of course. There is also a large number of non-commissioned officers and privates here, with eight from my battalion alone. This command came as a complete surprise to me. In the evening, I received a telephone call, and an hour later I signed off with the Count. All the experienced officers will be ordered to do this. Those of us who have already been here are Captain von Apell, First-Lieutenant Prince Lippe, First-Lieutenant Prince Solms, First-Lieutenant Mohr, Lieutenant von Wobeser, Lieutenant Oppermann, and various non-commissioned officers. Only active or reserve officers who have served for a year are taken; in other words, no former war volunteers who only received basic training at the time. In any case, you can endure it here for a while.

'A typical view of the gigantic area. The cattle pastures are all intersected by moats every 100 metres. Alongside these stand long rows of grazing and very tall poplar trees – Cysoing'.

114

Prince Lippe has already been behind the Front for many months. He is currently an associate of the commanding general. He will probably be the next to receive the Iron Cross 1st Class as a result. When the war will end — we haven't thought about this for a long time. It has no use either. We are satisfied when we are momentarily doing well again.

24.10.1915   We were alarmed on a drill basis at 4 o'clock last night, which was followed by a 16-kilometre exercise march. We haven't had a day without thick fog since I have been here, and sometimes you can barely even see your own unit during the morning exercises. I was very much envied by everyone for being given the command here, but I don't want to be behind the Frontlines long-term, as you do feel very different on the Front. I am happy to rest for one to two months though. We now also have enough officers on the Front since they are constantly being promoted. Unfortunately, I am unable to ride horses due to only a few puny ones being here for the people at the top.

31.10.1915   Here, we are efficiently working, exercising, entrenching, giving lessons and so forth. We are digging up a sequenced position — the foremost trench, and the reserve trench 30 metres behind with access trenches to both; with shelters, mine tunnels, and mirror-observation positions. So, with all shenanigans. Trees are being felled and trimmed in a neighbouring little forest. Something like that is a lot of fun. But just how difficult is all this work on the Front, where everything can only be built at night in constant danger to life and in the dark, and where all the material too can only be dragged forward for kilometres at night through the narrow, muddy trenches? Once we are finished with our sequenced positions, the entire duties of the trenches will be practised; replacement, alarm, throwing hand grenades and so on.

Tomorrow, there will be a big field-service exercise between the 2 companies against each other. Later come exercises in the night. The weather unfortunately continues to be very miserable. This winter will be even worse than the previous if it carries on like this. Attacks no longer seem to be feared here, as the company-commander courses have already been set up again. We will be assigned 30 officers tomorrow for this purpose.

We eat pheasants and rabbits very frequently here. Every unit has its own hunting ground, and whoever wants to hunt must obtain a hunting license. Everything is like during peacetime. However, the only big difficulty with this is obtaining shotguns and ammunition.

2.11.1915   It has turned out the way I thought it would with the Iron Cross 1st Class. Captain von Apell and First-Lieutenant Mohr received both that came to our battalion; not because they achieved something special in the last few battles, but because they are active officers, and it is their turn based on length of service. It is high time for this war to end, as the general dissatisfaction about the medal fraud is growing more and more. There are many people in the trenches on the Front who have been through a lot and who still haven't even got the Iron

Cross 2nd Class yet. On the other hand, the chef and the general's chauffeur have of course had it for a long time; not to mention the field-post officials, train-station commanders and similar folk who collect thick salaries, who live and reside marvellously and never get caught in the fire. They now bear the same award as someone who has put his life and health at risk every day for over a year. I am doing well so far, but it is raining non-stop.

8.11.1915   I was in Lille on Saturday and Sunday and visited Line. There is nothing going on there anymore. Everything closes at 9 o'clock in the evening and the streets are empty. We were both at the soldiers' cinema, but I unfortunately had to go to the train station in the middle of a scary detective story. Line wants to visit me here next time. The weather now isn't so bad anymore, but there is still a lot of fog every day, sometimes so thick that we have to stop exercising.

10.11.1915   Prince Lippe, who hasn't been in combat since Christmas and has always been behind the Front except for a few weeks, has now also received the Iron Cross 1st Class.

14.11.1915   We have now got a very unpleasant temporary captain who is disturbing the entire pleasant mood. He is just a typical, petty peace commission chief. Hopefully, he won't stay here permanently. As of today, we also have a band that now plays music daily during meals.

The sun recently shone for a few hours for once.

18.11.1915   We now have two companies of recruits here, and two companies of people from the Front in need of rest who will be exchanged for others after a couple of weeks. The recruits are also distributed to the Front as required. The ones we have had so far are already on the Frontline. 400 new ones have therefore arrived from Germany this evening. A new recovery department, which is under my authority, has now also been set up here for those released from the hospital. The commander told me this was a position of trust. I never would have dreamed of this either, that I would become a sanatorium director again *(a previous role before the war)*. This task is not easy because this society is as varied as possible — infantry, jägers, pioneers, artillerymen, Uhlans, pilots, and so forth; a completely undisciplined horde like all lightly wounded people who imagine that they are above everything, all because they were once wounded or sick. I first spoke to them to appeal to their conscience, and if that doesn't help, they will be given duties so that the guys will no longer know whether they are male or female.

We have a large house as our barrack that we have to completely refurnish since there was nothing there. We need to make our own tables and benches, and we also have to make our beds out of wooden frames with springs made of band iron. Ovens, wash bowls, utensils, towels — In short, everything has to be requisitioned because the people come out of the hospitals with nothing more than what they have on them. Everything needs to be created from nothing, and this is a devil of a job. We are working at full speed because there is a church concert here tomorrow that the commanding general will be attending, and he will surely want to see what we have achieved in two days. He will probably stay here to eat too, as he is a very close friend of our commander, Captain von Berg. There will be small gourmet meals on this occasion. Berg is generally a connoisseur. You rarely see him drinking anything other than sparkling wine with red wine. In his civilian career, he is a troubled agrarian from East Prussia!

'In the park of Chateau Cysoing – Left to right: Lieutenants Branscheid, Eskeldsen, Ferber, and Becker'.

'The surrounding area of Cysoing – December 1915'.

We find out what is happening on the Front through the army or division orders. Lieutenant von Wobeser from us was also present during the last company commander course, and now in my department, there is Lieutenant Treviranus, who got a piece of shrapnel in his hand during the big offensive near the church in Haisnes. It is now very cold here at times. It alternately freezes and rains just like last winter — no sun, and always foggy. As beautiful as it is here in summer, this cold, wet Flemish winter is just as horrible. It is very quiet on the Front. Both parties have enough to do with scooping out water. A breakthrough is now impossible since everything lies deep underwater, and you would simply sink into the swamp. All the meadows and even the roads are partly flooded. Back at home, you cannot even imagine what winter looks like in this flat country, where it rains almost non-stop for months.

'Cysoing – November 1915'.

28.11.1915 It has currently been freezing hard for a couple of days, which is very nice for us because you can protect yourself from the cold, but not from the constant wetness. There will be a big hunt here tomorrow, which will also be attended by the commander of the division, General von Altrock. Four of our gentlemen recently shot 16 rabbits in one afternoon. If only it weren't so difficult to obtain rifles and cartridges.

6.12.1915 I was in Lille yesterday and visited Line. I coincidentally met Werner Crienitz *(an old friend),* with whom I then had lunch at the Hotel Royal. With Line, Sister Maria and Lieutenant Eskeldsen, we were at the lace exhibition which had been organised to support the struggling local lace industry. I bought myself a laced collar. There were very nice things there. The showpiece was a laced dress for 2300 Mark. We then also visited a café and went for a walk.

'Me (left) with Lieutenant Eskeldsen in Cysoing'.

11.12.1915 There was a very lovely church concert here yesterday. We have now also set up a soldiers' cinema, and there is a lot of fun there. Like so, everything is being offered to bring people to other thoughts.

19.12.1915 I will probably be celebrating Christmas here. It will be more peaceful compared to the previous year at the Heckenhof. We will be having large feasts (with carp), as well as a hangover breakfast with oysters, caviar, sparkling wine and so on. It will all be for free from our board savings and penalty box.

26.12.1915 We celebrated Christmas here splendidly. In the afternoon on the 24th, there was first a communal celebration in the church. Then, at 6 o'clock in the evening, was the celebration of my department in the barracks in which 160 men took part, as well as the commander with the adjutant and staff doctor, and also 3 officers. There was first a piece of music, then a Christmas carol from the choir, and then I gave a big speech where I told the people how I spent the previous Christmas; saying to them how happy they should be that they can celebrate here, in such a warm and dry place. I have now learned how to give speeches. This comes from the lessons you have to give to people. In any case, the commander was very satisfied. Then came the gift distribution.

With the 240 Mark that we still had available, we bought apples, oranges, spiced cookies, small bottles of liquor, tobacco pipes, stationary, and so forth. Everyone received something. I donated three harmonicas which I bought on my last holiday, and I gave my attendant a small box of cigars and 10 Mark. There were 160 litres of beer at the celebration. There was then a large celebration in the mess hall at half past 7 in the evening, from which I didn't get home until 4:45 in the morning. The last ones left at half past 6 and then rode to the neighbouring village of Louvil, where they re-summoned the Uhlans who had just gone to bed after a long celebration, and then continued drinking.

'Cysoing – December 1915 – In the cage: Lt. Eskeldsen. Outside: Lt. Ferber'.

Right: 'Cysoing – December 1915 – Lt. Ferber and Stolzenberg'.

Left: 'Cysoing – December 1915 – At the top: Lt. Bresch and Ferber. At the bottom: Lt. Treviranus and Eskeldsen'.

On the first day of the holiday, there was a very good breakfast and another feast in the evening; and today, on the second day, things will be continuing in a similar way. Everything, including wine and cigars, is free and paid for from the penalty box. We namely have the following penalties at the table: Every foreign word — 10 Pfennigs; every violation against good customs or the use of indecent words, dependant on the severity of the case; standing up at the table, or reading and writing and so forth — 20 Pfennigs; arriving too late — 20 Pfennigs; unexcused absence — 1 Mark; not sharing milk and sugar — 20 Pfennigs; smoking before the light is on the table — 20 Pfennigs, and so on. A lot of money comes together this way, and sometimes over 20 Mark in one afternoon. Everyone is trying to fool the other. Like so, the non-commissioned officer was for instance asked to press the bell hanging over the table. Now since he is very small, he had to get up to do it, and along with overall joy, 20 Pfennigs were due.

I have been invited to the commander's for coffee this afternoon. It is now so warm here that you could walk without a coat if it weren't for the constant rain.

Right: 'Our donkey cart – Cysoing – December 1915'.

Left: 'In the park of Chateau Cysoing – December 1915'.

30.12.1915 I now always go hunting in the evenings with Treviranus. Yesterday's outcome was one rabbit and one wild pigeon. With two rounds, I recently shot seven pigeons which are plentiful here. They will then be eaten in the mess hall. There are also plenty of partridges, but they have already become very shy.

4.1.1916 I celebrated my birthday with Lieutenant Ferber along with champagne and burgundy. We are now having riding lessons on Uhlan horses again with Cavalry Captain von Platen, a famous jockey who only does it as a favour since he is often invited to our mess hall. Things are already going much better now than in Billy. Above all, riding without stirrups is no longer hurting my whole body. I have applied for three weeks of holiday. My request lies with the division.

14

8.1.1916   Nothing resulted from my holiday request because I was assigned to Lille, and it came like so — Several weeks ago, all military units received an appeal for experts from all possible industry sectors. I thought this could be a very nice position for me and volunteered for the textile industry. I hadn't even thought about it anymore when a telegram from the division suddenly arrived for me yesterday, telling me to immediately report to the Banque de France in Lille. I instantly packed my things and departed at 3 o'clock in the afternoon. From what I have learned so far, it seems to involve very pleasant and very independent work. You have to inspect the factories in Roubaix, Tourcoing, and so on; from the sea down to Valenciennes, and do surveys about everything possible — the owners, working capital, machines, supplies, war damages, the markets, and so forth. The completed questionnaires are then compiled and processed. Two men usually go together, and you are completely independent. I am still living in the hotel for the time being, but I am moving into citizen quarters tomorrow. I need to feed myself and receive 10 Francs a day for this, as well as my salary too, of course.

I visited Line yesterday. She invited me to the hospital for a birthday coffee tomorrow. The work should take four weeks, but it is believed that it will take much longer because there is a lot of material to process.

11.1.1916   Today, I moved into my private apartment on Rue de Bourgogne, a side street off the large Boulevard de la Liberté. A doctor who is in the war lived in the house. There is only one concierge with her 12-year-old daughter. I have all to myself one lounge, one bedroom, one toilet room, everything with gas stoves and electric lights, and a water closet. My attendant has a room too. I can endure it here already. Hopefully, I can stay here for a long time.

My activity is as follows — At 10:15 in the morning, I and my technician travelled to Tourcoing for 45 minutes with the electric railway, where we visited a weaving mill until around 1 o'clock. We then travelled back again for lunch. Today I had the roast goose made for me that was sent from home, along with strawberry compote and red wine. We are now making good use of my Christmas packages. I then filled out the questionnaires on the bench from 5 to 6 o'clock. It was very interesting today because we were in a factory that was only partially operational a month before the war. Everything was wonderfully arranged and equipped with the newest machinery. In the evenings, I eat at home or go dressed in my field-grey uniform, where there is military music and Bavarian beer in steins (1 litre for 40 Pfennigs). I came across Heinz Köchel *(an old associate)* as a pioneer vice sergeant two days ago, on the Rue Nationale.

A huge accident happened here tonight. The entire hotel shook as if from a strong earthquake, instantly followed by a terrible crash and clanging of glass panes. An ammunition depot had blown up, and people talk about there being 200 dead and wounded. It hasn't yet been determined who still lies under the rubble. An entire city district is supposedly destroyed. Many thousands of windowpanes and large shop windows have namely burst all over the city. You could see people sweeping up broken glass everywhere today. The glass damage alone runs into the many thousands.

16.1.1916   I have already recorded all kinds of factories — weaving mills, spinning mills, dye works, carpet factories, and hosiery and corset factories. You learn everything over time. I was at the site of the explosion a couple of days ago, and it is just awful. An entire city district is in ruins. Multiple large spinning mills larger than our factory have collapsed. We don't know how many people have died, but there are certainly several hundred.

The English fired approximately 15 heavy shells towards Lille tonight. I don't know where yet. In any case, the whizzing here in the middle of the city sounded almost more eerie than on the Front. All the French in the street were on their knees. I of course stayed calm in bed, as it would be too strange if my house were to be hit among the many thousand houses.

A Disaster in Lille

On the 11th of January 1916, at half past 3 in the morning, the city of Lille was devastated by the explosion of the '18 Ponts Munition Depot'. This was an old fortification consisting of 18 arches (the origin of its French name) used by the Germans to store explosives. There was a sudden big bright flash, tonnes of debris catapulted in the air, a shockwave streamed through the city causing devastation, and a sound so loud it could be heard in Holland where it was mistaken for an earthquake. It left a crater measuring 150 metres wide and 30 metres deep — 21 factories were destroyed, along with 738 houses within the Moulin District of the city. It also caused the deaths of 104 civilians and 30 German soldiers, along with almost 400 people wounded.

The cause is not known, but it is not thought to have been accidental. The Germans would blame it on sabotage, offering a 1000-Mark reward to whoever identifies the culprit. To show us the aftermath of this explosion during his time in Lille, Alexander kept a postcard that shows one of the large, destroyed factory buildings. In the 21st century, this disaster is commemorated by a monument on the Rue de Maubeuge, in the area where this took place.

'After the large explosion in Lille'

19.1.1916   I am always very tired due to the unaccustomed work. At 9 o'clock this morning, I took the electric railway to the suburban railway station of St. André; then at 9:30, took the train to Roncq via Roubaix and Tourcoing, where I visited three linen weaving mills. I then walked for one hour to Ponte de Neuville, where on the way I saw a French plane that had just been shot down by our fighter plane. Then I took the electric railway to Tourcoing, transferred, and continued to Roubaix where I had a very nice lunch in the 'Cercle de L'industrie' (a private club) at half past 2. After that, I took the electric mainline train to Lille. I then went to the bank after an hour and wrote three large reports. I had dinner from 7 to 8 o'clock (still from the Christmas parcels); read the newspaper and wrote home; and after that, went to bed very tired as always at 9 o'clock. This is how it goes day after day. I will be visiting carpet factories in Neuville tomorrow, and ribbon factories in Halluin later on. I have also already reserved the tapestry weaving mills in Cysoing, but I am not going there until the 1st of February so I can take this opportunity to collect my salary.

My previous attendant has been replaced, as all those capable of field service are to go to the Front; and as they should, because the strong, healthy people running around behind the Front alone would make a small army. My new attendant, named Ruben, is only fit for garrison duty. I would like to get rid of him though since the guy has nothing to do and gets lazier every day. My madame could take care of everything much better. I am just waiting for an opportunity to throw him out. It just isn't good when people are doing too well in the long run.

22.1.1916   From Halluin, I visited the pretty small Belgian town of Menin today, as you eat much cheaper there than in the French places. Everything is much cheaper in Belgium, including fruit. It is all barely affordable here in Lille, especially now that our food allowance has been reduced from 10 Francs to 5 Mark a day. I therefore need to completely feed myself. This is how much lunch is currently costing me. In Menin, on the other hand, I paid 75 Pfennigs for soup, roasted meat with potatoes, Leipziger Allerlei *(a German vegetable dish)*, and one bottle of beer.

The recent bombardment was rather bad. A house was shot into flames 200 metres from my residence. They have been shooting only towards the suburbs in the last few days though. On Monday, I will be visiting some large damask weaving mills in Halluin; and on Tuesday, the largest carpet weaving mill with 1000 weaving looms in Roubaix.

'Shot-up houses on the Railway Station Road – Lille.'

25.1.1916   I was in Halluin and Menin all day yesterday, and since I then took care of four factories, I will be skipping work today. It is much nicer and above all, much cheaper in Belgium than in France. The eggs cost 45 to 50 Centimes in Lille and only 18 Pfennigs in Menin. I immediately took a small supply with me, and together with my technician bought 20 pounds of apples, each pound for 15 Pfennigs. The people in Menin can barely understand French. They are all Flemish and have already learned German very well. It was wonderful spring weather on Sunday, and I wanted to pick up Line. She couldn't leave though, so we have now arranged to meet this afternoon. I want to show her my residence, and then we are going on a walk. Finally, we will probably end up in a coffee shop or the soldiers' cinema.

Our work was actually meant to be completed by the 1st of February. However, since the textile department is the most extensive and has over 1200 establishments to deal with, our deadline was extended to the 15th of February, and now even to the 1st of March.

27.1.1916   Yesterday, I bought several pretty things in a large upholstery fabric mill in Roubaix, namely a large colourful tablecloth and two sofa cushion covers. I believe I made a very cheap purchase at 13.15 Francs. Tonight, for the

Kaiser's birthday, there is a feast for the Industrial Commission in the officers' mess.

31.1.1916   I now frequently work together with Lieutenant Harnack from the Brösel Company in Greiz. I am travelling to Cysoing for my salary tomorrow. I very urgently need to purchase a new uniform and a pair of leather gaiters, which will probably cost 150 Mark. The good clothes suffer much more here than on the Front, where you always wear only the oldest stuff in the trenches. You also need to look decent here where there are so many troops represented, especially if you belong to such a distinguished battalion.

    Yesterday, on Sunday, I was in Tournai, a very small and pretty Belgian town, but there was unfortunately thick fog so you couldn't see much. I only went and saw the wonderful cathedral from the inside, and then ate very well and very cheaply compared to Lille. I also bought a week's supply of eggs again.

'Tournai (Belgium) – A view towards the belfry and cathedral – February 1916'.

'Tournai (Belgium) – Le Pont des Trous, an old fortified bridge – February 1916'.

3.2.1916 Line and Sister Maria visited me very unexpectedly this afternoon and then had coffee at my place. My new uniform made a grand impression. I supposedly look very slim in it. They also really liked my residence. I conveniently got my uniform here in the Army and Navy House, but it was very expensive: frock coat — 75 Mark; epaulettes — 2 Mark; trousers — 47.50 Mark; gaiters — 28 Mark. I was in Cysoing on the 1st of February, where two companies had gone to the Front to dig trenches. Otherwise, everything was as usual. Nothing has changed in Billy either.

20.2.1916 I have happily arrived back in Lille. I was in Germany for a few days, and it came like so — With a lot of skill, I explained to the head of the Industry Commission, Major von Weinberg, that it would be of great advantage and would certainly make a good impression if the relevant authorities in Germany, for example, the Wool Industry Office in Berlin and also the Weaving Association in Greiz, were given an oral presentation about our activities. I would be willing to do this, especially since I am well acquainted with the gentlemen concerned. He fell for it, and I got a one-week holiday. I immediately travelled to Weida, where I stayed for a couple of days and visited our association chairman in Greiz. I then travelled to Berlin with Hanne *(a relative)* and visited the concerning location, and then travelled back to Lille from Berlin. The train was so sparsely occupied that I could lie down from Cologne onwards.

Nothing has changed here, just it is much warmer here than in Germany. I am travelling to Tournai with the butter-and-egg transport this afternoon.

'Lille – The view from the train station into the Railway Station Road – February 1916'.

'Lille – La Grande Place – February 1916'.

25.2.1916   Since I have free travel everywhere in the occupied territory, thanks to my identification card as a member of the Industrial Commission, I will take a few nice trips to Belgium. I was in Antwerp today, a large city but with nothing else of interest. What is particularly striking is the population, which looks completely different to the French. It is unfortunately cloudy, and it has been incredibly cold for a few days. I am travelling to Brussels in the afternoon and then back to Lille in the evening.

27.2.1916   I visited Bruges and Ghent. It is wonderful in the ancient city of Bruges, where I strolled around all day. It was also very nice in Ghent, where there is an old castle and many nice old houses. The weather was unfortunately bad. I then travelled back along the very interesting coastal fortifications via Heist, Zeebrugge, Blankenberge and Ostend.

'Ghent – A view of the St. Nicholas Church and belfry – February 1916'.

Left: 'Bruges – Smedenpoort'.

'Bruges – Marketplace with the provincial court. At the front is a unit of marines – February 1916'.

1.3.1916 After my work in Lille ended, I travelled back to Cysoing today, where I received the order from the division to report back to the battalion. I thereupon travelled to Billy via Lille on ***3.3.1916***, where they were very happy that I was back. I have been given the command of the 1st Company in the trench. The actual company commander, Captain von Apell, alternates with the Count at the battalion command centre. I therefore have a completely independent post and no longer need to do regular night watches. I thus have overall supervision in the trench day and night, must specify what needs to be constructed and monitor the execution, and I am responsible for the expansion and security of the position.

I am going into position for one day tonight and will then be resting again for four days. Our replacement is now eight days in the trenches and four days of rest. The weather is currently horrible. It rained heavily yesterday, and it has been snowing and storming non-stop since this evening. This will create a lovely mess tonight. My old residence at Albertine's was occupied. My current room is of course just a dog hole compared to my Palais *(palace)* in Lille, but I have lived much worse. I at least have a bed, an oven, and electric lighting. Even that is a lot. The riding lesson here is from 4 to 5 o'clock on every rest day. The food is impeccable as before, and there is even draft beer for 20 Pfennigs a glass; for the enlisted men too, of course. Nothing of importance has happened since I left here, apart from the usual trench shootouts. I therefore haven't missed out on anything.

15

5.3.1916 I haven't experienced such a mess like last night in a long time. If I wasn't an old, grey-haired trench warrior but still a novice in this field, I would be completely fed up now. However, the good mood doesn't leave me when I think of the much worse times I experienced earlier during the winter of 1914 and 1915.

Yesterday evening, I drove with the car to Haisnes via Douvrin on the road covered in deep mud and with water everywhere in deep shell holes. Not much of this village remains, and even Douvrin, which I remember as being almost undamaged, is now just a pile of rubble. On the road, there are countless wagon convoys that bring forward provisions, ammunition, timber, planks, barbed wire, concrete, and so forth — knee-deep swamps to the left and right. The troops that you come across are layered from top to bottom with dirt and look as though they have rolled around in the mud. Some of them come in very adventurous disguises — legs, arms, the head and rifles covered with all kinds of rags to protect against the wetness. They look more like vagabonds than soldiers. But I have the greatest respect for these people, who lead a life here that the communication-zone pigs cannot even imagine in their wildest dreams.

I had to commence on foot from Haisnes to Auchy, as it was still too light to drive on the road. I walked across the country through the sodden, torn and shot-up fields. Auchy is now just a pile of stones with underground life in the cellars, which are connected to one another via concealed communication trenches. I reported to Captain von Apell in such a cellar, who was playing solace with Lieutenant Nugel. Our previous battalion command post is currently being rebuilt because there was too much leakage through the ceiling. I then went forward through the many 100-metre-long trenches, some of which run under shot-up houses in parts. Anyone who hasn't seen them or helped build them has no idea of the work that goes into these trenches, which are over two metres deep. The walls are covered from top to bottom with thick planks and wicker and braced with beams to prevent them from sliding together. The ground is covered with duckboards. And yet, this entire huge work has been accomplished only in the dead of night, under the most unfavourable weather conditions and under enemy fire. I could retire if I had the money for all the wood that has been used. In these beautifully developed trenches, I found myself completely dry until I reached the battle trenches, which do look very bad in parts. It often nearly goes up to the knees in the tough mud, but I got through almost dry since I was still wearing my old leather gaiters over the wrap puttees.

I am living in a shelter that I remember from before, which is particularly supported by a dozen strong tree trunks. The oven heats well, I have a petroleum lamp, and the food is good too. That it drips through the ceiling in various places with monotonous regularity; that rats and mice rustle and squeak behind the ceiling and wall coverings; that the boys next door play the harmonica with more enthusiasm than skill — These are little things from before that I have long since gotten used to. The sun is currently shining, the snow is melting, the water is rising, and the trenches are becoming more groundless. There was just a lot of noise because we attacked the English with heavy mortars, to which they responded with shrapnel shells. Lieutenants Stachelhausen and Petersen are still in my company. I am living together with Vice-Sergeant Joerding, who was previously a marine officer and who had been swayed due to some dumb games or womanising affairs. He voluntarily re-enlisted as a common jäger when the war broke out. He came into the field back then with my transport and was wounded at Les-Trois-Maisons. He is a very nice and calm man.

7.3.1916   The mess here is once again huge because we haven't had such incredible weather in a long time. Today is the first nice day again after raining and snowing for days, but everything is floating. I was relieved on Sunday night and had to walk back to Billy with Lieutenant Stachelhausen. This was a great route — nothing but deep mud, with the road flooded in places like a lake. Even though it was pitch black, you had to hurry as much as possible to get out of the endangered stretch. The villages of Auchy, Haisnes and Douvrin are now just piles of rubble because they are being shot at, day and night. I then had a lovely bath in our magnificent spa the next morning. The spa is always reserved the next day for the relieved officers and men. You book the time the day before and can then use it for an hour. There is a bathtub for the officers and oberjägers and a shower room for the other troops.

'Lt. Stachelhausen, Adelina (the landlord's daughter) and me in Billy – The camera was unfortunately not properly adjusted – March 1916'.

On the second rest day, we threw live hand grenades in the morning, and exercised in the afternoon while wearing gas masks; an indescribable, laughable sight. I then went into the gas room with a dozen people. The gas round was fired, and we were let back out after some time. I didn't notice anything, which is a sign that the mask sits well and that no gas attack can harm me, as the gas within this trial room is stronger than the gas clouds in any attack. The effect was so strong that everyone else who was just in the affected building needed to rush out immediately. My eyes instantly started to water too when I took off the mask on the street.

This morning, I went on a short practice march to Annoeullin with my company in the most beautiful winter landscape. Everything was already a wet mess again on the way back. Everywhere along the paths, squads of captured Russians are busy repairing them. An English 2-man patrol, which had made itself unwelcome by throwing grenades, was shot down by us on the frontline tonight. There was of course overall happiness. Tomorrow evening, we are again going back into position on the Front for eight days. I am already dreading the journey to Auchy. Anyone who isn't wrapped up all around in the trench in weather like this doesn't know what war is. Last winter was ten times worse though, as we now at least have good shelters. Any major attack is ruled out given the current ground conditions. The close combat mentioned in the army report concerns the so-called 'Hohenzollern Redoubt', a forward-protruding trench system just to our left, which played a major role in the September battles and which is where the English detonated. They have occupied the craters of the explosions, and we are still in the process of pushing them back out with mortars, hand grenades and so on.

Everyone is sick here. No wonder given the miserable weather.

11.3.1916   I have now been in the trench again for two days. I am doing well, and I am already completely used to the activities again. The weather has also gotten slightly better. At least it isn't raining and snowing anymore. The ceiling of my shelter is now nailed with corrugated sheet metal, and food cans have been hung up where it is still dripping. You just need to be very careful with this though, as you receive the entire blessing all at once if you ever bump your head into it.

'In front of the kitchen entrance of my shelter. At the front to the right is me – March 1916'.

Left: 'In front of the kitchen entrance of my shelter – From left to right: My attendant Nöding, Lt. Stachelhausen, and me – March 1916'.

Right: 'Jägers of the 1st Company in the trench during lunch – March 1916'.

Yesterday on the 10th of March, the anniversary of Neuve Chapelle and the birthday of the English King, we expected an attack. Everything stayed calm though. We generally can't complain right now as far as the shooting is concerned. Things look wild ahead of us. Hundreds of the Scots from September are still lying in front of our obstacle, but the piles of corpses, which were metres high back then, have now collapsed together quite a bit.

Lieutenant Seemann is now building concrete shelters in Billy and is currently in Berlin on a gas course.

14.3.1916 It has been wonderful sunny weather since yesterday. You can thereby endure it in the trench. I sat in front of the shelter in my sleeved vest almost all day today and even had myself shaved outdoors. At home, people will be surprised that I write about the weather in almost every letter, but that is what concerns us the most out here. The enemy comes second.

133

'I am having myself shaved in front of my shelter – March 1916'.

Left: *'Jäger Friedel, a porcelain painter from Triptis – March 1916'.*

Top and left: *'Lieutenant Stachelhausen – March 1916'.*

We were just shooting at targets on our last rest day when a squadron of 26 English aircraft suddenly approached. The largest number I had previously seen at once was 14. We immediately afterwards heard the bombs falling down and exploding. They were dropped over Provin, Carvin, and so forth. Two of our planes are said to have attacked the large swarm, during which the deputy officer, with whom I flew at the time, was killed.

'A looted English machine gun is used by us to shoot at the aeroplanes – March 1916'.

There was huge activity in our trench tonight. Mining sounds were heard within our tunnels through our listening posts, on the very left wing along the Auchy-Vermelles Road. It was then decided to detonate. Our tunnels were loaded with 30 quintals of dynamite, and tonight, at half past 4, the matter was blown up with a crash of thunder. It sounded eerie as the huge masses of earth which had been thrown up rained down again. Our machine guns were deployed as soon as the explosion was taking place, and immediately when the last chunks came down, the crater was occupied by a detachment of our men who instantly dug themselves in at the edge and set it up for defence. Of course, a connecting route to the position was immediately dug, and a new mine tunnel was started from the crater to the front.

This morning, I was in the crater that turned out to be much larger than I had ever anticipated — 30 metres in diameter and 15 metres deep. It is circular with raised edges, just like a moon crater. Hopefully, a fair amount of English perished inside the squashed enemy tunnel. We haven't had any losses. Only the officer cadet in my company, who, like all newcomers, is far too curious and peeped over cover for too long, received a shot in the head and will hardly get away with it.

'The mine crater detonated by us a few hours ago – On the enemy-facing side, you can see a steep path at the top for the sentries. A new tunnel is immediately being pushed forward at the bottom'.

Tunnelling At The Redoubt

It is now almost 6 months since the Battle of Loos commenced, and both sides have initiated new tactics to become the victor in this battle area — Tunnel Warfare. The goal of this tactic is to destroy the enemy positions and eliminate the troops inside them from underneath. This results in gigantic craters which serve as new strategic strongholds to launch attacks from. These events are known as 'The Hohenzollern Redoubt Actions from the 2nd-18th of March 1916', involving the specialised German pioneers and the Tunnelling Company of the British Royal Engineers. My father was a Royal Engineer, which led to him being stationed in Germany and me later being born. The fact that Alexander faces this same branch of the British Army, but in a different era, makes these events extremely remarkable from my perspective:

"On the night of the 14th of March, it was time. The first bright glimmer of light shows itself in the east. The trench crew stand on the trench exit ladders. Hand-grenade troops crouch in the trench next to the detonation site ready to leap, and the machine-gun operators, mortars and batteries listen intently in the night — 4:50 is the ordered time of detonation!

Lieutenant Köllmann of the reserves and commander of the Tunnelling Company, releases the electric detonation cord. The ground opens up under a thundering crash, spewing out flames and smoke. With the heavy earth chunks still raining down, the hand-grenade troops throw themselves into the gigantic, house-deep crater."

- The War Diary of The 11th Kurhessian Jäger Battalion

18.3.1916   I was relieved last night and have just come back from the riding lesson. It is going very well, including the jumping over obstacles. The English have been firing at us heavily with 11cm shells over the last few days, but they cannot do anything against our deep holes in the ground. We also didn't suffer a single casualty despite more than 200 shells. This morning, I bathed, shaved and put on new underwear and the new uniform, and now I feel like a new person after 8 days of dirt.

1.4.1916   There has been a postal suspension as of late, and that is always a sign that something is going on. There had always been rumours that we would be replaced, but nothing ever came of it. At the end of the previous month, these rumours intensified more and more, and on the 27th of March, I found out in the morning in the trench that not only we but the entire army corps would be relieved. You could then hear the wildest speculations. One person even claimed that we would be going to the Dutch border because Holland had declared war on us. Others feared Verdun. Others again heard from the artillery that the horses were being fitted with winter hooves, so we could only be going to Russia. Little by little the truth came through, namely that we will all be going to Belgium for a few weeks to rest.

On the morning of the 27th of March, my successor came into the trench to learn about everything, and I had to show and explain everything all day long; ammunition, materials and so forth, via a receipt. He was a district judge from Zwickau, as we were replaced by the Reserve Saxon Jäger-Battalion 25. The relief in the evening went very swiftly, and it was with some sadness that we left the position in which we had lived for over a year and in which we had experienced so much. But it was very unpleasant due to the snow and rainy weather in the last few days. We were also continually attacked day and night with mortars and rifle grenades to such an extent that, especially in the afternoon, we could only move in the trench by leaping from shelter to shelter.

I arrived in Billy at 2 o'clock in the night, covered in mud from top to bottom. I packed up quickly, slept for an hour and set out on the march to Seclin at 5 o'clock in the morning. We moved into quarters there. Everything was overcrowded since there were 15,000 men in the small town. I lived in a pharmacy and slept in the same bed as Lieutenant Stachelhausen, which worked very well with the wide French beds. At 6 o'clock in the morning of the next day, we, that is, two companies and the bicycle company, advanced towards our other two companies which had been relieved a day later, and we carried out a big assault together. We then went back to Seclin along with music.

In the evening, there was then a large celebration in our quickly improvised mess hall, which was particularly notable because all officers were gathered together for the first time in a year. At 7 o'clock the next morning, the entire battalion then departed on an endless train with the field kitchens and luggage. Our colony of chickens throned in a basket inside the food carriage. We marched south under Lille, carried out a major attack on Fort de Sainghin along the way near Cysoing, and then continued endlessly towards the border. We stopped in a meadow near a village en route, brought out the field kitchens and ate while lying on the grass. It was marvellous, just like on a field day.

'Food distribution by the field kitchen while on the march from Seclin to Belgian Templeuve'.

'Food break on the march from Seclin to Templeuve – From left to right: Lt. Petersen and Stachelhausen, Captain von Apell and Junior-Doctor Stark'.

At 4 o'clock in the afternoon, we finally reached our destination, the small Belgian town of Templeuve between Roubaix and Tournai. I am living in a very nice room at a brewer's residence. Our mess hall is inside a castle with a wonderful large park teeming with wild pigeons and rabbits. There are no traces of the war here, and you can bear it here, especially since the weather has been wonderful since we left Billy. It is generally said that it is far too beautiful here for us to stay for long. I was called by my name when I marched in. It was Fritz Rössler from Weida, who too had come here with his company of pioneers. Von Hammacher the Uhlan also visited me yesterday, with whom I was in the hospital of Valenciennes and who is now the civil commissioner in Tournai.

138

*'Castle Templeuve –
April 1916'.*

'Belgian Templeuve'.

We have staunch duties here; at 6 o'clock in the morning mostly marching exercises combined with combat drills, and then sports, lessons and so forth in the afternoon. We are also happy to have riding lessons three times a week. These duties are pure enjoyment in this pleasant weather. Of course, no one knows what will become of us later. Perhaps we will relieve another corps that will then be able to rest.

'Templeuve – Left to right: Lieutenants Otto, Schmelz, Stachelhausen, and Bode; Captain von Apell and Lieutenant Pötsch'.

'Templeuve – Horses of the jäger battalion in the marketplace. In the background is the canteen. The officer is Captain Conrad'.

7.4.1916 There is still a postal suspension due to the movement of troops. We have a large battle exercise near Tournai tomorrow, and on Monday, the Count is inspecting the 1st Company. Unfortunately, Captain von Apell is currently in Germany on a gas course, and so I have to present the company and set out battle instructions for the platoon leaders. Riding is a lot of fun for me now that I can see progress every hour. I am now in the first riding class.

10.4.1916 Yesterday, six of us went on a wonderful 3.5-hour horse ride across the Scheldt *(river)* to Mont St. Aubert. The area there is superb and very similar to ours at home. Nugel said it was like being upon the 'Käseschenke' near Gera. The hill is 150 metres high and stands all alone in the great plain. You can see infinitely far from there, far beyond Lille.

I have just come back from a leisurely ride. Since the captain is away all week, I take turns riding his two horses every day and also take part in the riding lesson. You learn something this way. There will be a large battalion exercise tomorrow, which I will take part in on horseback.

'Prince Solms and Lieutenants Oppermann and Weber'.

17.4.1916 I rode a lot last week; in a single day from 6 o'clock in the morning to 2 o'clock in the afternoon. But I have now also reached the point where I feel safe on every horse. Yesterday, on Sunday morning, there was a field prayer service in the castle park. We visited a cockfight in the afternoon. Four pairs emerged, and the fights regularly ended very quickly with the death of a rooster. The animals have a 5cm-long sharp steel needle strapped to each leg, and they attack each other with indescribable rage. Many residents watch with some of them sitting on the roofs. High bets are made in the process. Whilst it was very interesting, it was also so brutal that we won't be watching it again. The representatives of two places usually fight against each other. Yesterday, Templeuve had 1 win and 3 defeats. One winner is said to be worth 85 Mark.

18.4.1916 This afternoon, I received a telegram from home with the terrible news of Dieter's death. The Count immediately gave me 10 days of leave.

Note: Alexander's son Dieter sadly died of Diphtheria at just 3 years old.

16

'Templeuve – A view from the marketplace towards the main road and steam tram to Tournai. I am living on the left inside the house with the small tower – May 1916'.

1.5.1916   I have arrived back here again. On the return journey, I caught a carriage in Magdeburg that went through Brussels where I used the 2.5-hour layover to eat. There is complete peace here. There is a holiday until the 15th of May, so we will probably stay here for a long time. The weather is wonderful today, and it is amazing how everything has turned green in the last 10 days. This instantly makes the area look much prettier. There was a large May Day celebration in the mess hall last night, but I already went to bed at half past 9 and got up again at 5 o'clock in the morning.

6.5.1916   I am the company commander again until the 15th of May, as Captain von Apell is replacing the brigade adjutant who is on leave. I am sitting on horseback for half the day. The day before yesterday, we came back from big exercises at 5 o'clock in the afternoon, and yesterday at 3 o'clock.

23.5.1916   We are constantly carrying out large exercises here. I was on an exercise march in Cysoing with my company yesterday and visited my old acquaintances.

'From left to right: Lieutenants Lagner, Lingelbach, Bode, and me – May 1916'.

'Explosion of 3 hand grenades – May 1916'.

'The bridge over the Scheldt by Pont-à-Chin which is the access to the training ground, and which plays a big role in our exercises – May 1916'.

27.5.1916   The holiday is extended until the 15th of June, and the general opinion is that we will be staying here for a long time. I have nothing against this, although there are exercise operations like in peacetime. We leave three times a week at 6 o'clock in the morning at the earliest, and we don't come back until 3 o'clock in the afternoon. Captain von Apell is on a replacement yet again, so I have the company and therefore the two horses for another 14 days.

1.6.1916   We now have marvellous weather again. This afternoon, I am travelling to the 'Source des Mottes' with several friends, a very nice garden restaurant in Tournai.

9.6.1916   A lot has changed here again. Our corps has namely left for Verdun. Only we stayed behind, but tomorrow we need to make room for other troops and are then going to Kain, a small village a few kilometres north of Tournai. We are to be trained as a storm battalion and will therefore probably stay behind the Front for another three to four weeks. I don't know where we will end up then.

11.6.1916   We marched over Tournai towards Kain in the most beautiful weather yesterday. Kain is a half-village and half-suburb of Tournai. I am living very nicely with the Catholic priest. I have the tram stop in front of my door, and

I am at most 15 minutes from Tournai. It is very wonderful here with one castle next to the other, all surrounded by the customary moat and huge, ancient parks. The entire area is a large garden. The many asparagus fields are especially pleasant for us. The people here are very hardworking. You see them working in their fields all day long, picking out every bit of weed. My company is accommodated like never before in the war. Every man has his own bed. We are all of the same opinion that the next 14 days will be the nicest in the entire war, especially because the Count has been assigned to a training course for 14 days. It was no longer tolerable with him lately. As nice as he was as long as we were in the trenches and he was dependent on us, he became just as unpleasant behind the Front. Then came the old military spirit back to the surface, which shouted all day and complained about everything. Now, thank God, we have been free of him for some time.

Our mess hall is again within a chateau in the middle of an endless park with gondola rides, a tennis court and so on. I am now up to speed with my riding because you learn a good deal by riding on the grounds, especially on a horse as good as Lissi, where you constantly have to be prepared for anything with her.

'La Tombe by Tournai – The church and to the left the rectory, my accommodation – June 1916'.

Right: 'Our staff quarters – June 1916'.

Left: 'Our mess hall – June 1916'.

14.6.1916   Our holidays are unfortunately completely rain-swept. Even today it has still been pouring down with rain.

18.6.1916   There are now only sports activities here; no more exercises, but just gymnastics, gymnastic games, races, hand-grenade throwing, and overcoming obstacles. The entire battalion is being reformed. The old and stiff people are coming out, and we are therefore receiving the young replacements. We are even receiving special equipment — the 'Stahlhelm' *(the new combat helmet of the German Army)*, a blouse, laced shoes, wrap puttees, and trousers with leather trimming at the back and on the knees. The battalion is to become a force consisting only of very skilled people who don't shy away from any hindrance, and who can throw hand grenades with complete confidence. For this training, we will probably stay here for at least four weeks.

22.6.1916   Our corps has arrived at Verdun. Our old division lies out there in reserve, and the other division is in position on 'Height 304' *(a place of heavy fighting)*. We will certainly be going there too later, but that is still a good way away because our specialised training still necessitates at least four to six weeks. The utilisation of a storm battalion is something completely new. The entire battalion doesn't storm, but instead, individual squads are formed which are assigned to the infantry as hand-grenade specialists, flamethrowers and so on to support them. These troops are immediately pulled back again after the assault.

     We are never permanently in the trenches, but rather 20 to 30 kilometres behind the Front on our training grounds, and are only partially brought forward when required. The losses are said to become much lower than usual as a result of the special training. Since it is my turn again, it isn't out of the question that I will get a holiday in the next four weeks.

     We are now commencing large exercises here.

17.7.1916   I have happily arrived back from my leave. The train was only slightly occupied, so I was able to lie down to sleep through the night. Nothing has changed here in the meantime, except that the bicycle company will still likely be leaving us today. Our training will last at least four weeks. When you see the work and the vast amount of material that goes into our training grounds, you would almost think that we will keep our headquarters here permanently.

20.7.1916   Big news! — We are to be transported to the Carpathians tonight. We are extremely happy about this because at first, we thought we were going to the Somme. People in the East will be amazed when we arrive with our steel helmets. I am extremely happy that we are finally going to another theatre of the war.

22.7.1916   Our transport has been slightly delayed. We will be combined with two other jäger battalions to form a jäger regiment and will become a Carpathian Corps. Therefore, we will probably be going to Bukovina; hopefully very high up in the mountains, then what I have always wanted will be fulfilled. This deployment came as a big surprise to us all. Nobody would have thought it possible that we would end up anywhere other than the Somme or Verdun. It isn't known which route we will take through Germany. We are departing on two trains this Saturday. I am just happy that I had my full holiday, as the current holidaymakers have been recalled back after a couple of days via telegram. Along with music, we will be marching to the train station of Tournai tonight, where we will be loaded.

So off into the Carpathians!

A NEW JOURNEY BEGINS
(The Eastern Front)

"A telegram from the highest command of the army, Lieutenant. The adjutant is to personally answer the phone." — Like so, the adjutant of Jäger-Battalion 11 was called to the telephone on the 20th of July 1916, at 10 minutes past 5 in the afternoon. After days of great anticipation, the decision now had to be made as to which point along the large German Fronts the battalion, which had been newly trained to tackle difficult tasks, would be deployed to. There can be no doubt that this call has been made during a focal point of war events — The Battle for Verdun is still raging with undiminished violence, within which the VII Corps has now been bleeding for weeks. In addition, the mighty new battles around the Somme are becoming more significant, with the flashes from the intense artillery exchanges being visible as far as Mont St. Aubert on clear evenings. In the East, the Brusilov Offensive has overrun the Austro-Hungarian Front in Galicia, and masses of the Russian Army have surged up to the ridges of the Carpathians. The hopeless Austrian offensive in Italy had to be sacrificed already, and yet the allies were not able to stop the Russian advance...

Would the battalion join the VII Corps to continue the offensive at Verdun, or would it follow its bicycle company into the war of attrition on the Somme?; or will a new theatre of war be determined? — Nevertheless, no one could doubt that the battalion would be more than ever up to any task after seeing the neat, taut companies marching to their training grounds with impeccable equipment and the most modern weapons; once again led by the officers in full force, all while knowing of the precise detail of work that had been accomplished in these past few months. Fate has approached — the fate not only of Jäger-Battalion 11

146

but also that of each one of its jägers — The telegram of the general staff officer of the 6th Army thus stated in a cool, business-like voice — "Jäger-Battalion 11 and Reserve Jäger-Battalion 6 are to stand by immediately. Together with Reserve Jäger-Battalion 5, you will be unified as Jäger-Regiment 4 under the command of the Carpathian Corps. The transport will be arranged by Field-Railway Chief von Falkenhayn – Chief of the General Staff of the Army."

- The War Diary of The 11th Kurhessian Jäger Battalion

Almost two years have passed since the first diary entry in Weida in the summer of 1914, detailing Alexander's departure to the notorious Western Front and the experiences that soon followed. We have been part of his enthusiastic call to mobilisation and journey to the Frontlines; his first eye-opening, true taste of war, and also the regular fun and amusing times in the trenches and the communication zone. There were also times when he met his enemies up close after they had fallen in battle, getting a glimpse into their personal lives and stories through their letters, postcards, and pictures. These experiences will by now have made him realise that his enemies are not much different from him and that many could have been his dearest friends in an alternate reality. We have also tracked his journey to the rank of first lieutenant and company commander, as well as the deaths of his close friends, civilians, and common soldiers on all sides. After all of this, we are now about to follow him on his 'adventure' to the Eastern Front to fight the Russians.

During all this time, no significant gains have been made on either side along the Western Front despite the major offensives initiated, including the more recent ones such as at Verdun and the Somme. These are only accelerating the loss of life. Alongside this, the battles on the Italian Front, the Middle East, Macedonia and on the sea have continued to rage also. In Eastern Europe, the Brusilov Offensive, also known as 'The June Advance', which is the largest Russian offensive of the war as of yet, has been taking place since June 1916 in Galicia in modern-day Western Ukraine. The Russian success enabled a push all the way down into the Carpathian Mountains. This pressured the German Empire to send troops from the West to this new theatre of war, to aid the Austro-Hungarians and other allied forces. With the formation and integration into the highly-specialised Carpathian Corps (also known as the 200th Infantry Division), as well as the adoption of new equipment and training, Alexander's battalion is now fully prepared to begin the eastern battles in the high mountains.

The Conflicts in The Carpathians
& The Liberation of Bukovina
(1916 – 1917)

1

22.7.1916 We marched from La Tombe to the train station of Tournai along with music — 11:38 departure. With Lieutenants Fischer, Lingelbach and Kramer, I am travelling inside a very cushy first-class compartment of an old Belgian carriage.

23.7.1916 Food at 3 o'clock in the night in Brussels-Schaerbeek — cold cuts, ham, and lots of butter. In the morning, we have cold cuts and coffee in Herbesthal.

Continuing over Aachen, Düren, Neuss, Düsseldorf and Elberfeld. There is huge excitement everywhere. Everyone waves and cheers us on. Our carriages are decorated with green branches. We occasionally put on our Stahlhelms, which always summons great amazement. At the train stations, we are surrounded by hundreds of children who beg for "Foreign Money." Apart from this, you pass the time with sleep, card games, and by visiting each other.

Lunch in Holzwickede, and then further onwards over Soest, Paderborn and Driburg — dinner in Northeim.

24.7.1916 I wake up in the morning just before Leipzig, where we are superbly fed in the suburb of Engelsdorf. We journey across the Elbe by Riesa and go over Dresden and Görlitz (lunch). We hear from the railway officials that many jäger battalions have already travelled the same route before us.

25.7.1916 Supper after midnight in Brockau, Breslau. I wake up in Ratibor in the morning. We cross over the border near Oderberg where we eat breakfast.

The dawdling has begun ever since we have been in Austria. We are going through a wonderful area with high wooded mountains, but it is unfortunately raining. The population is very impoverished. All the women and children are with Polish headscarves and bare legs.

Journey over Teschen and straight through lovely mountain ranges towards Zsolna (Sillein), where we have a nice lunch. We are now already in the middle of Hungary. The Hungarians are very friendly people, and many speak German. Everybody shouts "Aufwiedersehen!" *("Goodbye!")* wherever we go through. We keep travelling in the valley of the Waag through the High Tatras *(mountain range)*. The scenery gets nicer with every bend.

In Rutka, I am gifted a bouquet of carnations from two young, blonde Hungarian women. It is unfortunately soon getting dark after this place.

'A farmer in the High Tatras'.

26.7.1916   I wake up in Poprad where we have very good coffee. The highest mountains of the High Tatras rise up like a wall, partly with small fields of snow, and included is the highest mountain — the Gerlsdorfer or Franz-Josef's Peak (2668 metres).

'Serbian prisoners in Kaschau, Hungary'.

Over Iglö in the deep valley of the Hornad towards Kaschau, where we have a nice lunch. The Hungarian farming women look very picturesque in their colourful attire with very short, crinkled skirts and bucket-top boots. There are many corn and poppy fields. The latter look very pretty with their multi-coloured blossoms. We are eagerly trying to uncover the secrets of the Austrian rank insignias. It was very nice weather today, but sweltering hot. Then came an intense rainstorm.

Continuing through Satoralja Ujhely where we come out of the mountains and into the deep Hungarian plains — dinner in Csap.

27.7.1916 We arrive in Maramarossziget during pouring rain at half past 7 in the morning. We go further into the valley of the River Tisza, up to where the Viseu flows into it. We are unloaded and we pitch our tents here. The place is called Visovölgy.

'A street view in Maramarossziget – Summer 1916'.

We train passengers are living in a blockhouse upon the height from where there is a wonderful view of both rivers and the high wooded mountains. Four of us sleep on our blankets inside a small room. The Hungarian women here wear delightful, patterned necklaces made from small, colourful pearls of glass. They unfortunately don't want to sell any though. You notice very little of the war here, apart from the endless Austrian wagon convoys driving up the mountain pass, which entail very small horses with small wagons or two-wheeled carts. One to two small foals run next to most of the wagons. Even a column of dog carts each pulled by two dogs came past.

I just bathed very nicely in the Viseu with the company. Unfortunately, the jäger, Fuchs, thereby drowned.

We sat on our porch for a long time in the evening, along with excellent food from the field kitchen.

28.7.1916 Before noon, there was a parade assembly of the 4th Jäger Regiment and an inspection by the Austrian heir apparent. He is a very good-looking and kind man. He shook the hand of every officer and asked some questions. We had field-kitchen soup at noon. The funeral of the drowned jäger was in the afternoon. Pleasant dinner — cheese bread, buttered bread with eggs, new potatoes with butter, one bottle of Rhine wine, and coffee.

My attendant is playing the flute.

29.7.1916 A very nice tour with the company in the morning, upon the 903-metre-high Obszyna Mountain — a magnificent view from all sides. The Carpathians in this area do not have any zagged rocks or bedrock walls like in Tyrol, but are instead composed of a row of high summits which are covered with large beech forests and wonderful, colourful alpine-like meadows.

There are suddenly a few claps of thunder every afternoon — the usual local thunderstorm. I bathed in the Viseu in the afternoon and packed my things. We are marching off tomorrow, but where to is unknown.

30.7.1916 Morning train departure in the valley of the Viseu towards Leordina, where the scenes are already becoming more war-like — barracks, many troops, and columns of pack animals. From here, we march on foot in the glowing sun with heavy baggage — a large break behind Huszkowa and food from the field kitchen. The inhabitants here look as brown as the gypsies.

Today, for Sunday, everyone is wearing their nice clothes consisting of very picturesque, colourful national outfits. The men wear short white shirts with wide sleeves over very wide white pants, sleeveless jackets out of goat or sheepskin, or either colourfully embroidered leather jackets; or thick grey felt jackets. On the long and black hair, felt caps. The women wear colourfully embroidered white shirts and white skirts, a colourful striped apron on the front and back, and very thick, colourful and patterned stockings. Furthermore, a pearl necklace, a dark headscarf with colourful braids or small straw hats; and colourfully embroidered leather jackets. Very pretty faces for the most part.

'A Ruthenian family'

Over Ruszkirwa towards the large place of Ruszpolyana in the wide valley of the Ruszkowa. There is huge activity here — a whole lot of jäger battalions, ski troops, mountain guns, field guns, howitzers, telegraphs, field bakers, a field hospital and so forth. The march was very exhausting due to the heat.

We are bivouacking by the road towards Luhi. I sat by the campfire for a long time in the evening, smoked my pipe, drank Rhine wine and listened to our choir — a very nice, starry sky. The night in the tent was rather cold. We lay in rubber coats on the bare ground, covered only with a blanket.

The Ruthenians

When reading Alexander's diary, I am always captivated by these people in the East who come across as being very mysterious and peculiar as though from a fantasy world or the distant past — The Ruthenians. The same applies to Alexander too, who talks about them every time he sees them, as well as regularly capturing them with his camera. The Ruthenians are in fact Slavic people who occupy the western slopes of the Carpathians, modern-day Ukraine, Slovakia, Poland, and Northern Serbia. They are thought to number around 900,000 to 1 million in the 21st century and speak a variety of East Slavic dialects. In Habsburg Austria, they were seen as 'faceless people', and there was little knowledge of their culture and ethnicity. In 1910, there were 4 million speakers of the Ruthenian language, who lived in primitive conditions in mostly rural and structurally disadvantaged regions, which had not seen the economic and social wave of modernisation compared to other parts of the empire. The Ruthenian national identity was determined primarily by the Greek-Catholic Church, and modern, national attitudes did not develop until the mid-19th century. This is thought to be due to the previous historic duty of maintaining a protective shield against the Asian hordes of the East.

Left: 'A beggar in Visovölgy'.

Right: 'Ruthenian girls in Ruszpolyana'.

31.7.1916 Almost all the houses are low one-story blockhouses with boarded roofs. As for field crops, you almost only see corn and potatoes. Our bread is made from cornmeal.

We continuously march in the valley of the Ruszkowa towards Luhi, and on a poor and muddy roadway in a nice, deep forest valley up until Klausura Rosasz Wielki. We pitch our tents in the forest here, namely on a narrow mountain edge between two rushing rivers, the bed of which is filled with boulders and huge tree trunks — height: 822 metres.

I sat by the campfire for a long time in the evening. I slept very well since we made the tent lower this time, and densely covered the floor with fir branches.

1.8.1916 We continue on a rapid climb in the eastern valley at 6 o'clock in the morning. The ascent begins after approximately three kilometres. The road, which was only built during the war, winds its way up the steep slope in countless wide windings. Around noon, we arrive close beneath the peak of the 1599-metre-high Copilasul whose grassy summit is lined with field fortifications.

We pitch our tents on the grassy ridge that forms the border between Hungary and Bukovina, and which leads to the 1655-metre-high Stog. It swarmed with jägers from various battalions on the way there. There is a lovely view here of the Pip Ivan (2026 metres) and the Corbul (1700 metres). On the higher mountains, the woodland suddenly stops at the top, and the summit is a green peak of grass. Our field kitchens can't drive to us at the top anymore. The food needs to be carried up in cooking crates using pack animals.

'The view into the valley during the ascent to the Kopilas – 1.8.1916'.

The last piece of bread has been consumed — nothing more to eat. I am sleeping in the grass during the afternoon. The field kitchens are to be dragged up via horse and carriage tonight. When it gets dark, an Austrian guard drives a large flock of sheep past and sells them for 1 Mark a piece. Many have even vanished unpaid. My company has pinched at least eight that will immediately be butchered and brought to the field kitchen. They were very beautiful animals with wonderful raven-black, shiny and long curly fur.

Dozens of watchfires are blazing up everywhere upon the heights, and you can hear singing from all around. It is a marvellous evening. Such a thing would be completely ruled out in the West, as the thick shells would be present within five minutes.

2.8.1916   I froze wretchedly in the night. No wonder on such a high and exposed mountain ridge. I immediately sat by the fire again in the morning.

The first post is arriving, and included with this is also the news that Ernst has unfortunately fallen near Verdun.

Note: Ernst Filler was the brother of Alexander's wife, Johanna. He was a professional pianist and music composer at the time.

Ernst Filler with his wife some time before his death

156

Rest day. Very good food — rice with mutton from yesterday's extra-slaughtered meat. Fried sheep liver in the evening.

The orders for the attack tomorrow: "After artillery preparation, our Carpathian Corps is to storm the Ludowa and Baba Ludowa mountains. We and the 6th Jägers are brigade reserves. The start of the infantry attack will be at 3 o'clock in the afternoon."

I sat by the campfire in the evening as usual. The Austrians generously provide us with tobacco. I have had 20 cigars and 100 cigarettes delivered to me since Visovölgy. We are alarmed at 11:30 in the night and the tents are dismantled.

'A view from the Kopilas towards the ridge leading to the Stog where we bivouacked on 2.8.1916'.

2

3.8.1916 At 2 o'clock in the night, we march several kilometres upon the long Ruski-Dil mountain ridges stretching from the Copilasul, and camp at dawn in a forest behind a battery of howitzers. The artillery fire commences at noon which becomes stronger from 2 to 3 o'clock, but nowhere near to what you are used to in the West. From the Ruski Dil, while sitting freely on an open crest of grass between the howitzers (also an impossibility in the West), we observe the impacts on the opposite-lying sunlit heights and watch how our firing lines advance in leaps and bounds from 3 o'clock onwards. First, the Hala Mihailewa (1610 metres) and then the Hala Lukawiec (1506 metres) are stormed. Both are long mountain ranges that have little or no forestation. An assault of this kind would have been completely ruled out in the West, but everything went as swiftly and smoothly here just like on manoeuvre. From 6 o'clock, the 15cm howitzers bombard the 1466-metre-high Ludowa which looks very much like the 'Hohentwiel' *(an extinct volcano in Germany).* It is fascinating to observe the impacts on the peak.

I stayed the night in a hut made of fir branches.

'Ruski Dil – The 15cm howitzers firing during the battle on 3.8.1916 (the assault on the Ludowa)'.

4.8.1916 Alarm at 10 o'clock in the morning — news that the Ludowa, the top of the pass south of it and beyond the Propina Valley, is in our possession. We march in many long windings deep down into the beautiful valley of the Czarny Czeremosz *(river)* and to the village of Szybeny, which only consists of a few miserable log cabins but is very scenically located. We camp here. Our people are helping the pioneers rebuild the destroyed bridge over the river. It is unfortunately very foggy and rainy. On the way, we met one officer and 350 Russians who had been captured yesterday. There are almost only conifer woods on this side of the mountains.

Russian prisoners are carrying past our wounded. Except for one company from the 23rd Jägers, our losses are very minor. The 5th Jägers have fulfilled their task and have even captured two artillery pieces, also without a single person wounded in the entire battalion.

Image from an old postcard – The Czarny Czeremosz by Szybeny

5.8.1916   Continued march at 5 o'clock in the morning, on the mountain pass south of the Ludowa leading east up to the Watonarka Pass; past 200 newly captured Russians and the two captured guns. The path is in terrible condition, alternating between deep, tough mud and log roads. The artillery cannot get through. We are therefore given the task of improving the road, which is done by shovelling away the mud and filling the holes with stones. Anyone who hasn't seen these paths has no idea of the transport difficulties here in these wild mountains. We are working like this until the afternoon. It is a pitiful sight how the poor draft animals are agonised to the top. There are four to six horses in front of every wagon, and even then they get stuck every few moments. How they will bring the heavy artillery guns up here is a mystery to me. There isn't such a miserable path in all of Germany, but we need to use it because it is the only crossing point for our entire corps.

    We are currently bivouacking on the top of the pass just south of the Ludowa. I had a look at the Russian fortifications on the pass and the Hala Lukawiec, and you can only be amazed that the Russians let this magnificent position be taken from them so easily.

6.8.1916   We went back to work on the pass at 8 o'clock in the morning. The artillery is being driven up; each being pulled by eight horses. There is huge road traffic. The ammunition, food, and equipment for people and animals of our entire army corps must be transported over this single, miserable pass which is 1000 metres high. What the little local horses can do is quite astonishing; in comparison much more than our large, heavy horses.

    We worked on the eastern side of the pass in the afternoon, which is much worse. We are cutting down trees along the road so that the air and light have access and dry the mud. The forest is an impenetrable jungle that is not utilised at all. What becomes old topples over, and so everywhere lies one tree on top of the other and decays.

7.8.1916   We worked on the western side of the pass all day. Artillery is constantly being dragged up with the greatest effort. This wretched pass is throwing all calculations out the window, as we should be much further by now.

But this way, the Russians have time to recover from their shock and bring reinforcements. Our foremost troops have reached the valley of the Bialy Czeremosz without significant fighting; so, the border of Bukovina. There is nothing left to see of the Russians apart from the Cossacks. Last night, a jäger of my company shot two feral pigs that were roaming around half-wild in the forest. This is again a very welcomed subsidy because aside from the field-kitchen soup, which we have for lunch, we only live on coffee and dry bread. There are plenty of provisions, but they cannot be supplied ahead of time.

We are suddenly alarmed at 3 o'clock in the afternoon. We march up to the mountain pass, prepare ourselves there and then march the same route back to the west. Everywhere along the way is full of artillery, ammunition wagons, pack animals, and wagons of all kinds. A large ammunition wagon of the heavy artillery topples over just as we go past. We are camping there where the passageway reaches the Czarny Czeremosz; that is, only the 1st and 3rd Companies and part of the Machine-Gun Company. Everyone else is marching down the river valley north to Zeleny via Jawornik, where a defensive position is taken up together with other troops and lots of artillery. The Russians are supposedly advancing with large reinforcements from Zabie and from Mount Kreta, in order to cut off our troops that have advanced eastwards over the Watonarka Pass.

8.8.1916   It rained in the night, and it was cold and rainy throughout the day. Provisions are becoming more sufficient — a tin of Hungarian goulash every evening.

9.8.1916   We had a small field exercise in the morning. I slept out in the open in somewhat better weather in the afternoon.

Alarm at 6 o'clock in the evening. At 7:30, we march north over Jawornik in the lovely forest valley of the Czarny Czeremosz and then take a left turn. At 5 o'clock the next morning, we go over the Skupowa (1583 metres) and reach the 1478-metre height between the Skupowa and the Kreta. The Austrians gave us a guide in the valley, but he continuously got lost. The ascent was very steep in places, and the path was only a narrow footpath which was especially dreadful at the end. The moon was luckily shining for at least the first few hours. An icy wind blew at the top of the ridge, which was twice as unpleasant because we had been sweating heavily beforehand. The entire march from half past 7 in the evening until 5 o'clock in the morning was extremely exhausting.

The opinions about our new theatre of war are very varied. Most are thrilled about this wild, adventurous, and truly jäger-like life, yet there are several who long for the cushy and less strenuous life in the West. Anyway, I am happy that I am here.

'Our tent for the day by Szybeny – From left to right: Captain Conrad, Field-Medic Wohlgemuth; Lieutenants Fischer, Lingelbach and Kramer – 9.8.1916'.

'View of the Czeremosz Valley by Szybeny – 9.8.1916'.

'The camp in Szybeny – August 1916'.

10.8.1916   Early at sunrise, we had a view from the ridge on all sides that I have rarely seen so beautiful — one mountain range behind the other, and one summit next to the other.

Just as we arrived at Height 1478, there was fierce rifle and machine-gun fire ahead of us. The Russians attacked our positions but were repelled. We camped on the opposite slope of 1478, but the Russians must have noticed us because they graced us with several shells and shrapnel. Oberjäger Schmelz received a shrapnel shot in the upper leg as a result. We are lying in the warm sunshine all morning and at noon.

We are supposed to take back two heights; the eastern foothills of Point 1385 that the Austrians have recently lost — Captain Conrad leads the storm battalion made from Austrians and our 1st and 3rd Companies. I lead the 3rd Company, and Seemann leads the 1st. While taking advantage of the very difficult and partly densely overgrown terrain, I move into a deep gorge with my company in the afternoon where we line ourselves up for the assault as our very meagre artillery fires. It is a miracle that the Russians didn't see us, as we would have fared very badly otherwise. We were thus only shot at slightly when we were already in the gorge. I likewise give the order to attack as soon as we see that the 1st Company is advancing to the right of us. Lingelbach starts with the first wave of the assault, and then Kramer. Both of them swarm out. I still stay back with the reserve platoon for the time being.

The ascent is incredibly high, steep, and troublesome with dense undergrowth and brittle trees everywhere. There is soon raging gunfire. Our artillery now shoots very well, and seven of our machine guns uninterruptedly pound the opposing foxholes. The Russians respond, and it is such an infernal racket that you can barely understand the person next to you. 15 minutes after our firing lines have advanced, I can't stand it anymore down below and order my reserve platoon to follow me. There is suddenly loud screaming halfway up. Jägers shout "Over Here!", and Russian voices yell in confusion. To the left of me, I unclearly see a large number of Russians through the bushes with jägers among them. I think that this is a flanking attack and even get the pistol ready to fire. I then see that the Russians have no weapons — they were the first captives.

I now continue ahead in all hastiness and arrive fully exhausted with my reserves at the 1200-metre-high ridge, which has been in our possession for 15 minutes. The 1st Company have also captured their height, and so have the Austrians to the left of us. My company has taken almost 320 prisoners. Some of the Russians defended themselves from our attack, but they surrendered without resistance for the most part. A large number had fled. Within the company, I have one dead, two heavily wounded and four lightly; incredibly minor casualties in relation to the Russian superiority and their brilliant position. Such a splendid success would have been impossible if there were only 50 Englishmen up here. The height was taken at 7 o'clock in the evening. There was then a lot of work — transporting the wounded and the prisoners, expanding the position to the other side, reorganising the company, pitching tents, setting up guards, providing food and so forth.

Our people are shooting a pig. There are also potatoes and kohlrabi *(German turnips)* up here.

I slept the night in the tent because the Ruthenian wooden huts stink too much and are likely full of vermin.

The Russians were armed with Japanese rifles.

'The height that was stormed on 10.8.16 by the 1st and 2nd Companies, on which 320 Russians were captured'.

11.8.1916 We received marmalade this morning for the first time since Belgium. There was overall joy as a result. The order has arrived for us to march back. The Russians have unsuccessfully been shooting at us with shrapnel and shells for a while, but aside from this, there is idyllic calmness with marvellous sunshine.

The march back to Height 1478 was very strenuous and hot because we were unable to take the convenient path considering the Russian artillery, and instead had to march under the cover of trees and wooden fences. We arrived back at 1478 by noon, where we somewhat rested ourselves in the most beautiful sunshine. We were to bivouac up there, but our joy was suddenly interrupted by the order to leave immediately — The mountain range to the west of 1385 is to be taken by our 2nd and 4th Companies and by the Austrians, and we are to help. There was of course a lot of anger because of this. Since they had it easier yesterday, the 1st Company is to attack along with them, and Lieutenant Fischer from my company is being provided as support along with his platoon. I and the other two platoons are to support the section on the right.

We orientate ourselves on top of a high mountain peak. The eastern half of the ridge is in Austrian possession, whilst the Russians sit on the western half up to the Czeremosz and beyond. We can clearly see the positions lying below us. We march in constant cover of the forest, up along the western ridge from 1478 in the following sequence: 1st Company, 3rd Company, and a Hungarian company. We then finally come to a bare area where there are Austrian positions. We march several metres further beneath the ridge to protect ourselves from the north side. The 1st Company is already far out, and I simply follow when we all of a sudden receive heavy fire from our flank. It is too late to go back. We therefore throw ourselves down on the spot and make ourselves as flat as possible since there isn't any cover. The Russians shoot at us like mad and the projectiles swish away over us or strike between us, and we have to endure this defencelessly — an awful situation.

By crawling and leaping, I finally manage to reach my company and the cover of the forest again. We now cannot go any further from here, so we try to head north over the ridge and down into the valley. However, this is not possible for the time being because the Russians are maintaining lively fire on the Austrian positions west of 1385, and all the shots currently fired too high hit the valley slope that we need to go down. After about one hour, they calm down and we climb in constant cover against the Russian positions in the forest, deep down into the gorge of the Zmyenski Stream, a tributary to the right of the Czarny Czeremosz. We fortunately arrive at the bottom where we already discover the Hungarian company. Our 1st Company, on the other hand, which is supposed to advance to the left, is not there yet. They are forced to take a large detour because of the Russian gunfire attack. A heavy engagement takes place on the western side of the Czeremosz. It stays calm on our eastern side. Our attack commences while it is already getting dark. Barely one shot is fired since the Russians have cleared their high positions almost without any resistance. I remain at the bottom of the valley because I am not needed.

It gets dark and we burn a large fire to warm ourselves, make coffee, and to show any possible order bearers our current location. We haven't eaten anything all day long apart from some dry bread, and we are also exhausted. At 10 o'clock in the evening finally comes the order to head to Zeleny, north of Jawornik in the Czeremosz Valley. We march down the stream valley on a miserable footpath, through swamps and over large stones. There is luckily moonlight, as we would otherwise have broken our necks and legs. We finally reach the Czeremosz and march south on its eastern bank on a wet meadow trail, past the village of Skupowa where there are many Russian foxholes; and to Zeleny where we cross over to the western bank via a makeshift wooden bridge. It took two hours to get here. We receive the order here to march even further south to where we received the guide on the 9th of August. Hungry, dead tired with wounded feet and feeling battered all over, we finally arrive at our field kitchen after another three-quarters of an hour, where we hear, to our great annoyance, that the food, coffee, bread and schnapps had been sent to us with pack animals. The column didn't find us, of course.

After midnight, we pitched our tents and slept marvellously. We learned beforehand that the 2nd Company had a heavy engagement on the western side near the village of Skupowa. Captain Thielmann and Lieutenant Kellerman fell. Lieutenant Hitzeroth is lightly wounded, as well as Lieutenant Möller from the 4th Company. Our battalion has again captured some 100 Russians.

12.8.1916   I woke up at 10 o'clock in the morning. All my limbs are shattered. I wrote the combat report. Thunderstorm — it has been raining all day long. Captain Conrad is being assigned to the headquarters personnel. I am to become the company commander of the 3rd Company.

14.8.1916   The night was very cold, and I froze. It is the loveliest weather during the day — the purest summer freshness.

15.8.1916   Alarm at 4 o'clock in the night — 6 o'clock departure in the Czeremosz Valley over Zeleny towards Skupowa, where we turn west into the valley of the Skoruszny Creek. We then go very steeply up to the bare, sharply-sloping, roof-shaped peak of the Skoruszny (1566 metres) where we replace two companies of the Austrian 28th Jäger Battalion — a wonderful view from all sides. The Russians lie several kilometres north on the mountain of Kreta and west beyond the Dzembronia Valley, upon the long and strung-out mountain ridge of the Stepanski (1137 metres).

'The view from one of our trenches on the Skoruszny – August 1916'.

There is complete peace up here. We don't have to expect any infantry or artillery fire. We cannot starve either because there are a lot of feral cattle and sheep, as well as lots of blueberries. There are also said to be deer, bears, and lynxes in the woodlands. We are securing ourselves with far-advanced field guards and patrols. Together with my attendant, I am living in a grass-covered stilt hut dug into the slope on the summit, with a table, bench, hay storage and fireplace made from pieces of grass. Apart from my company, there are still three of our machine guns up here, as well as two German mountain guns. We will hopefully be staying here for a long time. The other companies are upon the heights to the east of me. You can at most only see the smoke from one of their fires rise up from them.

'My shelter on the Skoruszny (1566 metres) – In front of it is my attendant'.

Through His Eyes

As you may have realised, this new theatre of war has become an opportunity for Alexander to further enhance his documentation via detailed photography. These photos, from the Carpathians, are today preserved in numerous envelopes and a large album with an Iron Cross on its front cover. Almost all have a detailed description with a date on the rear, which goes with the matching diary entries. However, some do not have this. Below is a compilation of these unidentified photographs, which were taken on various days in Alexander's current surroundings while on the march:

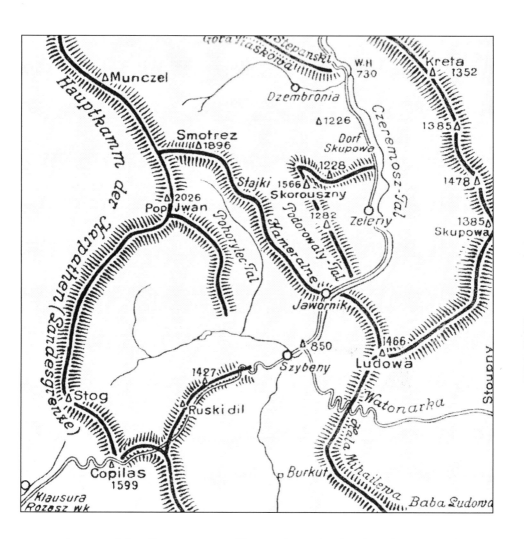

*A map of the Czeremosz Valley and nearby landmarks around
Alexander's current position.*

3

16.8.1916   It is nice and warm inside my grass hut. I most likely would have frozen a lot in the tent at night. Before noon, I visited the far-forward-deployed field guard, Fischer, and observed the Russian trenchwork on the Stepanski. Two companies of the 6th Jäger Reserves will be arriving towards the evening, who are to secure the sector to the west of me. Our post upon the 1750-metre-high Stajki will become overabundant as a result.

'Me (left) in front of Fischer's shelter on the Stepanski – 16.8.1916'.

17.8.1916   Wonderful weather. You can see how the 6th Jägers are winding up the steep slope of the Stajki in a long single file. You can see many old familiar landmarks from up here — Deep down in the Czeremosz Valley lies Jawornik; behind it, the Ludowa; to the right of it, the Hala Lukawiec; and in between is the Watonarka Pass where we were entrenching from the 5th to the 7th of August. Also, further right is the Ruski Dil with our encampment from the 3rd of August, and the Copilasul with our encampment on the ridge. Everything is clear to be seen. In the east, you can see the entire way over the Skupowa to Height 1478 (night march from the 9th to the 10th of August); Height 1385; the bare plain before 1478 where we received fire from the flank on the 11th of August; and also, the Zmyenski Valley and the Russian positions which were stormed on the 11th. Further to the left is Mount Kreta upon which the Russians still sit, which rises only a little from the mountain range.

    A very hefty storm in the night.

'View from the Skoruszny towards the Smotrez and the Munzel – 17.8.1916'.

'The shelter of the staff on the Skoruszny – Captain Conrad, Lieutenants Lingelbach and Kramer, and a captured Russian horse – 18.8.1916'.

19.8.1916   It is very hot. The mountain ridge with Mount Kreta is to be taken this afternoon, and we are therefore supposed to storm the Stepanski Ridge together with other companies tomorrow.

12 o'clock noon departure from the summit that we are reluctant to leave, as we would have liked to stay up here until the peace settlement —

Down into a stream valley in constant cover from enemy sight, until just before the mill in the Dzembronia Valley which lies approximately south of the Stepanski Summit (1137 metres). I stay here in camp with three squads and two machine guns, whilst Platoon Fischer and Kramer occupy the Dzembronia Valley from the mill up to the right towards the mouth of the Mala Drestunka. To our right is the 1st Company, and to our left are the 6th Jäger Reserves.

Towards the evening comes the news that Mount Kreta has been captured — 500 prisoners and 8 machine guns.

20.8.1916 We wake up at 3 o'clock in the night. I too march into the Dzembronia Valley with my battalion under moonlight and send out patrols, who report around 7 o'clock in the morning that the Russians have evacuated their positions. I report this to the battalion via telephone and immediately send several squads ahead to occupy the summit. I then slowly follow with the rest of the company and arrive at the top at 10 o'clock. You can only be amazed that the Russians have voluntarily left such a well-developed position. This is presumably because of our success at Mount Kreta, from where the Stepanski can be bombarded with artillery from the flank and rear. At 11 o'clock, long Russian convoys and pack animals come up the valley road from Zabie, which we shoot at from 1600 metres with our visors whereupon they quickly dash sideways into the bushes. There is a magnificent view from up here — The Skoruszny and the other high peaks of the Czorna Hora to the south; to the east lie the long mountain ridges of Mount Kreta; and to the northeast, the wide Zabie Valley dotted with individual farmsteads where we see the Russian artillery depart.

The Russians shoot at us heavily but unsuccessfully with artillery. My post pulls back from a strong Russian patrol to the outermost peak of a mountain ridge that stretches to the north. But the field guards, which lie further back, repulse the attack accordingly. Far to the left of us is heavy firing — the 6th Jägers are storming two heights.

21.8.1916 A very uncomfortable, dark and rainy night. We were expecting a counterattack, but it did not happen. It is raining throughout the day. The Russian artillery is shooting at us constantly. Our people have dug themselves foxholes as far as the rocky ground allows. Before noon, my 30-man-strong field guard repulsed a strong Russian assault with rifle fire and grenades. We do have several wounded though.

The enemy artillery fire keeps getting stronger. In the afternoon, the field guard was attacked by large Russian columns, two to three companies strong. After brave resistance that cost the Russians very heavy losses (also due to our flanking fire), the remaining approximately 10 men, a few of whom are still injured, had to retreat back to the company due to the large numbers of the enemy. Their courageous leader, Vice-Sergeant Wels, fell due to a headshot. The Russians are now sitting on the ridge that runs northeast from the main summit. The Stepanski Ridge itself is completely in our hands.

The night passes in anticipation of further enemy attacks, but everything remains calm. A house on the ridge is shot into flames by our mountain artillery. We have 2 dead, 6 wounded, and 7 missing.

22.8.1916   Nicer weather, but very cool. The Russians are keeping quiet. In the afternoon, our mountain guns shot at the mountain ridge that was occupied by the Russians yesterday. Kramer and I are having a small blockhouse built for us which will be finished today.

I have now adopted a small Carpathian dog; a young, lively animal, white with large brown spots. The knowledgeable have not yet agreed on the breed. I gave him the nice name, 'Ruski'. I don't get to ride my riding horse here, as it is standing below in the Dzembronia Valley. There are otherwise no living creatures here, luckily neither rats nor mice which almost ate you up in the trenches in France. I haven't had any bugs yet either since we never camp in the Ruthenian houses.

23.8.1916   It is chilly with occasional rain. The enemy near us is keeping quiet, but it is constantly pounding to our left. The large number of cattle has now stopped because the Russians have taken all the residents and the cattle with them. We instead have very nice potato fields directly behind the position.

24.8.1916   Everything is calm. I have to extend my Front again by 300 metres to the left, which means the occupation keeps thinning out.

25.8.1916   There was thick fog during the night — the ground is littered with fireflies — an enemy patrol is being driven out.

The food is good and plentiful, but it usually only arrives late in the evening when it is dark because the road lies under artillery fire. There are three different types of field-kitchen food — Pearl barley with mutton, beans with mutton, and dried vegetables with beef. Besides this, we also get half a loaf of bread every day, and alternately some lard substitute, Dutch cheese, canned sausage, and marmalade. We also get cubes of coffee daily, and sometimes tea.

The night before last, we caught a Russian officer's attendant who had gotten lost and came to us with the food and coat intended for his master. He was very surprised at how he was suddenly captured by us.

26.8.1916   Wonderful warm, sunny day. We are now living rather well because we have been brought up several boxes with all kinds of things from the canteen. For breakfast this morning, we had tea with marmalade bread, liver sausage, and Swiss cheese; and for lunch, asparagus spears, fried potatoes, one egg, roasted meat, and 1901-dated Tokay wine. We eat out of the field kitchen in the evening.

Two Russian patrols are being shot at in the night.

28.8.1916   The declaration of war by Italy and Romania was reported to us via telephone this morning. Maybe now we will reach the Romanian border. There was shooting from patrols on several occasions during the first half of the night.

Heavy rain. It is raining into my shelter, so I am having a wooden roof put on it today.

29.8.1916   The weather is nice. I now have a medium mortar in my sector, which launches mortar shells with a diameter of 18 centimetres and a weight of one quintal. We just zeroed in on the field-guard summit with four shots. Those things have a huge impact; the Russians will have run away nicely as a result. They have constantly been shouting "Hurrah!" since yesterday evening, and have also stuck out a signpost on which Romania's declaration of war is most likely written. They probably think that this is being kept secret from us, or they want to annoy us with it. Our mortars are the correct response to this.

30.8.1916   There was artillery fire to our left for several hours from 4 o'clock in the morning onwards, the likes of which I have never heard in the East. The volleys follow one another without interruption. It must be within the vicinity of the Jablonika Pass where the Austrians have retreated to in the last few days. We are always happy when we don't have Austrians next to us, as you can't sleep peacefully otherwise. As kind as the Austrian is as an associate, he is just as unreliable as a soldier — Always according to the motto: "Make room. The Germans want to attack. The Germans are braver people!"

I was just guiding the Count through my position which the Russians must have smelled, because they sent over plenty of shells and shrapnel from 10 to 12 o'clock at noon, although without success. Since my hut doesn't provide enough cover against artillery fire, I am now having a stronger shelter built in a more protected area where the sun also shines all day, as it is well needed up here.

The strong artillery fire to the left of us is continuing all day.

31.8.1916   The Russians have been shooting at us heavily with artillery and mortars since half past 5 in the morning. Four jägers have been wounded by a single mortar. During the morning, accumulations of strong enemy forces are reported on the 3 ridges running northeast from the Stepanksi and in the ravines between them. An attack is not carried out on the ridge furthest to the east. On the middle ridge, which runs from the Stepanski to the mouth of the Bystriz in the Czeremosz, a heavy assault is repulsed through our rifle and mortar fire. The attackers flee down the gorges to the left and right.

It becomes clear around noon that the main attack will be carried out on the left wing, which is why I send my two reserve squads to march over there. Before they arrive, the enemy attacks the small-protruding piece of forest with the strength of two companies, which is occupied on the left wing by the squads Oberjäger Trömper and Oberjäger Peter. After a long period of resistance, these

16 men need to retreat to the open height to the left of the fortified house; about 100 metres further back to the line of the Uhlans lying to our left, with a loss of 1 dead and 3 wounded. These squads are extended by the two reserve squads that take up positions to the right of the fortified house. Lieutenant Fischer pulled a machine gun to the left in the meantime and installed it so that it could fire on the flank of the forest now occupied by the Russians. For the same purpose, I also reinforce the squads positioned there. The entrenchment squads of the mortars take part in the attack around the main summit, and then also in the assault on the left wing.

I proceed according to the following plan to bring the small forest piece back into our possession — In response to a white flare, the squads on the wing and the machine gun take the forest under heavy flanking fire. Squads Trömper, Peter, Rumpff and Gaentzsch, as well as the mortars, storm head-on at the same time. The assault succeeds as concerted. The Russians flee in complete disarray after a short resistance, leaving behind many rifles and pieces of equipment. They suffer very heavy losses due to our fire during the retreat down the slope. All parts of the position are now in our possession again.

The awaited night attack did not occur. Our losses are 1 dead and 11 wounded. A captured Russian stated: "The regiment that arrived from the north five days ago attacked with two battalions in the front line, and two battalions in reserve." — They must have believed that they were dealing with Austrians.

1.9.1916   In the morning, I inspected the recaptured forest piece where a few dead and wounded Russians still lay. I heard on the way back that we are to take back our entire line and that the Stepanski is to be cleared. My company is to go back up to the Skoruszny. During the afternoon, we destroy everything that we cannot drag along with us, and we also burn 25 captured rifles. We leave the position in groups at 8 o'clock in the evening. Only a couple of squads from every company stay behind to hide our retreat from the enemy for as long as possible — Miserable descent into the Dzembronia Valley, where we are waiting for the other parts of the battalion.

2.9.1916   We continue our march at midnight, along the same route we came a few days ago. It is raining and it is pitch black. With every step, we are in danger of breaking our necks and legs or plummeting into the engorged mountain stream. The path itself has transformed into a raging stream in many places because of the rain. The notorious night march over the Skupowa was like a boardwalk in comparison. We finally reach the cloud-enshrouded summit at 6 o'clock in the morning. The shelters are occupied by artillerymen, and no fires are burning due to the few amounts of wood being damp. We are completely soaked and exhausted ourselves. We also discover the Count at the top with his adjutants, Captain Conrad, and Lieutenant Poetsch. I then finally find accommodation within a small, draughty shelter. All my things are oozing from the wetness. The squads we left behind arrive in the afternoon and report that the Russians noticed our decampment around noon due to the likely betrayal by the

Ruthenians, and that they have occupied the Stepanski. We see the first Russians immediately after, and single shots fall all afternoon.

The Russians entrench themselves 300 metres below us during the night, which we disturb by shooting. Prisoners testify the next day that they wanted to attack us at midnight, but were prevented from doing so by our fire.

A lovely starry sky, but a poignant cold wind. I froze wretchedly.

3.9.1916   At the crack of dawn, the Russians try another attack but are so shot at that they can barely get out of their dugouts. A mountain gun is brought forward and fires directly at the Russian positions at 300 metres, whereupon the Russians immediately break away and are fired upon by us. The same happens again in the morning after they settle back into their dugouts in the fog.

It is foggy, cold, and very uncomfortable up here. The Russian artillery shoots at us in the afternoon, which tries to target both of our mountain guns. The third shell immediately explodes directly next to the shelter of the Count, whereupon the entire staff quickly evacuates the premises and pulls further down the valley.

4.9.1916   The night proceeded very calmly. It is a nice warm day. We are shot at heavily by artillery around noon. The artillery fire increases little by little, and at 4:30, the Russians attack but are repulsed with casualties. From now on, they continuously try to work their way forward but cannot do so as long as it is light. Our mountain artillery, machine guns and rifles inflict great devastation. Many dead Russians lie before their trenches. The Russians constantly shoot like mad at our positions. At around 7 o'clock in the evening, they managed to break into our right wing and then also into the middle — wild hand-to-hand fighting. Lieutenant Lingelbach receives a bullet through both arms, and Vice-Sergeant Mager receives a heavy shot in the thigh. Through counterattacks with hand grenades, we throw the Russians back out. We then need to pull back, go forward again; and like so, it goes on throughout the first half of the night.

Our losses increase terrifyingly. I utilise everything that I still have left. My three combat orderlies seize a Russian machine gun. The situation keeps getting more critical. We lie only 15 metres away from each other in some areas. The Russians bring two new machine guns into position, and without interruption, they direct violent rifle and machine-gun fire upon us, with us partly receiving fire from three sides. At 10:20 in the evening, Captain Conrad telephones me that he believes the position is unable to be held and that I am to retreat at midnight. He retreats himself immediately afterwards, and I now sit alone out on a limb. I hear over the telephone that reinforcements are on the way. I then promise the regiment via telephone that I still want to keep the position for as long as possible; but if the reinforcements do not come before daylight, I would need to retreat since we would otherwise be in danger of being completely defeated or cut off. The regiment then expresses its appreciation to me for my holdout.

The eagerly awaited reinforcements are not coming, and the losses are increasing rapidly. It is getting more and more critical. If the Russians carry out just one more attack, we are lost.

It starts to get fairly light at half past 2 in the morning. The firing from the Russians keeps getting more unpleasant. With a heavy heart, I give the order to retreat. We leave the summit bit by bit from 3 o'clock onwards. The Russians do not notice anything of this but instead continue to shoot stupidly. We move back down into the valley and back up to the opposite slopes of the 1750-metre-high Stajki, where we arrive at dawn and dig ourselves in. The Russians first notice that we have left when it gets light. They flood over the summit in thick droves and shout "Hurrah!" like mad until a couple of shots from our mountain guns quiet them down. Only a few of them are now walking around, and you can see through the binoculars how they are looting our dead. Even the 2nd and 4th Companies situated to the right of me needed to withdraw.

My company has heavy casualties. I now only have 90 men left, but a few dispersed people may still return. I saved my belongings, but only my small dog, Ruski, was left behind. This night has been one of the most horrible that I have ever experienced. The Russians are shooting at us occasionally with artillery in our new positions. We destroyed the captured Russian machine gun before the retreat. The Russians attacked our 250 men upon the Skoruszny with the 125th Regiment; so, with at least 3000 men. You can just be surprised that we have lasted this long. I probably would have held the summit if I had just 150 men left.

6.9.1916   The night was very calm. Today is the most beautiful warm weather. The Russians were entrenching tremendously during the night. They have dug a continuous trench across the entire Skoruszny. We are yet again in the middle of wild and uninhabited high mountains. Directly behind us lies the strung-out mountain range of the Czorna Hora with the 2026-metre-high Pip Ivan. The nice potato fields have stopped here. Regarding the attack the day before yesterday, prisoners are saying that the Russian losses were extraordinarily high. The companies, which were 150 to 200 strong, now apparently number only 30 to 50. The eastern slope of the Skoruszny is said to be littered with corpses.

' The view from my current position on the Stajki – To the left is the Smotrez; in the middle, the southern ridge of the Nameless Mountain (in our possession); and to the right at the rear is the northern ridge of the Nameless Mountain, from where the Russians are entrenching towards me at the time I took this photograph – September 1916 ' .

The Renowned Jäger Battalions

A section about the jäger battalions may seem long overdue by now, but I believe there is no better part of Alexander's diary to truly demonstrate their efficiency, skill and distinctiveness than that which you have just read. The battle by the Skoruszny is for me one of the most incredible feats carried out by Alexander and his company — 250 jägers against 3000 Russians — outnumbered 12 to 1, holding the position for as long as possible, and yet still almost annihilating the attacking enemy. This is just one example of why the jäger battalions are overall highly respected and consistently utilised to pull off what would be considered impossible. To fully understand why this is and how they are involved in fully evolving infantry tactics as a whole, we will delve deeper into their history.

The story of the German jäger battalions begins around the early 18th century, a time when troops moved in lines and fired in close formations. They were primarily sons of gamekeepers and recruited from the forests, standing out not only for their exceptional marksmanship and stalking abilities but also for their unwavering loyalty. Unlike others who were deceived or forced into military service within the line-infantry battalions, the jägers were native Prussians who could anticipate retiring to esteemed positions on royal and private hunting grounds. Whilst other infantrymen were often disciplined through harsh corporal punishment during that time, the most severe penalty a jäger could face was being reassigned to a line unit. Their proficiency was well demonstrated during the Battle of Jena-Auerstadt in 1806 between Prussia and France. The German forces suffered a catastrophic defeat which led to a brisk French pursuit of the retreating forces, with many German officers and large line-infantry units giving up well-defensible positions. Despite this, the jägers proved their skill and loyalty by successfully pushing their way through enemy territory in small groups, or even as individuals, inflicting casualties against all odds and yet still reporting for duty.

The introduction of new firearms during the latter half of the 19th century brought about alterations in the tactics employed by line infantry. However, the core principles of iron discipline, composure in the face of enemy fire, and synchronised volley fire remained prevalent in many German infantry units. At the same time, there was however the opinion of many in the German military for the infantry to fight in a more individual way, and that moving on the field in small groups and firing separately was more effective. Their belief was also that the infantry should focus more on developing intelligence and initiative similar to the jägers, rather than relying just on immediate, unquestioning obedience. The hunting grounds of the aristocracy remained the ultimate training ground of the German hunter, consistently providing skilled woodsmen to jäger units throughout this period. But overall changes in infantry tactics, and the organisational challenges confronting the jägers, led to a decrease in jäger battalions, with many such as from the Kingdoms of Bavaria and Saxony converting to infantry units. By 1902, the number of infantry battalions numbered 607 whilst there were just 18 jäger battalions.

In the 1890s, proactive measures were already being taken to counter the threat of organisational extinction and to make them separate from the infantry. This was a success, with them becoming a modern and irreplaceable type of unit that was previously considered outdated. This was achieved by conducting trials with innovations aimed at completely enhancing their traditional abilities, such as scout dogs, bicycles, and experimentation with machine guns; as well as specialised units which were able to carry out difficult long-range raids. Now considering their clear distinction from the vast majority of the army and the fact that they entailed the upper class and nobility, the jäger battalions would be admired and regarded with utmost respect. When mobilisation commenced in 1914, these battalions raised additional reserve battalions entailing men like Alexander, who had previously served as jägers and were only called up when needed. At the start of the war, they upheld their traditional function as elite skirmishers and scouts, but they were soon required to act as ordinary infantry with the beginning of positional trench warfare. However, to tackle all tough Fronts in this ever-evolving war, they would later be trained in the newest effective battle tactics, and utilised to form specialised formations such as the Carpathian Corps, Alpine Corps, ski units, and elite storm battalions.

Alexander's courageous resistance by the Skoruszny is a shining example of this loyalty, skill, and all other qualities that have consistently made the jägers stand out from all the rest. It also demonstrates the true effectiveness of the recently adopted stormtrooper (shock troop) tactics; using brainpower and agility to rush and infiltrate the enemy positions in small groups — storm, pull back, recover and repeat — causing severe casualties, fear and confusion, and leaving the enemy with shattered morale. Alexander did of course need to retreat with his remaining 90 men considering the odds, but not without leaving behind over 1500 fallen Russians and earning respect and an excellent reputation within the battalion and beyond. We can only imagine his many experiences that were obviously not possible to capture on camera, but items that accompanied him during many of his experiences are still in existence today; his 11th Jäger-Battalion shoulder epaulettes and his used and worn belt buckle — true witnesses to these horrors.

4

7.9.1916   A nice warm day. Everything is calm — only a couple of shrapnel shells. I am having a warm hut built for Fischer and me, made out of stakes, spruce branches and pieces of grass. At each summit, you have to build according to a completely different system depending on the soil conditions and the available building materials. The ground here is covered over stretches with a low, dense lawn of a kind of arborvitae with small blueberries.

To our greatest joy, the great Bulgarian victory over the Romanians was communicated to us in the evening. Captain Conrad also said to me that the regiment had expressed its appreciation to the battalion for my tenacity — Another step closer to the Iron Cross 1st Class.

8.9.1916   I slept nicely in my new hut. It is yet again a nice sunny day. Two pack animals are coming up with things from the canteen.

I purchased things worth 7 Mark, but you barely notice anything of it because everything is so wickedly expensive. One small bar of chocolate costs 2.10 Mark. Since I became a company commander, I now also receive the company commander's allowance of 60 Mark.

I now have a very good reputation in the regiment. Yesterday in Szybeny, the regiment commander, Colonel Lehmann, asked my non-commissioned transport officer which company he belonged to; the horses were so well cared for. To the reply of "The 3rd Company", he said that this was the company that held so well on the Skoruszny.

11.9.1916   There is complete calmness. A Russian aeroplane, which is a great rarity here, is flying along our Front.

We are to be replaced by Landsturm-Regiment 38 today. Where we will be going is unknown. Officers from it were already up here this afternoon to view the positions when we suddenly received the counter-order to stay. We are already very used to the air up here. Everyone who comes up here from the valley freezes, whereas we consider it nice and warm.

12.9.1916   It is said that we will be staying in this position over winter. We are working day and night on its development — shelters, trenches, and wire-and-branch obstructions are being built. We will also be receiving special winter equipment soon. The Russian artillery shoots at us now and then. It is too far for infantry, as the summit of the Skoruszny lies approximately a 2-kilometre linear distance from us.

Thick fog and rain in the afternoon. It seems as though the uncomfortable period is now commencing.

13.9.1916   Thick fog. Heavy storm in the afternoon, which intensifies during the night in a way that I have never experienced before. You have to hold on to something to avoid being blown over.

We have been unfortunate with the food for a few days because when things started to get a bit uncertain at the start of this month, the Austrian depot officials in Szybeny just took off. The troops of people and other communication-zone folk located there had then of course looted the provision depot. We frontline troops now obviously need to suffer as a consequence. We now only receive field-kitchen soup once a day, a half of dry bread, and coffee. Captain Conrad received the Iron Cross 1st Class yesterday. I would just like to know what for, as I and many others have taken part 1 and 3/4 years longer in the war than he has.

14.9.1916   The storm continues to rage day and night. Along with this also comes cold rain. On top of that, the Russians fire at us in the afternoon with around 40 heavy shells. Life in the mountains is bleak in this weather.

15.9.1916   The storm subsides in the morning, and it starts to snow — everything is white. It melts again later on, and now everything is dripping wet.

Thick fog. You dread every step that you must take outside.

16.9.1916   Within the night, our patrols report the gathering of large masses of Russians in the deep gorge between the Skoruszny and the Stajki. The Russians shoot at us heavily with artillery from 10 o'clock in the morning. I need to head out of my light shelter since the 12cm shells explode just a few paces away from it. I set up our telephone station out in the open behind a steep slope. My attendant next to me gets hit on the head with a stone that was thrown up by a shell, but he luckily had on his steel helmet which obtained a deep dent. A shell strikes into a shelter — one man dead and two heavily wounded. Apart from that, the heavy shelling that lasted for hours did not cause us any harm.

It is bitterly cold. The Russians attack to the right of us at 12 o'clock noon. From 600 metres, we can clearly see about 100 clay-yellow guys working their way through a clearing. We place them under fire from the flank, whereupon they disappear back into the dense forest. Moreover, the attack was easily repelled by our companies on the right. The artillery fire starts to subside in the late afternoon, but it begins to sleet in return.

There is again a strong storm in the night with rain, snow, and hail. The expected night attack fails to materialise. The weather was probably too miserable even for the Russians. I just feel very sorry for my poor people who are suffering in this weather, as the winter equipment has still not arrived. Just what could it possibly be like here in winter, when there is already such weather in the middle of September?

17.9.1916 Snowstorm, fog, and wetness. I was just upon the 1750-metre-high summit of the Stajki, and it is terrible up there. You need to hold on tight to not get blown down. The Russians are shooting heavily with artillery again. At 4 o'clock in the afternoon, they work their way forward under the cover of the snowstorm and attack the Landsturm company to the right of me, as well as the right half of my company. They are thrown back with rifle fire and hand grenades, as is a strong patrol in front of the centre of my left-wing at 5 o'clock. The attack was accompanied by strong gunfire and again cost me one dead and six wounded. Apart from small shootouts between patrols, the night proceeded quietly.

'The Stajki – 1750 metres'.

18.9.1916 At 6 o'clock in the morning, they again attack the Landsturm company in strong numbers which has heavy casualties; the same must somewhat retreat. We fire at the Russians from the flank. Just as I am about to pull out a squad on my left wing to support the Landsturm, the Russians attack me in this spot. We have heavy losses, and the Russians position themselves firmly upon a summit. Together with one squad of the 1st Company, my people carry out a counterattack with hand grenades and throw the 30 Russians back down again, who leave behind six to seven dead. A prisoner is captured from Regiment 125.

The position on the Stajki Ridge is entirely back in our possession again in the evening. On the other hand, the report comes that the 1900-metre-high Smotrez to our left has been taken away from the 6th Jägers, which is very unpleasant for us because the Russians can fire artillery directly into our rear from the side from there.

'The Smotrez – 1900 metres'.

19.9.1916   Calm in the night. There has been the usual harmless artillery fire since 9 o'clock in the morning. It is marvellous clear winter weather with sunshine. We are all more or less snow-blind. The snow-white summits look wonderful all around, only you have to be a tourist and not at war. But this way you lead a completely humane life.

I am having a fireplace built in my shelter from pieces of grass. It was very cosy and warm there in the evening and at night. The last three days of combat have again cost me 23 men including 10 dead. My company now only has a fighting strength of 85 men, whereas the other companies still have at least twice as many.

20.9.1916   A wonderful, clear sunny day. We have been under unusually strong artillery fire since 10 o'clock in the morning. At around noon, a Russian company attacks the left wing of our 1st Company, comes within a few steps, but is then driven back down the steep slopes with hand grenades. The Smotrez is also taken back by the 6th Jägers in the evening. The flashes of the bursting shrapnel shells looked marvellous in the pitch-black night.

21.9.1916   There is very unusual calmness in my sector — no artillery fire. There is only firing to the left of the Smotrez at times. Serious fighting must be taking place further on the other side of the Czeremosz, as you can see countless white shrapnel clouds far away over there and hear distant machine-gun fire.

The Russians have yet again conquered the Smotrez.

22.9.1916   You can hear the Russians entrenching in front of us along the entire Front in the night, and you can also see many Russian campfires.

It is raining again for a change — no shots of artillery.

There is fog and snow in the evening. The night is very cold. It is raining through the roof of my shelter like a sieve. It is a good job that I have my rubber coat to cover myself.

23.9.1916   Everything is white again this morning. It is very cold, but the sun comes later on. The Russians are acting very quietly. They built a trench in the night, deep below us with barbed-wire obstructions, which suggests that they have given up their intentions to attack us. This ought to be fine with us.

I am having the ceiling of my shelter made considerably thicker; it is hopefully more waterproof now. In accordance with a tried and tested method, empty food cans are hanging in the worst parts. We are leading a completely unbelievable life here. I have not slept any way other than fully clothed since Belgium. I haven't seen my suitcase in many weeks. You only have to rely on what you have inside your backpack. I haven't shaved in four weeks. There was often no opportunity to wash for several days. I haven't seen most officers in the battalion for six weeks now because everyone is scattered in the mountains. To reach the next company commander requires one full hour of strenuous climbing. Whoever hasn't experienced this cannot possibly comprehend how we reside here. It is lovely up here when the weather is nice, but it is much worse when it rains. You thereby have to crawl into your low shelter, and if you have to close the door because of the cold, it is pitch-black inside since there are no windows, and you have to be very sparing with candles. You then feel very gloomy.

24.9.1916   Finally, a nice warm day again. It froze barbarically during the night.

Just now came the following radio message through: "His Majesty the Kaiser has occasionally expressed his special appreciation and gratitude for my lectures on the excellent conduct of the troops fighting in the Carpathians; and has deigned to order that the troops be informed of this right up to the Frontline — Signed by Hindenburg, Chief of General Staff and Field Marshall."

We are putting all our things in the sun for them to dry.

5

25.9.1916   It is the loveliest weather again today. There is another engagement taking place again, all the way to our right around the Baba Ludowa. Our 1st Company is also being heavily shot at to our left, and approaching columns of Russians have been reported there too. From noon onwards, we also receive some very heavy shrapnel fire. Our 15cm howitzers finally shoot now as well for once.

A Russian from Regiment 125 deserts in the evening, and tells us that they wanted to attack at noon but had too heavy casualties because of our artillery. The attack will now probably take place at dusk the next morning.

26.9.1916   Everything is calm; nice day. No artillery shots — an almost frightening stillness after yesterday's racket.

27.9.1916   For the purpose of questioning about the jäger who drowned in the Viso, I need to go down to the regiment in Szybeny. I walked 7 hours there and back; very strenuous on the horrible paths, for the condition of which there is no expression at all. Dead pack animals are lying everywhere that have perished due to overexertion. Szybeny has changed a lot. The entire valley is full of barracks, stables, and blockhouses.

Szybeny – 1916

28.9.1916   The weather seems to be getting bad again. We are shot at with heavy mortars from 7 o'clock in the morning onwards — 2 wounded. My large new blockhouse shelter is complete. As the pinnacle of its luxury, it even has a window in the shape of a triangular shard of glass.

Heavy fog towards the evening. A few mortars.

'My first shelter on the Stajki – September 1916'.

29.9.1916   It is cloudy and cold. Swarms of snow geese are flying over us. The Russians and we are shooting at them, although without success.

     A strong storm in the night.

1.10.1916   Miserable weather throughout the night — fog and rain. After my company had dwindled to 75 men due to the daily losses, I am getting 70 replacements today. They arrived in very terrible weather and immediately got the right perception of the Carpathians. By the evening, only 16 of the 70 men made it to the top. The others got stuck in the dirt along the way and arrived one by one until noon the next day, obviously thoroughly wet and frozen. Among the replacements was also Felix Niese *(an old acquaintance)* from Weida, who has come to my company.

     It is raining nonstop.

3.10.1916   I am receiving a section to the left that is a couple of 100 metres larger, and the highest 1750-metre-high summit of the Stajki now belongs to me. Three very frozen Russians defected yesterday evening.

     The winter equipment has now arrived, including thick winter clothes. On this occasion, I am having a potbelly stove and roofing felt for my shelter brought to me from the valley, as well as planks for a double door. The food is now plentiful again. Every other day, we now even receive a quarter of extra 'Kommissbrot' *(German rye bread)* and are also getting schnapps delivered which we can put to good use.

4.10.1916   Lovely winter weather. I went to the summit of the Stajki in the morning, which was a proper mountain tour given the deep snow. I received a small metal stove for burning log fires today, as well as a hanging carbide lamp *(an acetylene gas lamp)*. It is now very cosy within my robbers' den. Hopefully, we will stay here over the winter, as we have settled very nicely into our position.

5.10.1916   Very nice sunshine weather but with an icy storm. Lovely view towards the snow-covered peaks. We are completely adjusting ourselves for the winter. We have marked out the small footpaths along the position with four-metre-high poles so that no one gets lost in a snowstorm or fog. Firewood supplies are being hauled up out of the woodland starting 300 metres below. However, I can already predict that when we are finished and have made ourselves comfortable with a lot of effort, we will be replaced, and others will take up residence in the finished warm nest.

'Stajki – 1750m – In front of my shelter from left to right: Captain Conrad, me, and Lieutenant Fischer – October 1916'.

6.10.1916   The snow starts to melt towards the morning — fog and rain.
Two Russians from Regiment 125 are defecting; young and strong guys with tall felt hats.

8.10.1916   Storm — half rain and half ice needles. A heavy mortar hit a shelter in the evening — 2 dead, 1 heavy and 4 lightly wounded.

9.10.1916   Storm and fog. You can barely stand on your own feet. We are all growing full beards out of boredom.

11.10.1916   Strong storm, but occasional sunshine. Towards the evening comes the appalling news that a heavy mortar shell destroyed the company-commander shelter of the 1st Company, and that all situated in there (Lieutenants Stachelhausen, Bode, and Le Roi) are dead, as well as one telephone being destroyed. The shelter was nevertheless not very strong, but rather more of a log cabin.
The storm is turning into a hurricane in the night. We have already experienced many storms here, but certainly nothing like this yet. It is not possible to stay on your feet.

12.10.1916   The storm raged all night long. For safety, I am having my shelter reinforced with several strong support beams.

15.10.1916   Between 4:30 and 5 o'clock in the morning, the Smotrez is stormed along with the so-called 'Nameless Mountain' which lies between the Smotrez and the Stajki. My company supports the assault through heavy rifle, machine-gun, and mortar fire to deceive the Russians about the actual point of attack. The shooting doesn't stop all day in this area.

It is wonderful warm weather, and I don't need to heat the shelter for the first time in a long time. Along with loud squawking, large swarms of snow geese are again migrating south. The food is very varied; it depends very much on the weather. The day before yesterday, for example, a pack animal was thrown down the slope due to the storm, and almost all of the bread was thereby crushed.

17.10.1916   Cold wind and rain. Due to the daily losses, my company has already dwindled down to just 108 men, with whom I have to occupy a Front of over 1 kilometre. There has been a strong blizzard since noon, and everything is white again in a short amount of time. We luckily lie on the south side, whereas the Russians are on the northern slope. They will suffocate directly in the snow in winter.

During the night, my shelter gets so covered in snow that the door barely opens. The snow lies over one metre high in some parts.

18.10.1916   Nice sunny winter weather, but the wind is blowing terribly. You have to shovel the entrance free every few moments. You sink up to the torso in the snow outside. From the afternoon until late in the night rages a terrible snowstorm — it is unbearable outside. I only appoint a few guards outside and replace them every hour, but despite the thick winter attire, the people are half-dead each time. The storm is luckily blowing all the snow down to the Russians.

In the newspapers, it says that trucks full of doors and windows are being made ready in the back of the country and are being brought to the Front. We haven't noticed anything of this, unfortunately; everything will probably get stuck in the communication zone. We have fortunately learned how to help ourselves. My door has been cobbled together using roof shingles from a Ruthenian house. Two shards of glass have been placed in a hole in the middle as a window, and the rest is covered with burlap with moss stuffed behind it. Fischer made a door out of small boards from ammunition boxes, and based on my recommendation, attached three 9 x 12cm photographic plates as windows. Others reuse oil paper from the mortar-shell boxes as windows or layer empty white bottles on top of each other; the spaces in between are filled. My shelter is nice and warm since it is stuck deep in the ground on all sides. The only unpleasant thing is that it already gets dark here at 5 o'clock, but it is therefore light again at 5 o'clock in the morning.

I am ordering myself a washbasin from home, made of waterproof material. For this purpose, I until now have been using an empty rollmops *(pickled herring fillets)* tin, which has unfortunately disappeared since yesterday. Of course, we also don't have plates and glasses; the cookware lid and the aluminium drinking cup are used for this purpose. But today I will be receiving an empty mustard jar which is very valuable. I did have a couple of colourful Ruthenian plates on the Stepanski, but they were unfortunately lost on the Skoruszny. Things are extremely primitive with us here because you cannot get anything. My bed consists of a layer of sticks covered with pine branches. There are also no chairs, of course; ammunition boxes are used for this. However, it is still nice up here anyway.

21.10.1916   Thaw — the snow has almost completely disappeared in a short amount of time. A Russian patrol of 11 men was shot down by my posts in the morning.

Heavy rain in the evening. The transport difficulties are already so great that it is hard to understand what things will be like later when winter really does set in. The snow and cold are still acceptable, but the worst of all are the days of terrible snowstorms that come over from the Pip Ivan and pierce through everything. Luckily my shelter, which is buried deep beneath the snow, is very warm. I can only heat with long breaks, otherwise I cannot tolerate the heat. The view of the snowed-over mountains was wonderful this morning, but most of the time you can't see 50 paces away.

'Stajki – The view northwest from my shelter towards the valley end. To the right is the Smotrez – October 1916'.

23.10.1916 It snows again, melts, and then rains — all shelters are underwater, and mine is dripping through in countless places. This morning, I shot a Russian who was very cheekily working on the wire obstacle 150 metres away while fully standing up. One of my oberjägers shot a rabbit and gave me a leg from it. I never tasted a rabbit as good as this Carpathian rabbit.

The winter here will probably last until May, so we expect to need to endure over six months of winter up here, cut off from the rest of humanity. There are sure enough no inhabitants here in the wildest high mountains. The last living thing I saw other than soldiers was on the Stepanski, which was an ancient Ruthenian woman who smoked from a clay pipe all day long like a factory chimney. We will hopefully get some snowshoes delivered soon so that we can do a little bit more exercise.

25.10.1916 Dense fog and thaw weather. My left wing is being taken over by the 2nd Company. My long frontline will thereby become shorter by a third, and to my great joy, I will also be getting rid of the highest Stajki peaks. For the current surplus of people, I am having two large barracks for 20 men each built 200 metres below me.

I again shot a Russian at 7 o'clock this morning from a distance of 500 metres. Following the shot, he plummeted together and screamed in great sorrow. I could clearly see through the scope how two others bandaged him and carried him away. I now lie up in the cliffs for hours every day and shoot at the Russians below us. It is a wonderful sunny day today. To the west, there are beautiful clear views of the snow-capped mountain range; and to the east, the mountain peaks emerge like islands from the sea of clouds, a view like the one from the 'Großvenediger' today *(the highest peak of the Venediger Group mountain range in Austria)*.

26.10.1916 Wonderful warm sunshine weather. I have been placing a Russian shelter, which I spotted 100 metres from my trenches, under constant rifle fire since this morning. From a rocky cliff, we can shoot directly into the entrance from the flank. The four to five Russians, who are inside and have constantly annoyed us at night with their constant shooting, are unable to move all day. I have fired at least 50 bullets myself.

27.10.1916   I again kept the shelter under rifle fire from the morning onwards, and then I let my small mortar fire 20 shells at it. The tenth shell ripped apart a corner of the shelter, whereupon one Russian fled. The last shell was a direct hit right in the middle, which completely destroyed it. We later observed how two paramedics carried away two dead or heavily wounded. In front of my section still lie perhaps a dozen such shelters, which you can best recognise from the smoke in the morning. I now systematically shoot them to pieces one by one, as the Russians get too cheeky otherwise.

Sudden thick fog in the afternoon. A patrol of mine has just brought in one of the Russians shot down on the 21st despite heavy fire. He is from Regiment 125, our old friends.

6

28.10.1916   Fog. In the afternoon comes the order that I am to take over the position on the far left by the Nameless Mountain. Anyone who has seen how much effort and work we have put into expanding our current position will understand our anger. I immediately went to the left wing in dense fog to have a look at the new position. It looks dreadful there — everything neglected — a sufficient trench only in some parts. The existing shelters are practically unusable, and the entire section is dirty and abhorrent. I gave Captain Conrad, who told me that I was going to a wonderfully constructed position, a vent about my feelings via telephone. I am surprised that he put up with it.

'My current position – In the background to the left is the Smotrez, and to the right the Nameless Mountain – 28.10.1916'.

29.10.1916   At 8 o'clock in the morning, we relocate with doors, ovens, lamps and so forth. We immediately get to work from noon. I am having two solid blockhouses built on the foremost line behind two rocky peaks, and one large barrack somewhat further below for the reserves; as well as a shelter for me and my orderlies by the Nameless Mountain. The work is very troublesome because of the rocks. We constantly have to blast them with hand grenades. The weather is luckily nice, and the clouds enshroud us only now and then.

30.10.1916   Work is being carried out strenuously all day. I am currently living in a hole in the ground that you wouldn't stick a pig in at home. I cannot even sit in it, and it is also pitch black. My new position lies approximately 1700 metres high in the wide hollow between the Stajki and the Nameless Mountain; upon the latter lies the Austrian Landsturm. In front of us, after the Russians, lie dense mountain pine fields. After the Nameless Mountain comes another large hollow with dense pine bushes, and then follows the 1900-metre-high Smotrez. The Russians lie 400 metres away from me, but only on the far right where I bump into the 1st Company. They are up to 30 metres apart there, and you can hear them speak in their trenches. Several dead Russians from the 15th of October still lie there too.

'Austrian blockhouses in the cliffs of the Nameless Mountain'.

'To the left next to the boulder is the cave in the ground that I am occupying until my blockhouse is complete'.

'My blockhouse under construction. Behind it is the Nameless Mountain'.

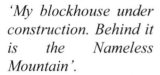

31.10.1916   My new shelter is dug out, or rather blasted out by noon. For this purpose, I used about 30 hand grenades which blew out the gigantic boulders. In the evening, nine thick trunks are placed as supporting pillars and connected at the top by three trunks, each 5.5 metres long. There is banging in all corners. Everywhere, you hear the cry: "Heads up! Detonation!", and then the boulder fragments fly through the air. The Russians won't be able to explain what is going on here with us.

I have a marvellous view from my shelter. Straight ahead of me, I can see deep down into the long valley of the Pohorylec Stream, the other side of which is formed by the elongated, dark Czorna Hora with the 2028-metre-high Pip Ivan. To the left, I can fully see down into the valley up to Szybeny by the Czarny Czeremosz, as well as plenty of high summits behind it in the direction of Kirlibaba. Directly to the left of me is the steep double-peak of the 1750-metre-high Stajki. To the right is the Nameless Mountain (approximately 1700 metres) and the 1900-metre-high Smotrez which is furrowed with trenches.

'The 3 peaks of the Stajki seen from the Nameless Mountain. In between is my current position – November 1916'.

'The northernmost Stajki peak seen from the tree line. Between these trees lies the graveyard – November 1916'.

'A view of the Smotrez – November 1916'.

_1.11.1916_   Yesterday's lovely weather has unfortunately stopped again, and we now have the customary wet and thick fog. It does get nice again though in the afternoon.

_3.11.1916_   Lovely weather. The Russian artillery is firing quite strongly. A jäger, standing next to me by my shelter, received a shrapnel ball to his thigh, but it only tore a hole through his trousers without injuring him.

_4.11.1916_   A Russian from Regiment 125 defected during the night. It is lovely weather yet again, and I am currently writing at 8 o'clock in the morning while sitting outdoors. There was still metre-high snow lying 14 days ago.

'A deserted Russian – 4.11.1916'.

_5.11.1916_   I was upon the Nameless Mountain at noon. It looks wild over there. The entire summit is streaked with trenches, and everything is rumpled from shells and mortars. Nothing will be growing up there anytime soon.

In the evening, we once again orchestrated a little fire magic to frighten the Russians. At 9 o'clock, the artillery fired 50 shots into the trenches lying in front of me and the 1st Company. All machine guns simultaneously started to rattle, the mortar fired 30 shells, our people chucked hand grenades, the hornist blew all the signals that he could; everybody screamed "Hurrah!", whistled and hooted; and flares also went up. The Russians, who had to assume that we wanted to attack, opened up barbaric fire, which did us no harm because we of course stayed well under cover. It was a hellish racket, and we were greatly amused. On the other hand, we really spoiled the Russians' night of rest because they most certainly also alarmed their reserves in the valley.

_6.11.1916_   I am moving into the new shelter.

9.11.1916 I received the washbasin and an air cushion today which I ordered from home. It is a whole different thing, washing with the sink instead of a rollmops tin. I can also make good use of the air cushion, as I have always been using the knapsack as a cushion up to now. The weather has been so nice in the past few days that you could lie in the grass for half the day. My new shelter is the nicest one that I have ever built. Of the two rooms, one belongs to me alone and the other is for my three orderlies and the telephone.

We are now in the middle of preparing for our large attack taking place the day after tomorrow, together with the 1st Company. The enemy position needs to be precisely scouted and the break-in points need to be determined. Stormtroopers are being put together and must be instructed in every detail about their tasks and their conduct.

In the afternoon, the 4th Company in my previous position attacked, capturing one machine gun and 60 prisoners.

In the evening comes news that our attack has to be postponed until the 14th, as the mortars must first bring up some more ammunition. These operations have been ordered to deceive the Russians about our strengths, or rather our weaknesses, and to bind the strongest possible forces to our Front. Things have been pretty peaceful in my current position so far. I have only had 2 wounded up to now. Here, we can freely walk around behind the ridge that we occupy, whilst the Russians below us are condemned to a permanent life in the caves.

'The arrival of the pack animals with ammunition and provisions. In the background to the right is the Smotrez, and to the left is the path to the Czorna Hora – November 1916'.

'The distribution of food after the arrival of the pack animals – November 1916'.

14.11.1916   Fog and snow. The artillery is not able to set their range because of the fog — they have shot into our own line and wounded several people. Our assault is temporarily cancelled as a result.

16.11.1916   The view is occasionally somewhat clearer. Our artillery and mortars are setting their range.

I have been lucky once again. I was standing with the artillery observer and was helping to set the range, when a shell, fired too close, burst directly above us without causing any harm.

17.11.1916   It snows heavily at night and continues to snow during the day. However, we decided to carry out our attack — From 3 o'clock to 3:20 in the afternoon, our artillery and mortars batter the Russian trenches and then our hand-grenade troops push forward. Despite the artillery fire not being effective, and the barbed-wire obstructions being fully intact, all the shock troops penetrate into the enemy trenches in spite of the very strong resistance, especially in my sector. My troops are only unable to make any progress on the very left wing, as the Russians have positioned two machine guns behind a rock and the trenches are very heavily occupied. The invading troops destroy everything that they find in the trenches and return in the darkness with 45 captives and two machine guns. We would have captured many more if most of them had not run away.

Towards the evening and throughout the entire night, there is a terrible snowstorm.

The regimental statement from the 17th of November: "After short and effective artillery preparation this afternoon, shock troops from the 1st and 3rd Companies of the 11th Jägers, under the command of Lieutenants Hungerland and Pfeifer, infiltrated multiple enemy trenches by the northern slope of the Stajki, dispersed the Russian garrison, took 45 captives, captured two machine guns and inflicted bloody losses on the enemy during their retreat. I express my full appreciation to all those involved for exemplary brave behaviour and the will to win, which could not be broken by the tough enemy resistance. Once again, Jäger-Battalion 11 showed the enemy, who was far superior in number, who the master in the battle area of the Stajki is — Signed: Colonel Lehmann."

18.11.1916   All the snow has blown over to the Russians due to the strong storm. It is again very cold, but a lovely winter's day.

The division statement from the 17th of November: "During an advance into the enemy position, ordered by the 4th Regiment, parts of Jäger-Battalion 11 were completely successful today for the third time in a short space of time. Over 40 captives and two machine guns were taken. The enemy suffered heavy, bloody losses. Their own casualties are small. It is to be announced to all troops that with very special joy, I can once again express my warmest appreciation to the brave battalion. All mortar and artillerymen, who participated in the preparation and execution, deserve full praise. Success lies in the understanding cooperation of all weaponry and the valour of the jägers. To be announced to the subordinate troops — Signed: The 200th Infantry Division."

19.11.1916 Snowstorm. Half snow and half rain — disgusting weather. Our people have now been equipped with long sheepskins, rabbit-fur vests, and snow goggles. Even the food is now outstanding since we are receiving extra rations as mountain troops. For yesterday's assault, ten of my people are to receive the Iron Cross 2nd Class. I have also recommended an oberjäger for the 1st Class.

22-25.11.1916 Lovely weather. At half past 10 in the evening, the adjutant, Lieutenant Otto, telephoned me to say that I had received the Iron Cross 1st Class, as well as Oberjäger Euler from my company. 10 jägers are also to receive the Iron Cross 2nd Class.

26.11.1916 It is starting to rain in the afternoon. Yesterday, I was down in the valley and observed the shingle production and the charcoal kilns by the 6th Jägers, as well as the lovely blockhouses of the Styrian Landsturm. We are miserable bunglers in comparison.

27.11.1916 It is lovely weather. In the evening, both 1st-Class Iron Crosses are being celebrated in Fischer's shelter along with a lot of red wine.

We were alarmed in the night. A Russian defector has said that they want to attack tomorrow.

28.11.1916 Since the morning, the Russians had been firing like mad with artillery and mortars until 2 o'clock in the afternoon, but they didn't come out of their trenches here near us. On the other hand, they attacked the 6th Jägers twice between the Smotrez and the Nameless Mountain but were smoothly repelled.

Thick fog in the afternoon. My company only has two lightly wounded despite the heavy firing.

29.11.1916 The Russians were very quiet in the night. It snowed, and now everything is white again. The Russians will probably keep quiet now for this year when they see that they cannot get through to us.

The Iron Cross 1st Class was awarded to us along with the following statement: "By order and in the name of His Majesty the Kaiser and King, His Excellency, the Commanding General, has awarded the Iron Cross 1st Class to the Lieutenants of the Landwehr, Hungerland and Pfeifer; and the Oberjäger, Euler, of the 11th Jäger Battalion — For exemplary bravery and the strong will to win throughout an operation by the Stajki, during which they inflicted heavy losses on the enemy."

One defector said that when the Russians were supposed to attack yesterday, they outright mutinied.

Top and Below: Alexander working on a shelter with his men.

7

30.11.1916   This morning, Seemann with the 2nd Company also threw himself at the Russians, after blowing up the strong barbed-wire obstacle by pushing a toboggan sled underneath. This was loaded with 50 hand grenades and lots of explosive ammunition. Loot — 2 machine guns and 41 prisoners. No own losses.

1-2.12.1916   It is the nicest sunshine weather. The Russians are again firing at us like mad with artillery all day, especially at the Smotrez and the Nameless Mountain. At 12 o'clock noon, you could suddenly see many hand grenades bursting upon the Smotrez, and the summit was immediately afterwards swarming with Russians who kept shouting "Hurrah!". We could hear this all the way over here despite being three kilometres away. The 6th Jägers retreated back to a trench that lay behind them. They carried out a counterattack between 3 and 4 o'clock in the afternoon. The Russians swept out in clustered droves, then faltered, turned back again, were pelted with hand grenades, and then whizzed down the steep slope like greased lightning. This was a wonderful scene. We all shouted "Hurrah!" with joy.

    The night has passed quietly.

3.12.1916   The weather is splendid again. The Russians are shooting a great deal with artillery; equally so from the 4th to the 7th of December.

11.12.1916   At 1 o'clock in the night, the 1st and my 3rd Company once again attacked the Russians. Gaps were detonated into the enemy obstruction using two elongated charges, and through these, we forced ourselves into the trench. Our shock troops returned with seven captives. The enemy also suffered very heavy casualties, mainly from our hand grenades.

12.12.1916   During a terrible storm at 2 o'clock in the night, my company once again blew up the enemy obstacle in the same way as yesterday, and my shock troops brought back five prisoners from the trenches. The Russians barraged the Smotrez very well yesterday, and they attacked three times judging by the strong machine-gun fire. They didn't achieve anything though.

    Our battalion is now highly respected as a result of our multiple successes. We are receiving one recognition after the other from the top and were even mentioned in the army report on the 1st of December. But we have therefore raided the Russians seven times in one and a half months, and have taken seven machine guns and almost 300 prisoners from them. The 5th and 6th Jägers are bursting with envy. For yesterday and today, my company again received nine 2nd-Class Iron Crosses. Raudonat from Forstwolfersdorf *(a village near Weida)* is also included. So, in the space of three weeks, two 1st-Class Iron

Crosses and nineteen 2nd-Class Iron Crosses, just like that. This is something I can be proud of as a company commander.

'We received the Iron Cross 1st Class in the Carpathians – From left to right: Lieutenants Otto (Adjutant), Totzek, me, Seemann, Weber, and Hungerland – December 1916.'

13.12.1916   An icy storm rages through the night and all day, the likes of which I have never experienced, even here in the Carpathians.

14.12.1916   The storm finally subsides somewhat around noon.

The regimental order: "The 11th of December is once again a day of honour for the regiment, which achieved great successes over the enemy on the entire Front. Strong patrols from Reserve Jäger-Regiment 5 attacked the enemy on the right and left of the Czeremosz, partly bypassing their bases, partly penetrating their obstructions, and inflicting considerable losses on them. The established courageous shock troops of the 11th Jäger Battalion (the 1st and 3rd Companies) invaded the enemy positions twice without preparation, cleared several trenches, inflicted a loss of approximately 150 men on the enemy, and took 17 prisoners. The 6th Reserve Jäger Battalion caused three enemy assaults to fail upon the Smotrez, after a short but very fierce Russian pre-bombardment. To all those involved in these activities, I express my full appreciation and gratitude for your bravery and belligerence which is once again proven, as well as your tenacity in persevering in the face of enemy attacks. Unfortunately, the day of battle also cost victims everywhere, but they are small compared to the success. This achievement is not just seen locally; it is the means to bring about the great final outcome in Romania. I am proud of the regiment's actions, and I am confident that we will continue to be the terror of our enemies. Signed — Colonel Lehmann."

15-16.12.1916 Intense storm. There is a snowstorm in the afternoon, making you unable to see ten paces ahead. A Russian patrol that broke into our foremost trench, which we didn't occupy because it was fully snowed in, is immediately thrown out again and two Russians are shot down.

The night is pitch black. The storm is terrible. I have metre-thick walls of earth surrounding my shelter, but the wind still whistles through everywhere. The entire interior is layered with finger-thick snow dust in the morning.

Many of us here are sick. They have the Carpathian fever, which is seemingly harmless though, and only lasts for a couple of days. It probably has something to do with the thin air. I personally haven't noticed anything of it yet. It is now very boring since you only leave the shelter when absolutely necessary, sticking one log after the other into the oven all day long. The remaining 12 hours are spent sleeping.

18.12.1916 Blowing snow. The Russians keep getting calmer.

20.12.1916 Icy wind and snow. My blockhouse is covered in a crust of ice. Nobody goes outside if they absolutely don't have to.

22.12.1916 It is marvellous weather again. The Russians are noticeably quiet. There have been no shots of artillery for several days now.

23.12.1916 At noon, we were relieved and placed in reserve below my previous position. I am now living in the company commander's quarters of the 4th Company with Lieutenant Weber. It is significantly warmer down here in the forest, and the wind doesn't blow for as long. I am exercising here as shock troops with my company until the 6th of January. Count von Soden is on leave and is unlikely to return to us because he will probably receive a regiment. Who our new commander will be is still undetermined. Hopefully not Captain Conrad.

24.12.1916   Fog and snow. I celebrated Christmas with Weber, Hermes, and Jenner. The four of us drank one bottle of wine and one bottle of sparkling wine, and then went to sleep at 11 o'clock. The expected Russian attack did not materialise. On the contrary, the Russians were very calm. On the 29th of December, my company will be going to Szybeny for a number of days where we are to exercise on the frozen lake. This way I can at least see our nice mess hall for once and finally eat from porcelain plates at a white-covered table again for the first time in half a year. These are all just small things that do not exist up here.

25.12.1916   It is lovely weather. There will be a religious service down in the valley this afternoon. However, the pastor came up to us due to a mistake while we were waiting for him at the bottom. We did at least have a very nice 3.5-hour walk in return.

30.12.1916   There has been a snowstorm since last night. It is snowing all the time, but the snow isn't particularly deep. There are of course many deep snowdrifts, but they are on average no higher than half a metre because the storm blows everything into the valley. The snow doesn't bother us, but the permanent storm is terrible in contrast — it blows through the metre-thick earth walls. We don't have anything like this at home. It is thereby not even particularly cold either, but the icy wind blows through and through. You need to come to a stop every few steps because you cannot breathe.

31.12.1916   Calm wind and snow. The food arrived two hours late because the pack animals got stuck in the snow and had to be shovelled out.
        I celebrated the New Year until 1 o'clock in the morning with Weber, Hermes, Jenner and Schmelz.

1.1.1917   9 o'clock departure into the valley. I am living with Lieutenant Sander by the Large Star *(a local landmark)*.

5.1.1917   The inspection by Colonel Lehmann in the presence of the brigade commander, Colonel von Below, went well.

6.1.1917   We have taken over the old position again during strong snowfall.

7.1.1917 I submitted a leave of absence with the permission of the battalion. I walked to Szybeny and back to get a medical certificate for a recreational holiday.

9.1.1917 It is very nice, sunny, and windless weather. We went snowshoeing behind the position in the morning and afternoon.

17.1.1917 Yesterday evening came the news that my holiday has been authorised. I left the position at 5 o'clock in the morning and walked 2.5 hours down to Szybeny. At 8 o'clock, I rode the postal sledge (a large box on runners) up the Kopilas (1600 metres), and from there I walked down into the valley to the end of the cable car and the beginning of the field railway. This took me 2 and a half hours; the last half hour on the sleigh of an ammunition convoy.

'Our postal sledge in the Carpathians'.

At 4:30 in the afternoon, I travelled to Ruszpolyana via the field railway in a meat transport wagon, where I arrived at 6 o'clock in the evening and, after a long search in the darkness, finally found our valley squadron with the officers' overnight accommodation. I met Captain Conrad here, who is waiting for his holiday to be approved.

18.1.1917 At 10 o'clock in the morning in the open carriage of the field railway to Leordina, and then on the slow train to Visovölgy. Then at 4:45 with the Budapest train to Maramarossziget and Satoralja Ujhely, where I arrived at 3 o'clock in the night.

19.1.1917 I took the slow train to Kaschau at 4 o'clock in the morning, arriving at 9 o'clock. Now continuing home via Oderberg, Breslau and Dresden.

HOLIDAY!

Boredom On The Front

As you may have realised, the writing style and length of Alexander's entries have temporarily changed and become somewhat shorter compared to before. Because, unlike popular belief, soldiers often had many days and weeks of boredom with nothing to do, where the change in weather was the only thing worth talking about. These diary entries have been maintained to show that this was in fact the case. During extended campaigns, soldiers often had prolonged free time which they spent lingering in their trenches while awaiting the next big assault.

These living conditions, within claustrophobic spaces and dire environments, meant that there weren't many activities or entertainment to pass the time. Soldiers were therefore limited to eating, sleeping, cleaning their equipment, writing diaries and letters, as well as creating trench art. With a surplus of scrap wood, metal, shell casings and other items to hand, soldiers were able to craft various items for amusement, practicality, and other uses. In Alexander's case, he did the exact same thing and even had a small wooden tobacco box carved as a reminder of his time in the Carpathian Mountains:

8

25.1.1917   I received a telegram this morning, saying I have to arrive in Ruszpolyana on the 2nd of February.

31.1.1917   At 6 o'clock in the evening, I travelled over Leipzig, Dresden and Breslau towards Oderberg, where I wasn't able to catch the connection to the morning train. In the afternoon on the 1st of February, I continued towards Kaschau where I arrived on the 2nd. I used the long stay to take a look at the city. I continued to SataraljaUjhely in the afternoon, and towards Maramarossziget in the night where I arrived at half past 6 in the morning.

Captain Conrad, whom I met on the way, continued on whilst I visited Lieutenant Prüsse from Köckritz with the regimental adjutant, Lieutenant Hackbarth, who invited us to lunch and dinner in the mess hall of the communication-zone headquarters. I visited a charity concert in the evening that was organised by the communication-zone command, where I saw General Kövess and Archduke Albrecht. The civilian population was in full dress. We then went to a café with gypsy music, then to the mess hall once again; and then finally to the delegate of the Red Cross until 2 o'clock, where we drank shots of schnapps.

Hint: General Hermann Kövess is the current Commander-in-Chief of the Austro-Hungarian Army. Archduke Eugen of Austria is a Prince of Hungary and Bohemia, as well as a Field Marshall.

The journey here far exceeded my worst expectations — hour-long delays everywhere and no connection, as well as the carriages in Germany being proper ice cellars, and sweatboxes in Hungary in return. I arrived one day late as a result, but this wasn't noticeable at all. Nothing special happened here in the meantime, only it is said to have been a coldness of minus 28 degrees up in the emplacement.

4.2.1917   A lovely car ride to the foot of the Kopilas at half past 6 this morning via Visovölgy, Leordina and Ruszpolyana. On the way, in Ruszpolyana, I had a half-hour breakfast break with First-Lieutenant Bieneck, the leader of our regiment's supply transport. Such a winterly car ride through the lovely mountain valleys is wonderful. We then drove over the Kopilas Pass in the sleigh and arrived down in Szybeny at 4 o'clock in the afternoon. We luckily had very nice weather. There is much less snow up to the Kopilas than at home, but it lies enormously high at the top of the pass. I then spent a very comfortable evening in the mess hall of Szybeny, which lasted until 2 o'clock in the night along with gramophone music.

5.2.1917   With the sleigh in the morning, through the Pohorylec Valley up to the foot of the Stajki and then with much difficulty up to my old position along covered pathways — fierce and cold wind. Everything is the same as before up here, but the communication with the superiors just seems to have become very uncomfortable. A Russian patrol had in fact infiltrated the position of the 1st Company a couple of days ago, and people at the top got very uptight about it. This resulted in stricter guard and work duties. Everyone complains and is dissatisfied.

Nugel from Gera was on holiday with me at the same time and is now a platoon leader in my company. After his pleasant life behind the Front, he is now very unhappy about our icy desert and the more-than-primitive conditions in which he now has to live. And yet it is downright lavish for us here compared to the conditions in September and October.

11.2.1917   It is a lovely day. Since I was deprived of part of my holiday due to being called back early, I applied for a new holiday today with the consent of the battalion, because I don't see why I should miss out.

14.2.1917   It is a nice sunny day, but the wind is bitterly cold. We are starting to blast bomb-proof tunnels into the rocks. The Russians have again been firing at us with 12cm shells for a long time, although without any success.

Storm in the night.

16.2.1917   Sunny, but a strong storm — impossible to work. The oven is smoking to the point where it is unbearable.

The storm subsides in the night. When there is no storm, you don't feel the cold up here as much as you do on the plains.

24.2.1917   It is sunny, but there is a very icy wind. In the afternoon, I received a telephone message that I have been commandeered to Felsoviso for a 14-day machine-gun course.

25.2.1917   I walked up to the Stajki at 9 o'clock in the morning, and then with the sledge towards Szybeny.

26.2.1917   At 8 o'clock in the morning, I walked up to the Kopilas Pass in 3 and a quarter hours and ate lunch there. At the top, the last hour and a half was very difficult due to the heavy snow and heavy snowdrifts. Everywhere are large groups of Austrian workers who are constantly busy shovelling the pass clear of snow. I then went down with the sledge to the foot of the Kopilas, and with the automobile to Ruszpolyana where I am spending the night within the officers' home; a large wooden barrack with dining rooms and bedrooms, and eight very nice bathing cubicles.

'The officers' home in Ruszpolyana'.

27.2.1917   I bathed in the morning and then went to Leordina with the car at 9 o'clock. The train, which was supposed to leave at 10 o'clock, was delayed by the local norm of two hours.

With the train towards Felsoviso at 12 o'clock noon, a large Hungarian Jewish nest, half village and half town. There are huge numbers of Jews here with tendrils of hair, as well as Romanians and Ruthenians. I am living on the Jewish street with a Jewish family — very primitive and dirty. We eat together in the mess hall; very little and expensive.

28.2.1917   The first lesson was from 9 to 11 o'clock in the morning — an explanation of the machine gun. Duties — three hours in the morning and one hour in the afternoon.

We generally have nice weather during the course. It was very cold at first, but it is now thawing later during the day.

6.3.1917   I am now completely familiar with the difficult mechanism of the machine gun. We have been live shooting every day since yesterday. It is otherwise very boring here. There is only very expensive wine available in the mess hall — no bottle under 4.50 Mark. Then there is also a Jewish café, and that is all. We still have to pay out 2.50 Mark a day in addition to the food we are entitled to. I purchased 20 eggs for 8.50 Mark today. People don't like to accept money, but on the other hand, you can get everything in return for tobacco, schnapps, and so forth.

13.3.1917   Through an inspection by Major von Altrock, the course has come to an end today. I had to demonstrate the explanation of a machine-gun part and fire live at targets. In the evening was a fun, long-lasting farewell celebration.

14.3.1917   In the morning, all jägers (11 men) went on a truck to Ruszpolyana via Leordina, where we are now eating lunch.

We stayed overnight in the officers' home.

'Machine-gun course in Felsoviso'.

Alexander is 9th from the left.

Life in Felsoviso

While in Felsoviso, Alexander took many photographs showing the daily local activities there. What strikes me is how personal some of these are, having been taken of individual people who are long forgotten, but whose split-second moment in life has been captured for us to see.

15.3.1917   It is pouring with rain — groundless mud. In the afternoon, I received a telephone message that I am on leave from the 16th of March to the 5th of April — Immediately to Leordina with the automobile, where I only just catch the train.

16.3.1917   After tedious slow travelling and endless delays at every station, I arrive in Kaschau at noon. It goes somewhat faster from here.

It is marvellous weather — magnificent view of the snow-covered High Tatras. Despite a one-hour delay, I still manage to catch the connection to Breslau at 9 o'clock, where I arrive at 1 o'clock in the night.

17.3.1917   The train to Leipzig is gone. I am spending the night in the waiting room, 1st class.

I continue in the morning via Dresden — Arrival in Weida at 4 o'clock in the afternoon.

HOLIDAY!

2.4.1917   Towards Gera at 10:22 in the morning. Then onwards within huge, overcrowded trains at 1 o'clock in the afternoon through Dresden, Breslau and Oderberg, where I needed to wait for the connection from 12:40 in the night until 9:50 in the morning.

4.4.1917   Through the Tatras yesterday in good weather, arriving in Kaschau at 5:30 in the afternoon. Today, from Kaschau to Maramarossziget where I arrived early. I was the only German officer on the train, whilst yesterday there were hundreds of officers travelling in the direction of Lemberg. I was even able to lie down that night.

Lunch in Leordina, and further on to Ruszpolyana with the field railway. I have just occupied a bed, drank coffee, had myself done up at the hairdresser and then took a bath. It is the nicest warm weather.

5.4.1917   Towards the base of the Kopilas with the car in the morning. The mountain slopes are dotted with snowdrops. Then, to the mountain pass on foot, where huge amounts of snow still lie. The road is even covered up over the railings. I rode down to Szybeny. It is the purest spring weather here, and the air is much nicer than at home. Snow only lies on the highest mountains, but even more so there. I instantly feel better here, and I no longer have the headache that I always had at home. Everything is still the same as before in the emplacement.

'The road over the Kopilas shortly before the mountain pass – 5.4.1917'.

'The climb to the Kopilas along the footpath – Lieutenant Schulz of Jäger-Battalion 17, and my attendant, Oberreich – 5.4.1917'.

6.4.1917   The purest summer weather in the morning. Long stretches are often completely violet from a type of crocus *(flower)*. In any case, it is wonderful here now, and nobody wants to leave here again. After my meal, I rode up to the foot of the Stajki. The last stretch from the Ölser Square *(a local landmark)* is in an awful condition due to the melting snow. The paths are better on the Stajki itself. There are now fields of snow only in the sheltered areas, although some of which still being 1.5 metres deep.

'Szybeny – The mess hall of Jäger-Battalion 11 – Left to right: The paymaster, Lieutenant Jenner, and Lieutenant Seemann (on horseback) – 6.4.1917'.

214

'Szybeny – Bridge over the Czarny Czeremosz. On the slope to the right is the start of the Kopilas Road – 6.4.1917'.

7.4.1917 Strong wind, fog, rain, and snow. At 8 o'clock in the evening, under the cover of heavy artillery and mortar fire, our 1st Company and the 6th Jägers by the Smotrez broke into the Russian positions and brought back several captives. These say that the troops opposite us have been relieved in the last few days and replaced by new formations. This explains the numerous fires that have been observed everywhere behind the Russian Front in recent nights.

There is an intense storm in the night.

8.4.1917 There is an extremely violent snowstorm. It is very uncomfortable holiday weather. The whole company had pancakes today, which were cooked in our kitchen.

Everything is deeply snowed in again now.

9.4.1917 The storm has slackened — strong snowfall. We are now in the middle of winter again. It is snowing so much that you cannot see ten steps ahead.

9

13.4.1917 It is windy but warm and sunny. This afternoon, the Russians suddenly started to wave, and our people waved back. People showed themselves more and more on both sides, and in the end, everybody stood out in the open on top of cover. Entire Russian squads then came towards our obstruction where bread and cigars were exchanged, as well as "Milo" (soap) for "Wutki" (schnapps). Both parties stood everywhere on the cliff tops and upon the Nameless Mountain and waved — it is namely Russian Easter today. We received orders this morning to only shoot in the event of an enemy attack until further notice. When several Russian shells and shrapnel approached, the fraternisation quickly came to a stop again and everyone disappeared back into the trenches.

14.4.1917 Lovely weather in the morning. Everyone on both sides has been standing back on top of cover again since the break of the day. My entire company is collecting the many thousands of fired bullet casings lying around in front of the trenches, which will then be handed over to the waste material collection point.

Fierce wind and rain in the afternoon.

15.4.1917 In the morning, we distributed several leaflets to the Russians in the Russian language that have been delivered to us, which say that we will not interfere in their internal affairs and so forth. I also sent another Russian letter over in the afternoon.

It seems as though the same ceasefire is occurring along the entire Eastern Front. If our diplomats don't fail again now, then we will have the best

216

prospects for peace with Russia. If we then throw some of the many freed corps into Tyrol *(a region in Austria)*, the Italians will then immediately declare peace too. What could the French and English possibly do to us then, when we release the millions that are currently bound to the Eastern Front? In my opinion, we should now comply with the Russians in every respect and possibly give them Galicia, Bukovina and part of Romania. We can then deal twice as much damage against the French and English. The pathetic Austrians can hand something over by all means. In any case, the Russians are greatly fed up with the war. We therefore hope for the best.

No shots are being fired. Everyone is walking around in the open, but when too many Russians stand on our side, the Russian artillery fires a couple of warning shots since they are most likely concerned that people will desert.

'The Russians visiting us on the Stajki'.

17.4.1917 It is warm and sunny in the morning. It suddenly gets cloudy and cold in the afternoon — weak wind. The ceasefire still holds. The Russians are brewing their tea outside their trenches, as they are probably filled with water.

18.4.1917 It is a nice sunny day — profound peace. We have informed the Russians that we will immediately reinitiate hostilities if their artillery shoots once more. We have had complete peace here since then.

'A hidden observation stand from where I shot at the Russians daily who lie deep below us – 18.4.1917'.

'The view from the southern ridge of the Nameless Mountain towards the northern ridge occupied by the Russians. In front is our barbed-wire obstruction, and in the background are the mountains by Zabie. Very small on the ridge, you can see a few Russians – 18.4.1917'.

20.4.1917   We are having pigs' liver today. Each company was given two adolescent pigs that were to be fed with the kitchen scraps. However, it seems as though the animals could not tolerate the mountain air, and we had to slaughter them.

23.4.1917   I am handing over half of my emplacement to the 1st Company today, the so-called 'Commanding Height', and will be taking over half of the Nameless Mountain; the sector occupied by the Austrians up to now. We have named all the important area points. There is a 'Commanding Height', a 'Goat's Ridge', 'Brown Earth', the 'Kramer Nose' (a rock that closely resembles Lieutenant Kramer's head), and the 'Bottom-Beater Rock'; named like so because a platoon leader, who is a teacher, has his shelter there.

'The Kramer Nose – A group of rocks in my position developed into a base. At the front is a trench that has been started. The rock looks like 2 faces behind one another'.

218

24.4.1917 It is warm with a lot of snow and fog. We tore down the old and lousy Austrian huts in the morning, and are currently excavating for my new shelter which is being built very deep into the rocks behind the Nameless Mountain.

27.4.1917 Sunny, but a very sharp and cold wind. The spot for my shelter is now completely blasted out. The large 30-centimetre-thick supporting beams are being dragged 300 metres up from the forest today.

'The construction of my new shelter by the Nameless Mountain'.

'The shelter of a machine-gun crew on the Nameless Mountain. At the top left is the officers' shelter of the 6th Jägers'.

'One of my blockhouses by the Nameless Mountain'.

Right: 'Blockhouses of the central mortar crew between the Stajki and the Nameless Mountain'.

Left: 'Our barbed-wire obstruction by the Kramer Nose – April 1917'.

Right: 'During blockhouse construction'.

Left: 'Nugel in front of the mineshaft'.

Right: 'Blockhouse Kilian by the Commanding Height'.

28.4.1917   A very large snowstorm has been raging uninterruptedly since yesterday afternoon. It was extremely terrible this morning. I was upon the Nameless Mountain with Captain Gräffendorff, and we were half solidified after half an hour. He will not be coming back again any time soon.

30.4.1917   I walked into the valley during a fierce and cold storm in the morning, and I rode to Szybeny where there is lovely and warm summer weather and no snow. In the afternoon, I rode for one hour up the Czeremosz Valley to the dentist in Borkut. The paths are in an indescribable condition. Where there is no boardwalk, you sink up to your knees in large holes of mud and water. Riding is directly life-threatening.

A long May Day celebration inside the mess hall in Szybeny in the evening.

1.5.1917   Back into the position during the nicest warm thaw weather this morning. In the evening, Nugel gave me a punch bowl because he had acquired the 2nd Company.

2.5.1917   It is lovely warm weather, and it is very wet following the melting snow. The Russian artillery has been shooting quite a lot since yesterday. On the other hand, we are still living in profound peace with the infantry.

3.5.1917   Fog and snow — it has gotten colder again. We are still living in profound peace with the Russians. Some of them come through the thick snow up to our obstruction every morning and fetch themselves Russian newspapers (printed by us for the captured Russians), schnapps, tobacco and so forth. Just recently, someone by the Nameless Mountain got so filled with schnapps that he lifelessly rolled down the steep slope. Only the artillery fires at times.

My new house is complete and has been named 'House Gudrun'. The signpost is already being drawn.

4.5.1917   It is a wonderful sunny day. The Russian artillery bombarded us fairly heavily from 10 to 12 o'clock noon.

'The Smotrez seen from the Nameless Mountain. You can only see the top third of the gigantic mountain – 5.5.1917'.

7.5.1917   Strong snowfall at night, but the weather gets very nice again during the day. The Russians are giving us leaflets calling on us to fraternise and abolish the monarchy.

8.5.1917   It is a very nice day. Our new regiment commander, Major von Bünau, observed the emplacement today. Considerable Russian shrapnel fire started just as we were on the Nameless Mountain.

'The Skoruszny (1566 metres) seen from the Nameless Mountain – 9.5.1917'.

'A view from the Nameless Mountain towards Szybeny in the south – 9.5.1917'.

15.5.1917   There was tremendous artillery fire taking place to the far right of us this morning. The Russians held a large gathering of people towards the evening. Someone held a big speech, and you could hear him all the way over here. He was presumably a deputy from St. Petersburg.

17.5.1917   It is the proper weather for Ascension Day. The ceasefire still continues on our end which is a great advantage, as the huge amounts of ammunition, which will thereby be saved on the Eastern Front, will come to good use in the West.

Note: Ascension Day (German: Himmelfahrt) is celebrated 39 days after Easter Sunday and commemorates Jesus Christ's ascension to heaven.

At half past 6 in the morning, with Lieutenant Nugel, I climbed over the large mountain pine hollow onto the Smotrez, where you get a very strange impression seeing the Russians below you from just 20 metres away from the front trench. As I waved at them with the camera, they stood up, postured themselves and smiled for the photograph.

'Russians on the Smotrez – 17.5.1917'.

We then continued going along the ridge, partly through a snow tunnel that the Austrians had dug through a large amount of metre-thick snow because their access to the trenches kept getting covered. It was superb upon the summit of the 2026-metre-high Pip Ivan. We lay there for over one hour in the sun and admired the wonderful, endless panoramic view. Even the gigantic mountains of the Transylvanian Carpathians were to be seen. We made the descent very comfortable for ourselves, as we simply sat on our lederhosen and set off down the steep snow fields and into the Pohorylec Valley like greased lightning. From the Bülow Square *(a local landmark)*, we climbed up to our position where we arrived back again at 2 o'clock in the afternoon. It was a marvellous outing for the occasion of Ascension Day.

My new blockhouse is the nicest that I have built so far. My room is panelled with shingles, and I even had myself a proper washstand made. I also have a real window to open with a shutter, and in front of it I have a desk. Outside on the veranda with railings, there is also a bench with a table.

An Outing on Ascension Day

When I first read about Alexander's hike in the mountains, I imagined the fun that he would have had with his friends during this time. Luckily for us, he took a dozen photographs on this single day for us to see, describing the scenes on the back in writing. Here they are in order:

'The ascent to the Smotrez (1900 metres). At the front is Lieutenant Nugel – 17.5.1917'.

'On the Smotrez – A view of the Russian trench only 20 metres away with a few Russians'.

'The view of the Stajki from the Smotrez. To the left in front of it is the double ridge of the Nameless Mountain (to the right German; to the left Russian). Behind it is the Skoruszny, and right at the back is the Skupowa'.

'The view of the Pip Ivan from the Smotrez'.

'The rock at the peak of the Smotrez'.

'Wandering the ridges from the Smotrez towards the Pip Ivan – A rear view of the Smotrez'.

'The view towards the Nameless Mountain from the Pip Ivan'.

'The view towards the Stajki from the Pip Ivan'.

'The view from the Pip Ivan towards the Koverla (2058 metres) in the northwest'.

'The lookout post of the mountain artillery upon the Pip Ivan'.

'A view from the Pip Ivan to the northwest. The long ridge to the right is the Mihailecul, to the right next to it the Farcaul; and to the north, Leordina'.

'Upon the peak of the Pip Ivan (2026 metres) – In the centre is Lieutenant Nugel – 17.5.1917'.

19.5.1917   In the afternoon, during light rain, I went down into the valley for an evening meal in the regiment's mess hall. Among others, Prince Joachim Albert of Prussia and the Hereditary Prince of Hohenzollern-Sigmaringen were there. I spent the night in the mess. The adjutant of the regiment told me on this occasion that I had been put forward for the Wilhelm-Ernst War Cross in mid-April.

Note: The Wilhelm-Ernst War Cross was a decoration of the Grand Duchy of Saxe-Weimar-Eisenach, awarded for exceptional military valour. The recipient had to hold the Iron Cross Second and First Class and was eligible if they were a citizen of the grand duchy. Only 366 people were awarded this between 1915 and 1918, with Alexander being one of those.

20.5.1917   I walked 2.5 hours back up to the emplacement during lovely warm weather in the morning. In the afternoon: storm, thunder, and rain.

23.5.1917   The Russians keep coming up to our obstruction wanting schnapps and tobacco. I have already exchanged several bars of soap that I will be sending home. Our people already know some by their names and are learning Russian. For example: "Milo" — Soap; "Mir" — Peace; "Dobre" — Good. It is very strange how fast they are communicating with just a few words. In any case, the friendship is great, and it is a lot of fun to see. I photographed several of them and gave them the pictures which they were very happy about.

'Russians from Regiment 665 coming to our obstruction for trade. For soap and sugar, they are receiving schnapps and tobacco'.

The Russian Revolution

As you may have noticed, the morale and overall organisation within the Russian army is collapsing. The troops are mutinying, they are having consistent heavy losses, and significant events seem to be unfolding at home. This is namely due to the affairs surrounding the February Revolution, which took place from the 23rd of February to the 3rd of March (Julian Calendar). This was the first of two revolutions that took place in Russia in 1917. Russia was an autocracy before the revolution, with Tsar Nicholas II holding absolute power. But compared to other countries, the structure of its economy, society and politics were rather undeveloped. Despite the revolution's manifestation at the peak of WW1, its origins can be traced further back to the 1905 Revolution, caused by the state's failure to modernise the country and better the lives of its citizens. These problems developed into protests, riots, strikes, and military mutinies at the time, which led to some reforms. However, these events would shape the future outlook and sentiments of the average Russian.

At the outbreak of the war in 1914, most Russians supported it, with almost all political deputies voting in favour of entering. This actually encouraged a restoration of nationalism and even somewhat reduced internal turmoil. As the war progressed, its infrastructure and economy would struggle with the demands of the war, and the country's military would be no match for industrialised Germany. The Russian army did have some success, such as with the Brusilov Offensive in 1916, but they did suffer some crucial defeats; most notably the Battle of Tannenberg in 1914, the Battles of The Masurian Lakes, and the loss of Russian Poland. By January 1917, Russia had suffered almost 6 million casualties. Russian morale reached significant lows because of all this, with mutinies becoming common. Newly made commanders and officers were also incompetent, and the army had inadequate supplies. One could say that matters led to chaos.

At home, a famine started to materialise, and production became limited due to the overstrained railway network. Refugees from German-occupied Russia also arrived in their millions which added further strain. The industry did not fall apart, but it was struggling tremendously, and wages could not be sustained when inflation increased. With the populace losing its faith in the Tsarist regime and the overall discontent growing, the first major protests began in Petrograd (St. Petersburg) on the 18th of February, followed by further growing strikes and demonstrations against the government and the war. On the 23rd, these developed into mass riots, and up to 250,000 people were on the streets of Petrograd despite gatherings being forbidden. Clashes often turned violent, and many of the soldiers sent to control the crowds even sided with the protesters. As events continued to unfold, Tsar Nicholas II abdicated on the 2nd of March (Julian Calendar), ending the Tsarist regime after almost 500 years. However, the war would continue for the Russians. With these events having taken place, it is evident why we are seeing the Russians finally lose hope. Alexander now directly experiences for the first time how these men, whom he has been fighting against for all this time, could be his good friends under alternate circumstances. However, no matter what we, Alexander or the soldiers think — "The War Must Go On".

10

24.5.1917   The weather is wonderful. At 10 to 11 o'clock in the morning, the Russians shoot at the Nameless Mountain like mad with shells and shrapnel, and they damage my foremost trench quite severely as a result of several direct hits.

'My shelter at a height of 1700 metres upon the   Nameless Mountain   – 25.5.1917'.

'Our trenches need to be blasted into the rocks – Engineers seen drilling the detonation holes – 25.5.1917'.

'The trench-covered Stajki seen from the Nameless Mountain.   In   the foreground is part of my position – 25.5.1917'.

27.5.1917   Lovely weather. Since the Russians are again shelling the Nameless Mountain with artillery, I call for retaliatory fire, whereupon our 10 and 15-cm howitzers fire at the northern summit.

Compressed air is now being drilled into the trenches and bomb-proof rock caves here. To do this, I have a petrol engine, a compressor, a drilling machine, a demolition worker, eight Hungarian miners and several pioneers. I also have at least 20 jägers occupied with drilling and detonating. It is blasting all day long as though my position is being heavily bombarded. Creating trenches in the mountains is too tedious because everything needs to be blasted into the rocks.

'Pentecost Sunday – An afternoon concert performed at a height of 1700 metres by the Carpathian Band of the 3rd Company, Kurhessian Jäger-Battalion 11 – 27.5.1917'.

28.5.1917   It is nice weather in the morning. Since the Russians are shooting at the Stajki, our 10cm howitzers fire 18 shots at the northern ridge. As the Russians themselves tell us, they had 7 dead yesterday and 5 dead today. We, on the other hand, had no losses.

Lightning and rain in the evening.

30.5.1917   Because the Russians are bombarding us heavily with artillery, I am yet again initiating retaliatory fire which is even stronger and better than yesterday this time. It was a rather violent cannonade, especially since the Russians responded vigorously.

31.5.1917   Very nice weather. Light rain in the afternoon as usual due to the distant thunderstorms. The Russian artillery is very quiet today. They only fired a few shrapnel shells over the Nameless Mountain in the evening.

3.6.1917   The alpine roses have been blooming since today. Heavy rain in the afternoon. The Russians shelled the Smotrez, followed by the usual retaliatory fire.

6.6.1917 The general of the division, His Excellency, Lieutenant-General Boess, visited the battalion's emplacement. He did not come to me though, because he turned into the valley directly at the company boundary. The Nameless Mountain seems to have a very bad reputation — none of the higher-ups dare go up.

There is a heavy storm in the afternoon with otherwise nice weather. The Russian artillery is quiet.

11.6.1917 There was heavy shrapnel fire at the Stajki in the evening. On the way back from the class at the light signal station, we thereby had to make our way through the Stajki hollows in leaps and bounds.

16.6.1917 It is foggy and rainy — dreadful weather. I received news in the evening that I am going to the recreation home in Trebusa for 14 days.

17.6.1917 I left the emplacement at 4 o'clock in the morning during fog and rain and walked for seven hours to the foot of the Kopilas, which was no fun because of the paths that were groundless due to the constant rain. Then, with the car towards Ruszpolyana where I am staying the night. It is very warm — rainstorm.

18.6.1917 I was in Ruszpolyana all day long. Very hot — thundery showers every few moments. In the evening, the field cinema. The nature is completely different here. On the side of battle by the Kopilas, there are solely conifer forests, whereas it is all a large beech forest here on the communication-zone side. There is also tropical heat on this side, whilst it has been really cold over by us in recent days.

From an old postcard – The southwest foot of the Kopilas.

19.6.1917   To Leordina with the field railway in the morning, and further with the train to Erdesvölgy Station via Visovölgy. After that, with the ferry across the Tisza *(river)*, and 15 minutes to the recreation home that lies wonderfully in the Tisza Valley in the middle of infinite beech forests. It used to be the hunting lodge of some archduke, which was fairly ravaged by the Russians and has now been simply restored. There are 18 officers here from the entire Carpathian Corps, and there are three nurses who are leading the place. Included is the commanding-general's daughter who is currently ill, as well as the pretty 20-year-old daughter of a colonel. The food is impeccable, and I got a very nice single bedroom.

Tropical heat. There is almost only thunder in the afternoon with strong cooling. You can do whatever you want here all day long; go hunting or go for a walk, fishing, or whatever else. The home has only one flaw, which is that it gradually gets boring here since you can only do a few excursions because the mountains are almost pathless, very steep, and mostly forested right up to the top so you don't have a view. I have been upon the Polonski (1094 metres), the Tempa (1091 metres) and the Menczul (1242 metres) many times. However, it is so hot most of the time that you don't feel like moving.

Holiday in Trebusa

'The officers' recreation home of the Carpathian Corps'.

'A view towards the park at the recreation home'.

'Sister Erna and Sister Käte'.

'Our main occupation'.

'Our departure from the recreation home – 4.7.1917'.

'With the regional train from Leordina to Ruszpolyana – 4.7.1917'.

4.7.1917 After lunch, I drove with the carriage to Visovölgy, took the train to Leordina, and then the regional train to Ruszpolyana where I am staying the night.

5.7.1917 With the car up to the foot of the Kopilas, and over the Kopilas Pass to Szybeny on foot.

6.7.1917 Heavy artillery fire. In the afternoon, I took the truck to the Pohorylec Valley, but I soon had to send it back because the valley was heavily shelled. I then continued on foot since you can move faster this way, as you can only go dead slow on the log roads with the truck; and because you can immediately throw yourself down if a shell comes rushing towards you. I fortunately arrived back at my position. It had been reported that the Russians were bombarding up from the Jablonika or Tartar Pass towards the Ludowa, and that they wanted to attack in the evening. We laughed about it here and felt sorry for the poor guys, as our mountains have gradually become proper fortresses. The night passed without any disruption though. The Russian infantry probably refused to advance. It has become much livelier than before, however. The enemy in front of my company is still peaceful, but it is still banging consistently to the left and right of me.

I am just sitting writing on my veranda and the shells and shrapnel are constantly whizzing over me, but they cannot reach me behind my rock. I have again been given another sector while I was away. I handed over the Nameless Mountain and have again received the same sector that I previously had; the large hollow between the Stajki and the Nameless Mountain. I have luckily kept my nice shelter. The weather is different up here; rain, fog and quite cold, so I have to heat up in the mornings and evenings, especially since I am a bit spoiled by the tropical heat at the recreation home. It has also turned green up here, and you now only see individual patches of snow.

15.7.1917   Since yesterday evening, there has been another violent storm, thick fog, and rain. There isn't much hunting going on here, because where hundreds of shells, shrapnel and mortars explode every day, you cannot blame the wildlife for seeking out quieter areas. Recently, however, a guard from the 6th Jägers shot a roebuck very close to my shelter, and the sergeant of the 1st Company shot a bear close behind the position. We will soon be awarded the Carpathian insignia, which is to be worn on the hat between the cockades.

A Carpathian bear and Sergeant Dinter.

19.7.1917   Lovely weather but a strong, cold wind. There have been no shots of artillery yesterday and today. There was a very strong storm and rain in the afternoon and night.

20.7.1917   It is nice weather but very stormy. In the evening, thunderstorms. Patrol operations are being ordered following the major breakthrough to the north of us at Tarnopol. The 6th Jägers planned to do this on a larger scale at 3 o'clock in the night, against the northern summit of the Nameless Mountain. This was a complete failure though, as they had 15 to 18 dead and wounded from their own artillery fire and mortars, and achieved nothing. Perhaps the Russians here will leave voluntarily which we wouldn't be angry about, as we would then come out of the wilderness and into more populated areas. I don't want to go through another winter up here with its constant snowstorms. It just doesn't want to be summer here.

11

23.7.1917   Fog and a mighty storm. Something is going on here — Parts of the 20th and 5th Jägers have been pulled out, the 8th Mountain Battery has left the Czorna Hora, new troops are on the way, our field kitchens have moved over the Kopilas, all convoys are continuously transporting ammunition, and holidays have been suspended. Everything points to an advance in the Baba Ludowa region, probably in the direction of Kuty, Wischnitz and Czernowitz; in collaboration with our attack to the north at Tarnopol. The Russians to the left of us by the Jablonika Pass have already gone back. So, we will have been here the longest.

The Mountain Machine-Gun Detachment is moved away from the Nameless Mountain towards the evening.

24.7.1917   The weather changes between nice and cloudy. Our pioneers are being pulled out. Gunfire on the Russians has resumed again as of today.

The violent storm is continuing non-stop.

25.7.1917   The Russians are withdrawing, and we have occupied the cleared positions. There are fires everywhere in the valleys. There is one cloud of smoke after the other until behind Zabie. The Russians are seemingly blowing up all the crossings and burning down all the houses. We will follow them soon.

There is intense artillery fire to the right of us by the Baba Ludowa. Everyone is alarmed here — feverish activity. It is lovely calm weather. The Russian emplacements are so inferior and in such terrible condition that you can only wonder how they survived the winter there. There is no trace of such blockhouses as we generally have.

Order to march off at half past 3 in the afternoon. We march over the Skoruszny and into the Czeremosz Valley during rainy weather, where we are once again amazed by the Russians' miserable accommodations. We then go over the Czeremosz and reach the commanded point (1036 metres) southwest of the Kreta at 10 o'clock in the pitch-black night, where we light large campfires and spend the night partly lying around them and partly inside tents. It was high time that we arrived because my people were completely worn out, as we are no longer used to marching and because of the very heavy luggage.

'My company on the march towards Bukovina in the Czeremosz Valley'.

26.7.1917 7 o'clock ascent to the ridge of the Kreta where we meet our 4th Company. It is cloudy but almost always lovely weather. There is intermittent gunfire to the right and left, and several tremendous detonations can be heard. The Russians are probably blowing up bridges.

The news has come that the Baba Ludowa, Skupowa, Kreta, Zabie, and the Stepanski are taken. Our battalion has not seen any combat yet. The other three companies are moving further east against the Bialy Czeremosz in the afternoon, whereas I am remaining with the staff on the Kreta Mountain as a reserve.

27.7.1917 Departure in a northeasterly direction through a marvellous area at 8 o'clock in the morning. There are large Ruthenian houses everywhere and lots of cattle on the mountain pastures. The Ruthenians are very friendly and bring us milk without asking. We meet up with the other companies again down in the valley, and the battalion continues its march in the Zabie Valley. Things look bad here. The Russians tried to blow up the large wooden bridges but didn't quite succeed. The explosive devices with fuses are currently still hanging on the pillars. All the larger houses were burned, but only the Jewish houses, whilst the Ruthenian houses are intact.

'The Ruthenians bringing us milk at Mount Kreta'.

We march down the Czeremosz Valley via Krzyworownia, and towards Jasienow where we bivouac. These towns consist of widely scattered individual houses and are therefore many kilometres long due to the narrowness of the valley — lovely wooden churches. The Jewish houses are burned everywhere.

We go past the fire sight of a large ammunition depot with a huge crater from an explosion. Scattered around are quantities of exploded cartridges, mortar shells, hand grenades and so forth.

There is milk and butter everywhere for little money here. It is a completely different area than our lonely, wild high mountains. If only it wasn't for the strenuous marches. It is nice, somewhat overcast weather. Lots of dust.

28.7.1917   At 7 o'clock in the morning, the battalion continues its march past the confluence of the Bialy and Czarny Czeremosz and then further down the valley. We go over a half-blown-up bridge to the other riverbank at Usie Putilla, and towards Marenicze where we have a lunch break — very hot, dusty and strenuous. After the usual cold of the high mountains, we now feel this oppressive heat twice as much. Here we encounter the 5th Jäger Regiment (Jäger-Battalions 17, 18 and 23) and Jäger-Battalion 5.

We continue through Bialobereczka and towards Rostoki in the afternoon, where we arrive in the evening and pitch our tents. It was a very hot and strenuous day. Behind Rostoki, we see the first shrapnel shells bursting again and hear gunfire. The regiment commander congratulates me here for the Saxon Wilhelm-Ernst War Cross.

240

'The bridge by Usie Putilla in the Czeremosz Valley'.

29.7.1917   The Russians are holding the mountain ridge that stretches southeast from Rostoki. There was lively gunfire all night long. Our artillery arrived and started to fire in the afternoon. The 5th Jäger Battalion stormed these heights towards the evening, except for a few summits.

Heavy rifle fire again all night. In the middle of the most beautiful sleep, we are alerted at half past 11 at night.

30.7.1917   We march off down the western bank of the Czeremosz at 12 o'clock in the night. Since the Russians can keep the road under fire from the peaks already mentioned, we must march past in the dark of the night, which also succeeds. We then go back to the eastern bank and opposite Rozen Wielki on steep Ruthenian paths in great heat, and then up to the 800-metre-high mountain range where we arrive at 9 o'clock in the morning. The planned assault becomes obsolete since the Russians already disappeared beforehand. Steep and strenuous, we go back down to Wischnitz where we arrive at 12 o'clock noon. At 4 o'clock in the afternoon, we continue in severe heat and heavy dust along the road to Berhometh, which leads over a large plateau. After 8 o'clock in the evening, we bivouac a few kilometres from Berhometh where large clouds of smoke and firelight can be seen. It was a very exhausting day. I slept like a dead man.

31.7.1917 We are ready to march again from 5 o'clock in the morning and head into the Sereth Valley towards Berhometh, where we stay until noon and are heavily bombarded with shrapnel, heavy shells, and machine-gun fire. We are scheduled for an attack on the heights between Berhometh and Mihova in the afternoon. As I reach my point of attack after a strenuous, very hot march, the Russians have just disappeared. We follow them through Mihova and past the burning Sereth Bridge towards Moldauisch Banilla. We receive heavy rifle fire upon the height, and then the Russians disappear after short firing from our machine guns. My company captured an artillery limber with 75 rounds of artillery ammunition.

It just starts to get dark as we arrive in the village of Mega, and I stay in a Hutsul house. I was only able to sleep outside on a haystack for a short time because reports were constantly arriving or had to be made, and my advanced guards had several lively firefights with the Russians who lay on the road just before us. My people are utterly exhausted and overworked. For days, there has been little sleep and food, but endless strenuous marches in extreme heat instead. The inhabitants are glad that the Germans are here. They bring milk and corncakes without being asked. My company sadly had five wounded today.

'Hutsuls in Mega (Bukovina)'.

Note: The Hutsuls are an East Slavic ethnic and cultural group, who reside in the Carpathians between modern-day Ukraine and Romania. They speak what is considered a dialect of Ukrainian with Polish influences.

1.8.1917 At 6 o'clock in the morning, my company again takes the lead towards Moldauisch Banilla — terrible heat. The Hutsuls erect triumphal arches for us and distribute bouquets of flowers. Almost all of them have beautiful faces. As always, the Russians have looted and burned everything during their retreat. We again capture five dispersed Russians in front of Moldauisch Banilla.

'Triumphal arches are being erected for us by the Hutsuls in Moldauisch Banilla'.

'Russians captured by my company in Moldauisch Banilla'.

We continue further towards Moldauisch Banilla in the afternoon, which is very heavily occupied by the Russians. Because my company deployed three assault squads, I just have 40 men left and go in reserve. The entire jäger brigade attacks. I receive heavy artillery fire and have two wounded. Moldauisch Banilla is mostly taken towards the evening. This is a large place with a large German colonist quarter and a Jewish quarter. The residents had a bad day in the town, which was bombarded from two sides, with many being dead and wounded. Multiple houses burn. Late in the evening, I move into a Hutsul house in

Moldauisch Banilla, where we are given a very friendly welcome by the residents.

'Gypsies in Bukovina'.

2.8.1917 Forward march at 6 o'clock in the morning. An old Jew bangs like mad for joy on a Russian drum as we march past. The Russians have cleared the heights to the east of Moldauisch Banilla by morning — the thankful inhabitants kiss my hands while marching through. My company is taking the lead in our division today.

We march over a wooded ridge towards Czudyn. The last Russians disappeared into the forest an hour ago after being shot at by our patrols. It is tropical heat again today. My assault squad, under Lieutenant Fischer, surprises an enemy battalion bivouacking in the village of Neuhütte, which flees under fire and later retreats hastily; so that when we advance, we find the village no longer occupied. During the evening, the residents, who hid in the forests with their cattle for a week, return and kiss our hands with joy. I am staying with a Romanian farmer, and the whole family is touchingly looking after us. A neighbour even brought us a slice of honeycomb.

Just as we had made ourselves comfortable, we were alarmed at 3 o'clock in the morning and marched to Czudyn, an endless nest where the other companies took up outposts, whilst my company quartered itself as a reserve in Romanian houses.

3.8.1917　　　My hostess brings milk and eggs again in the morning. There are eggs, geese, chickens, milk, and an abundance of livestock here, and it is very cheap. I have drunk incredible amounts of milk in Bukovina so far. It was previously called "Mologa" by the Hutsuls, and now "Lapte" by the Romanians.

There is an incredible tropical heat again. At 8 o'clock in the morning, we continue to the church in Czudyn, and my company secures the place via field guards. Bouquets of flowers are presented to us everywhere, and all the horses and carriages are wreathed. We have been pulled out of the front line today and are now division reserves. The Russians are in a hurry to flee. They didn't burn anything apart from the bridges in Neuhütte and Czudyn.

I am living with Poles. My company is stationed as field guards.

'At a well in Czudyn'.

4.8.1917　　　I slept wonderfully in a proper bed. In the morning, I march behind the battalion that marched ahead over Idzestie and to Petroutz, where there is a longer lunch break. I then catch up with the battalion in Kupka. We encounter thunderstorms twice, the likes of which I have never experienced before. We attack Fantana Alba towards the evening, where the Russians want to prevent us from leaving the forested mountains. We stay in the forest as brigade reserves, where we can fortunately light large fires and dry ourselves. I was wet to the skin despite the rubber coat. I am spending the night on the stove bench inside a lonely Ruthenian forest keeper's house, inhabited by 1000 flies.

5.8.1917　　　It is nice weather but very hot. I am riding from today onwards, whereas previously I only used the horse as a packhorse and marched everywhere. My feet are now completely broken though, and I can really feel the old knee damage again.

Down into the Sereth Valley towards Kamenka, a large place composed of many small Ruthenian houses. I moved into a Ruthenian house, where two very pretty girls named Domka and Veranja are sleeping very uninhibitedly in the same room as me. I have put together small bits of vocabulary which are completely sufficient when communicating with the Ruthenians: Good Morning — 'Dobrédi'; Water — 'Wotá'; Milk — 'Mologá'; Egg — 'Jezá'; Eggs — 'Jeize'; Salt — 'Sil'; Potatoes — 'Barabule'; Butter — 'Maslo'; Plate — 'Tari'; Wood — 'Trewa'.

'In front of my house in Kamenka – The 2nd and 3rd girls from left are Domka and Veranja with whom I lived'.

My binoculars and luminous clock with an alarm caused the biggest stir, and when we brushed our teeth, the entire village stood there in amazement and couldn't explain what we were trying to achieve with this. Yet these people have the most beautiful white teeth.

The Kerensky Offensive

After a year in the high mountains fighting the enemy and nature, positional mountain warfare has finally come to an end for Alexander and his battalion. A rapid push towards Sereth in the Bukovina Region has begun. This advance is related to the recently failed 'Kerensky Offensive', which was the last great Russian offensive of the war; and this came like so:

Soon after Tsar Nicholas II abdicated in March 1917, a provisional Russian government was formed which was put in place to govern Russia until elections could be held. This new leadership instantly introduced some democratic reforms, which included removing Tsarist governors and granting certain freedoms and rights not previously imaginable. However, the country was still backward and deprived, and the war was draining the country of resources that would otherwise enable it to progress. The war was therefore one of the most urgent matters to address with three options — continue fighting, to seek peace without indemnities and reparations, or to completely accept defeat. The leaders of the Provisional Government, with Alexander Kerensky as its prime minister, decided to continue the conflict. During this time, and even after the Great War, Kerensky argued in favour of the offensive, believing it would revive national unity, military discipline, and Russian honour. He also hoped it would eliminate the shame of previous military defeats in the conflict. The Russians readied the offensive with 2 days of artillery pre-bombardment, but their enemies were already aware of the plans. On the 1st of July 1917, the Russian assault would begin with the intent to smash through the Austro-Hungarian lines and to take Lemberg (Lviv) and the rest of Galicia.

The Russian 7th and 11th Armies made some significant progress during the first few days. The shock battalions successfully penetrated the defences for a considerable distance in areas, capturing multiple lines of trenches within just 48 hours. Whilst the 11th Army managed to force back the Austrian 2nd Army and advance 2 miles into enemy territory, the 7th Army in the southern region faced a more sluggish advance due to the strong resistance from the German troops of the South Army. It wasn't long until there was a temporary pause in heavy fighting. By the time the Russians continued moving forward again on the 6th of July, German reinforcements had reached the sector of the Russian 11th Army; inflicting heavy losses and bringing the advance to an end. The loss of momentum was also due to poor organisation and the unwillingness of many soldiers to continue, leading them to remain in the positions they had taken. The Russian 8th Army was later more successful, but their advance also came to a halt. On the 19th of July, the Germans initiated their counteroffensive against the south-western Front. Possessing a significantly higher fighting capability compared to the Austro-Hungarians, they applied immense pressure on the Russian lines. The most dependable Russian troops suffered the heaviest casualties, and the ones that were left were unwilling to fight. The Russian armies were eventually in full retreat which turned into a complete rout while putting up little resistance, and they were so devastated that they couldn't launch a counterattack. By the end of the counteroffensive, the Germans will have advanced approximately 120 kilometres, pushing the Russians back to the original Austrian-Russian border. In the meantime, tensions are rising amongst the Russian people at home, and their soldiers are becoming more defiant. Furthermore, the Provisional Government's incompetence will be further exploited by the socialist Bolsheviks to further strengthen their path to power.

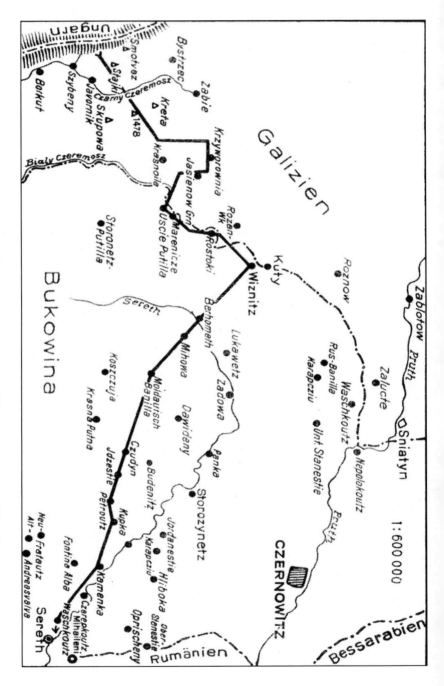

Alexander's march to the east through the Sereth Valley, in pursuit of the fleeing Russians.

12

6.8.1917 In the morning, we continue our march to the next village of Wolcynetz where we occupy alarm stations in the Ruthenian houses. At night, I sleep on straw in a barn with a platoon of my company. We slept a full night without disturbance for the first time since this offensive began.

7.8.1917 We stay in Wolcynetz all day. The town called Sereth is to be taken the next night. At 7 o'clock in the evening, we are alerted and first march to the next village of Bahrinestie where we move into alarm stations for a few hours.

8.8.1917 We continue to the village of Waschkoutz at night. The artillery fire begins at 8 o'clock in the morning, and the infantry attack begins at 9 on the steep, barren heights in front of the town of Sereth. The Russians defend themselves with unexpected tenacity, and we don't make progress despite repeated attacks by almost the entire division — very heavy losses. Our battalion is in the 2nd line. My company lies in a roadside ditch close to Waschkoutz all day under very heavy shell fire, but despite the heavy shells exploding directly between us several times, we have no casualties. In the evening, my battalion relieves the troops of the foremost line and entrenches itself. Nice weather; hot.

9.8.1917 I slept in a straw-filled hole dug into the edge of the road. It is a quiet day — no attack. There is little artillery fire compared to yesterday.

10.8.1917 It is quiet and very hot today. It looks bad in the village of Waschkoutz. Most of the residents have fled, and masterless dogs, pigs, geese, and chickens are walking around everywhere. There is therefore enough to eat for the time being. Many homes are shot up.

A swarm of many 100 storks is flying south over us and is unsuccessfully being shot at by the Russians.

Two men from my company have become heavily wounded due to a shell directly hitting a house. I have lost 11 men since the start of the offensive.

We are replaced in the night by Regiment Crown Prince. Our entire division is going more to the north.

11.8.1917 We march to Kamenka after midnight, where we arrive at 5 o'clock in the morning and move into alarm stations — Rain.

12.8.1917 The offensive is currently stalling across the entire Front. The replenishment of food and ammunition is too difficult, and the very favourable Russian positions along the Romanian border are unable to be taken without heavy artillery preparation. We will probably continue once the railway is in operation again in a few days. I am assuming that we will want to at least reach the Prut River.

13.8.1917   Lovely weather — church attendance in the morning. Like all border communities, the population here is much less pleasant than previously. At 4 o'clock in the afternoon, I rode to the village of Slobodzia with the other company commanders to scout the enemy position in Oprischeny. We received some rather unpleasant artillery fire in Slobodzia. On the way there and back, we rode through a ford of the Sereth River.

16.8.1917   We are now exercising daily for two hours in the morning. In the afternoon, lessons and roll call. We are having crab dinner tonight, as there are a lot of crayfish in the streams.

17.8.1917   During the night, we relieve Regiment Crown Prince in the position near Waschkoutz. We march off at 5 o'clock in the afternoon in heavy wind and rain, arriving in Waschkoutz at 11 o'clock in the evening. I received the section to the left of the road towards Sereth.

     The trenches are just being developed and are full of mud and water due to the rain. Shelters are not yet present, of course. The conditions here are similar to those in the first terrible winter in La Bassée. The Russian is luckily far away and isn't shooting much. I am currently living in a better Ruthenian house directly behind the position, but I need to move out during artillery fire. We will start constructing the shelters as soon as the weather improves. It really seems to be turning into positional warfare here.

23.8.1917   It is nice, cool weather. For three days, I have been working on a mined shelter for myself with two exits. The old chickens in the village have long been consumed, and I have gathered about 30 chicks that I want to raise.

27.8.1917   It was raining from yesterday afternoon until this morning. The weather is nice during the day. The Russian artillery has been much quieter for days now. To the north of us, in the direction of Czernowitz, there was a strong barrage of fire for several hours this morning.

28.8.1917   Yesterday's artillery fire was a German-Austrian attack on the village of Bojan to the east of Czernowitz. Loot — 1000 prisoners and 6 artillery pieces. The Russian artillery here has been much livelier today.

2.9.1917   The company commander of the 4th Company, Lieutenant Weber, was killed this morning. The same bullet also penetrated through the lung of Lieutenant Ernst who was standing behind him and who later died too. I am to become a company commander in an Austrian regiment as an exchange officer for 3 months. Captain von Gräffendorff, Lieutenant Hermes and Lieutenant Hitzeroth from us were already exchanged in the same way.

We have a big diarrhoea epidemic here. We are dependent only on food from the country due to the difficult supply conditions, and we therefore only have meat, potatoes, and bean seeds. Milk and eggs are now only available at the back, in the communication zone. But even the finest bowels could not tolerate bean seeds every day, and we are all suffering from terrible bloody runs.

The residents of Waschkoutz have been forcefully evacuated.

3.9.1917 Colossal barrage fire to the north of us at 6 o'clock in the afternoon. It is the long-prepared operation against the Czardaki Height (324 metres), located southeast of Czernowitz on the Romanian border, where 200 artillery pieces including 30cm howitzers and several mortars are involved. The large village of Oprischeny has been on fire since last night, probably set alight by the Russians. Perhaps they want to retreat there.

6.9.1917 The weather is nice. It is very boring here and much less comfortable than up in the mountains.

8.9.1917 We are going to be replaced in the next few days and will be going to Storozynetz, southwest of Czernowitz. Nobody knows yet where we will be going to then.

9.9.1917 We are replaced by a Hungarian regiment at 11 o'clock in the night.

11.9.1917 We march off at 12:30 in the night. We change our marching direction behind Kamenka and go over Suczaveny to Petroutz, where we arrive at 11 o'clock in the morning. It was an exhausting march. It is luckily cloudy and not hot. The inhabitants are very friendly. I am living very well with an impeccable bed.

'Petroutz – Girls that are handing us flowers'.

251

12.9.1917 We continue marching at half past 6 in the morning, across a very nice area through Korczestie and towards Neu-Fratautz. We set up camp in the village of Kostischa to the east from there at half past 1 in the afternoon. The last half of the march was very hot.

14.9.1917 At half past 7, we march back on the same path to Korczestie and then turn right to Kupka, where we arrive at 1 o'clock in the afternoon — rain and cool weather — good living quarters.

15.9.1917 At 3 o'clock in the night, we go over Karapzin-Iordanestie and towards Storozynetz, where we march past Commanding-General von Conta to say goodbye. There are many burnt-out houses.

Onwards to Panka, a miserable Polish village.

16.9.1917 We go further to Zadowa at 7 o'clock in the morning — many Germans. Good quarters and bed. Arrival at 11 o'clock in the morning. It is now always very cold in the morning.

17.9.1917 We march left, past Unterstanestie and towards Waschkoutz by the Czeremosz at 8:45 in the morning, through a very nice area and hours of beech forests. The Russians have burned down the train station and many houses in Waschkoutz. I am now living with a Polish chief miller.

20.9.1917 Forward march in glowing heat at 6:30 in the morning to Russian Banilla, a village that is many kilometres long. Most of the better houses are destroyed, but I still manage to find very good quarters.

Beer night with duck dinner at the staff quarters.

'Paraska, the pretty water carrier in Ilinse'.

252

24.9.1917   We continue marching over Dzurow and Ilinse at 5 o'clock in the morning. We cross the Czeremosz directly behind Banilla, and thereby the border between Bukovina and Galicia. It is very warm and dusty.

     Arrival in Zablotow at 10 o'clock in the morning. All the decent houses are just ruins, and the town is almost completely destroyed. The living quarters are very mediocre as a result. I am living in a proper Ruthenian hut. The plague of flies is appalling. The populace is very unfriendly. In this region, which has been plundered three times by the Russians, there is nothing but what grows on the fields. Matchsticks cost 1 Krone. You could still buy quantities of eggs in Russian Banilla; 6.50 to 8 Pfennigs a piece.

Life in Zablotow

'Zablotow   –   My accommodation'.

'Zablotow   –   My landlady breaking flax'.

Left: 'Zablotow – A blind beggar with a barrel organ'.

'Zablotow – Cattle market'.

25.9.1917   The cattle and weekly market is very interesting here. We will be loaded here at the train station tomorrow evening. Nobody knows where we are going yet, but based on the preparations, we are going back into the high mountains. The opinions vary between Macedonia, Albania, the Transylvanian Carpathians and Tyrol. My command to the Austrians has become obsolete as a result, as has any prospect of a holiday.

THE ITALIAN FRONT

It is the end of Summer 1917. The Russians in the East have been defeated, and Alexander and his battle-hardened battalion must now face another major theatre of the war — The Italian Front. In May of 1915, Italy launched an offensive against Austria-Hungary along the Isonzo River and in the Trentino region, aiming to seize lands that it considered rightfully Italian. However, the geography of the Italo-Austrian border presented significant challenges, making the direct conquest of these areas far from easy. In the northern Alpine region, the sole area showing potential for military operations was the easily reachable plateau called the 'Altopiano di Asiago'. This was surrounded by heavily fortified mountain ranges which obstructed the Italian advance towards Trento and the Tyrol region. Italy faced formidable military obstacles in the Alps. Stretching northeast from the Trentino region, the border traversed the virtually impassable Dolomites and Carnic Alps, leaving little opportunity for a successful attack. The most favourable option for an Italian offensive lay in the east, where the terrain flattens into a series of rolling hills and valleys along the Isonzo River; stretching from Plezzo (Bovec) southwards, passing through Gorizia, and leading to the barren and rocky Carso Plateau. The Italian command identified the Lower Isonzo, particularly the stretch between Gorizia and the sea, as the most probable location for a breakthrough. The optimistic plans devised by General Luigi Cadorna, the Chief of the General Staff, involved launching an attack eastward into Slovenia. The aim of this was to capture Ljubljana and Trieste, before redirecting forces northwards for an assault on Vienna. However, just like we have seen in the West and the East, an immobile and deeply entrenched war of attrition swiftly emerged, with both factions unable to achieve a breakthrough.

Attacks began in June and July 1915, with the First Battle of the Isonzo starting on the 23rd of June, delayed by Italy's inefficient mobilisation which allowed Austrian forces to establish effective defences. This battle resulted in an Italian advance that led to the second battle; then the third, and then a fourth. 11 Battles of the Isonzo had been fought by September 1917, with 5 Italian victories, 3 inconclusive, and 3 Austro-Hungarian victories – a total of around 1.1 million casualties. By the tenth battle, the Italians had managed to expand their presence at Gorizia and made some territorial gains on the Carso. However, these advances were minimal and came at a great cost in terms of casualties.

Given the Austro-Hungarian army's resilient defence and the costly Italian triumph in August 1916, initiating a big offensive was not feasible. These battles were therefore characterised by limited objectives and focused on wearing down the enemy through attrition, rather than seeking territorial conquest. Cadorna firmly believed that significant territorial progress could only be achieved once the enemy forces had been steadily weakened over time. Nevertheless, the utilisation of his outdated tactics, and the severe discipline imposed upon his soldiers, resulted in a disconnection between him and his troops.

The eleventh battle, also known as the 'Battle of Bainsizza', was launched in August 1917. Following intense and lethal clashes, the Italian Second Army successfully seized control of the Bainsizza Plateau and Mount Santo, along with various other strategic positions. This triumph dealt a significant blow to the Austrian defences. However, due to tactical blunders and the ineffectiveness of their artillery, the Italian forces suffered casualties nearly double that of their Austrian counterparts. The battle ended on the 12th of September 1917, with Cadorna fearing the imminent arrival of German support. In the meantime, national unrest has been growing in Italy with both Catholics and socialists becoming increasingly active against the war, and economic deprivation has been exacerbating social tensions to an even greater extent. Peace on the Eastern Front has opened up fresh opportunities for the Central Powers, allowing them to relocate three Austrian and four German divisions from the Austro-Hungarian sector of the Front to Italy. The Austro-Hungarian Empire is facing mounting political and economic challenges, making it crucial to swiftly finish the war. Also, the success of previous joint campaigns in the Balkans indicates that a synchronised offensive is the most favourable course of action.

'On the journey to the Isonzo Front'.

256

The 12th Battle of The Isonzo & The Triumph in Italy
(1917 – 1918)

1

27.9.1917   We were loaded in Zablotow and left at 7:45 last night, arriving in Stanislau this morning. We continue through Kalusz where there are particularly many old trenches and wire obstructions. There are a lot of graves between Dolina and Bolechow.

Lunchtime in Stryj. From here, we go south into the mountains via Skole. It is a wonderful area, but it is just a shame that we will be going over the Beskid Pass *(a mountain range in the Carpathians)* through the night. Very good dinner at 8 o'clock in Lavochne, just before the top of the pass.

28.9.1917   Via Munkatsch and Czap, we are already in the Hungarian plain by the morning. We have breakfast in Nyiregyhaza, lunch in Debrezin, and dinner in Oradea. The boring and sparsely populated lowlands seem twice as desolate following the Carpathians and the lovely Bukovina. The main type of tree here is the Acacia.

29.9.1917   Breakfast in Bekescsaba at 4 o'clock in the morning, and lunch in Szegedin — very warm. The wine region is very nice, but it is otherwise a dull area.

We are in Maria-Theresiopel in the evening and continue through Sombor in the night, crossing the Danube near Dalj.

30.9.1917   We wake up early in Slavonia, a very populated, pretty region with many oak forests. We have breakfast in Brod on the Bosnian border. The Sava, which forms the border, is a vast river on which paddle steamers sail. The weekly market is interesting, but everything is very expensive: beer — 50 Heller; ordinary shoes — 110 Krones; a kilo of peaches — 5 Krones; a kilo of plums — 1.20 Krones. A kilo of grapes cost 3.20 Krones in Hungary. This country is much more civilised than we think at home. The question of where we are going has now also been decided. Macedonia is no longer an option, so all that remains is the Tyrolean or Isonzo Front.

Lunch in Nova Kapela-Batrina. There are lots of fruit trees, especially plums from which the Raki Schnapps is made.

Across the Sava behind Novska — there are large herds of livestock everywhere. We then continue through Sunja. Dinner in Sissek — two-hour delay. Serbian national dances are taking place at a restaurant in town.

We go past Agram in the night, the Croatian capital.

1.10.1917   We wake up in Steinbrück in the morning, which lies in the beautiful, narrow mountain valley of the Sava. Through here we continue towards Salloch via Littai, a stop before Laibach where we are unloaded at 11 o'clock in the morning — very warm and dusty. At 2 o'clock in the afternoon, we continue our march 25 kilometres northwards via Mannsburg, in a wide valley basin to the village of Salog, south of the Kamnik-Savinja Alps where we arrive at 9 o'clock in the evening.

This is a very nice and rich region. The villages all have beautiful, large stone houses that you cannot find in our villages. I wouldn't have believed the Croatians to be capable of this. What is striking in the fields are the huge wooden racks for drying corn, hay, and buckwheat. The windows in the houses, which are usually very small, are all barred. Also, when beer is available in the pubs, there is a bundle of wood shavings hanging over the door. I am living in a mill. Everything is very expensive — one egg for 50 Heller.

2.10.1917   We will probably stay here for at least ten days. There are magnificent views of the high mountains. There are huge amounts of apples here.

10.10.1917   It is cloudy and rainy. The company is carrying out exercises with live hand grenades. The local population is very unfriendly. You feel like you are in the land of the enemy. The mob does not deserve to live in such a beautiful area.

12.10.1917   Division exercise in pouring rain in the forest mountains north of Stein. It is a shame that the weather is so bad because you are always amazed at the wonderful region. Stein is a small town with very nice ancient houses.

16.10.1917   Nice weather during the day; it starts to rain in the evening. Departure westward at 7 o'clock in the morning — pitch black. It rains heavily. We move into local accommodation in Senica, east of Bischofslack at 1 o'clock in the night.

19.10.1917   We march off through Bischofslack at 5 o'clock in the evening, which, as far as you can see in the dark, must lie beautifully. We then go further west in the valley of the Poljanska Sora *(river)* along with increasingly heavy thunderstorms; and then through Pölland and Goreinawas towards Kopacnica, which consists only of a few poor houses, hence why most of the battalion has to bivouac in the pouring rain. The river is swollen due to the constant rain. You are so dazed by the lightning that you are almost blind for several minutes. Two jägers from the other battalions plummet into the abyss next to the road and drown. A few others are rescued with a lot of effort. Even though I sleep on a warm tiled stove in a house, I am still completely wet the next day. We arrived in Kopacnica at 4 o'clock in the morning.

20.10.1917   It continues to rain heavily all day. We used to laugh about Cadorna because of his desperate weather reports, but we are now finding out firsthand how right the man was. The area is otherwise wonderful — deep, steep valleys covered with beautiful, colourful beech forests.

At 7 o'clock in the evening, we continue our march in persistent heavy rain, over the pass that forms the watershed between the Black Sea and the Adriatic; then down to the town of Kirchheim, deep in a valley. It is a shame that we only march at night out of consideration for the enemy planes, and so don't see anything of the beautiful region.

The rain is gradually subsiding. You can already see the beams of light from the Italian headlights.

2

21.10.1917   After a 13-hour march, at 8 o'clock in the morning, we arrive in the village of Prapetno Brdo to the north of Trebusa in the Idrija Valley; on a 700 to 800-metre-high plateau where we move into very poor quarters. From here, there is a wonderful view of the steep limestone mountains which are covered with beech trees. The wind is very sharp and cold like on the Stajki. The weather is nice. These two days are among the most unpleasant days I have experienced during this war. Everything that I have in my pockets and rucksack is wet, spoiled, and mouldy.

22.10.1917   The weather is nice. I am gradually becoming dry again. There is heavy firing at Italian planes.

Forward march at 3 o'clock in the afternoon, down into the Idrija Valley near Slap where the Italian shells reach. The houses, with their wine trellises and flat roofs, already have a very Italian character. We then go further down the valley to Sankt Luzia, which lies in a wonderfully picturesque location where the Idrija flows into the Isonzo, which flows in a deep and narrow, vertical gorge. Sankt Luzia is heavily shot apart, and you have to hurry to get through. In groups and by leaping, while always taking advantage of the pause between four shells arriving at regular intervals, we pass the stone bridge that leads over the deep blue Isonzo, on the floor of which there is a huge shell hole.

The rubble ruins of Sankt Luzia

From here, we go north past endless stacks of artillery ammunition; and also, past the position of two 38cm mortars, the shells of which are as tall as a man. We then head west again, and since it is quiet, not in the communication trench, but rather we risk marching on the road two kilometres south of Tolmin. The high, steep mountains look wonderful, the backs of which shine with hundreds of lights from the windows of the shelters and barracks built there for cover.

*From an old postcard –
Resting allied troops
outside of the attacked
Sankt Luzia in the Isonzo
Valley*

I arrive at our camp with my company without any casualties at 9 o'clock in the evening. The company goes into a huge cave that has been blasted into the cliffs, in which there is room for several hundred men. I go outside into a small wooden barrack. There is electric lighting everywhere, as well as a water line.

In the night, the Italians shoot close to us multiple times with thick calibres. The shells produce a frightening noise which is amplified due to the echo in these steep mountains.

23.10.1917   I was at the foremost position this morning during the nicest weather, where it looked very bad in parts. The trenches are shot to pieces by mortars and shells and have collapsed due to the constant rain. On the other hand, the large rock caves or caverns are nice, although they are very damp because the lime allows water to pass through. The Jeza, which we are supposed to storm tomorrow, is a very unpleasant mountain with steep, partly forested rock faces, and a 700-metre difference in altitude from valley to summit. In between also lies an almost one-kilometre-wide open plain that we have to pass before we reach the mountain. How we are meant to get over there and then up is still a mystery to me. None of us feel very comfortable with this thought.

24.10.1917 The shelling of the enemy position with gas shells begins at 2 o'clock in the night. At 6:30 in the morning, the shelling of the foremost enemy position in the valley, at the village of Ciginj, commences with 50 heavy and medium mortars; and the high positions with 46 heavy and the heaviest guns (including 30cm and 38cm mortars), and with a lot of field and mountain artillery. There is a lot of noise, especially since the Italians of course respond. It unfortunately starts to rain. The entire Jeza Mountain is so shrouded in clouds of gas and smoke that you can hardly see it.

According to the task, I advance through the communication trenches with my company at 7:30 in the morning, towards the foremost line and to our other companies, arriving there safely. The assault commences at 7:55. We climb down the steep slope through our wire obstacles, which were cut during the night, and then, as quickly as our heavy luggage and the many craters allow, we head across the 800-metre-wide coverless plain over to Ciginj. The Italian barrage fire luckily doesn't harm us much, as most of the shells don't explode in the swampy meadow. Only one man in my company was heavily wounded as soon as he left the trench.

Attack on the Jeza – the march through the ruins
of Kozarsce, east of Ciginj.

Our mortars have had a huge effect over in Ciginj. Trenches and obstructions have been destroyed, and we don't find any more Italians in the village ruins. We reassemble ourselves again in Ciginj to continue our advance. Some Italian machine guns, firing between us from the forests above, hold us up for a long time, as we can only leap from house to house one at a time until we reach the blind spot. We have several dead and wounded, including one from my company again. From now on, we march behind Reserve Jäger-Battalion 5 which is in the first line, and we go up the path north of the Jeza that leads to the ridge. Everywhere else is impassable due to the vertical cliffs. We encounter the first captives on the way there, who make a very good impression. On the path lie many heavy mortar shells and mortars that the Italians had dismantled for transport. The advance comes to a halt halfway up, due to us coming across a vertical cliff upon which the Italians sit in concrete trenches. It is so cloudy and rainy that our artillery cannot see the target signalled to them with flares. We are soon completely soaked, and we light ourselves a fire on the way to warm ourselves and cook food. Like so, the whole day goes by without us making any progress, especially since there is a halt to our right and left.

Our artillery continues to fire without interruption. While we are sitting around the fire fairly dry in the evening, there is a sudden whooshing sound and a terrible impact — pieces of wood and stones hail down on us, and we are all thrown apart due to the air pressure. A heavy mortar exploded right next to me. One dead and several wounded lie a few metres from me, including two men from my company who are lightly wounded from the falling rocks. I miraculously escape the horror. The revealing fires are immediately put out, and I move further up into the cliffs with my men where I spend the night in an open Italian shelter — very uncomfortable and ice-cold. The rain and the artillery fire subside throughout the night.

25.10.1917   It is the nicest weather. Our aircraft circle very low over the mountains. Our artillery fires again from 7 o'clock, and we are able to march further up the road to the ridge at 9 o'clock. We encounter long columns of captives on the way, and we pass a provision warehouse full of canned meat, zwieback *(rusk)*, lemons, soap, and wine. As we are in the process of stocking up on provisions, a heavy shell strikes right in the middle of us. My company again has one heavily and one lightly wounded. We finally reach the top while constantly being harassed by two heavy guns. You can only wonder how quickly the Italians were able to give up such a brilliant position, which only suffered little from the barrage fire, and which you could describe as being impregnable. We continue further northwest in a trench on the ridge to protect us against the constant heavy shell fire. We are endlessly littered with rocks from the impacts, against which our steel helmets provide good protection.

The view of the blue-green Isonzo, Tolmin, and the high mountains is wonderful. An Italian plane is being shot down by our artillery and is spiralling down on our side. It looks great at the highest point (1114 metres). Our heavy artillery had a great effect here. Our 30cm and 38cm shells tore open craters the likes of which I have never seen before. Endless prisoner transports are heading to the valley on every path. On this single height alone, 1500 men have surrendered with regiment and battalion commanders. The Italians are still sitting on the southwest slopes of the ridge, and opposite on the height (990 metres) by the villages of Clabuzzaro and Prapotnizza. Our 1st and 2nd

Companies, and later also two platoons of my company, will be taking action against these in the late afternoon.

Success — 860 prisoners, several trucks and eight heavy artillery pieces. The Italians are beside themselves with joy that they have been captured. Down in the valley, we find another warehouse with provisions, clothes, mountain shoes and wine. We didn't leave much of it. The baggage that you need to carry is already unfortunately so heavy that you can only bring a little with you.

Late in the evening, we climb up the steep rock faces of Height 1114, again under enemy artillery fire, and bivouac there. We are lying in the large shell craters. Rarely have I felt so miserably cold as now, on this icy cold night.

26.10.1917   At 3 o'clock in the morning, we continue northwest on the large road on the western side of the Kolovrat Ridge, which the Italians built during the war. This ridge is fortified in such a way that you cannot help but be amazed at how easily such a position has been cleared. Artillery has been installed everywhere, from the short and thick mortars to the long and heavy fortress guns. There are 20 pieces at least. Huge stacks of heavy shells stand everywhere. Trucks lie all over the place. The whole area is littered with all kinds of weapons and pieces of equipment.

'Campfire on the Kolovrat Ridge by Ravna (Isonzo)'.

We stop in the village of Ravna for a short time, by the 1243-metre-high Kuk — a wonderful high-mountain landscape. From here, we march in single file along a narrow ridge that leads southwest to Azzida near Cividale. We then go over Glava (933 metres) towards Monte San Martino (965 metres), where 300 Italians with several machine guns surrendered again after just a few shots. I wouldn't have thought the Italians to be such pathetic guys. They could have held us back for days in this wonderfully built emplacement upon the Monte San Martino, considering we have no artillery with us. The Russians are heroes in comparison.

We go further over Monte Bartolomeo and the village of Clastra towards Monte Vainizza, the last ridge before Azzida which lies down in the valley. Further behind, you can clearly see the large town of Cividale and the large, deep Lombardic plains. It was a very strenuous, troublesome march on narrow mountain paths, always uphill and downhill. On the way, we had to watch as Italian planes unfortunately set alight two German aircraft and brought them down within ten minutes.

It is already dark when we want to go down towards Azzida. A tremendous shootout suddenly starts over there. Since it is not our task to take Azzida, we stay on Monte Vainizza and pitch our tents.

27.10.1917   From the morning on, we observe the storming of Azzida and the battles for the heights to the east from there. The Italians set alight the warehouse in Cividale. There are large fires and black smoke towers everywhere from the exploding petroleum and gasoline supplies. Millions worth burn. In the meantime, our jägers bring in everything from the surrounding deserted villages — bacon, fruit, nuts, grapes, and large amounts of dark red wine. There are large barrels of it in every cellar.

We move down to Azzida in the afternoon, which looks very Italian — tall, angular houses with vine-covered verandas. Our 10cm howitzers are on the village road and fire up to the old, picturesque Castel del Monte, where the Italians are still holding out. You can see their trucks pulling away at top speed. We stay in a village near Azzida in the evening. There are huge amounts of wine here. I am sleeping on the litter floor inside a shot-up house.

28.10.1917   We continue at half past 12 in the night. It constantly rains heavily from now on. We go past the burning train station of Cividale, where the Italians have set railway carriages on fire. We have our lunch break to the west of the village of Ziracco. A pig and chickens are immediately slaughtered. In the smallest general store, you can find everything like in peacetime — soap, coffee beans, pasta, bouillon cubes, and all things that we have only known by name for many months. It is a shame that you cannot send anything back home.

Further westwards at half past 12. It is raining like a torrential downpour. We march through Remanzacco towards Godia. The large bridge over the Torre River is sprayed with machine guns by the Italians. People from the Alpine Corps individually cross over, and we then follow in leaps and bounds. Most of our people have acquired umbrellas. Me too, of course. It makes a strange impression to see a Prussian jäger battalion march with opened umbrellas. The Italians were fortunately no longer able to detonate the bridge due to our fierce pursuit. The Torre has become a wide, raging river due to the downpours.

We continue our march through Godia and Paderno towards Rizzi, two kilometres northwest of Udine which was taken in the afternoon. We take up field guard positions here. I slept very well in a bed.

The Battle of Caporetto

The recent and upcoming series of events are today known as 'The Battle of Caporetto' (The 12th Battle of The Isonzo), one of the most significant chapters of the Great War. When Italy declared war on Austria-Hungary in May 1915, they did so while influenced by the dreams of territorial conquest; and the desire to conquer the Italian-speaking areas around Trento and Trieste along their northeastern border. However, the Italian army had become fatigued towards the end of 1917. Insignificant progress had been made on its frontlines at the cost of severe casualties and a breaking economy. After 11 battles for the Isonzo in just over two years, the Italians anticipated a period of rest during the winter of 1917, but this did not happen. There were growing rumours of an attack by the Austro-Hungarians, and the Italians worked towards strengthening the mountainous combat areas around the town of Caporetto, today known as 'Kobarid' in Slovenia. Caporetto is positioned on the western side of the Isonzo River, with the frontlines lying six to seven miles east of the river as of October 1917. Due to the supposedly weakened Italian defence there, Caporetto had been chosen by the Central Powers as the main target for this significant offensive. The offensive, initiated on the 24th of October, would be seen as a complete disaster for the Italian army, also causing devastation nationwide.

In the early morning of the first day of the battle, the Italian trenches were smothered with poisonous gas, which left many occupants dead and caused others to flee. An intense artillery barrage would later follow, as well as mines being detonated beneath Italian strongpoints — Then, the infantry assault. The attacks were led by specialised stormtroopers who made full use of their light mortars, flamethrowers, machine guns and hand grenades. The Italians were in a state of complete disarray and fell into retreat due to this rapid and astonishing breakthrough. The attackers advanced up to 25 kilometres towards Italy on the first day without much resistance. By mid-afternoon, the command centre of the Italian army was still oblivious of the magnitude of this offensive, and Luigi Cadorna, Chief of General Staff, would not realise to what degree his troops were suffering until later in the evening — Munition shortages, wavering commanders, communication breakdown and lack of information — all working against the few trying their hardest to suppress the German and Austro-Hungarian assault. We know how these events unfolded from Alexander's perspective, but just what exactly was it like through the eyes of someone on the other side?

Colonel Francesco Pisani was the acting general of the Foggia Brigade, who was present at Caporetto on the first day of the offensive. With orders for parts of the brigade to reinforce other units under pressure from the assault, the left-over troops headed towards Caporetto while passing the retreating men telling horror stories of the battles ahead. Pisani was to defend the Eiffel Bridge over the Isonzo with his troops, with a retreat soon after being ordered. The control of the town was then handed over to the Foggia Brigade. This is how he afterwards describes this series of events in his post-battle debriefing:

"There was total confusion. The road was almost entirely blocked by a mass of troops, carts, horses, trucks, artillery pieces, mules, and supplies. Officers' cars were unable to make any headway, and it was very hard to execute or even transmit any orders. At this point, the various components of the Brigade became separated in the chaos, the freezing fog, and the rain. We also tried to organise transport for the wounded, many of whom had been abandoned in the road. We could hear them groaning through the fog, and it was imperative to move them since their presence was demoralising the defenders of the bridge."

This battle will continue until late November 1917, and will eventually lead to enormous Italian losses and setbacks. They will lose over 5000 square miles of territory, over 40,000 dead and wounded, and hundreds of thousands of soldiers left scattered who will either be captured or will have deserted. The Italians will not just be subject to losses of soldiers and land. More than 10 million ration sets and over 6 million tins of fish or meat will be seized by the attacking forces, as well as hundreds of tonnes of dried pasta, cheese, and coffee; and 5 million litres of wine. Many thousand pieces of clothing, bedding, boots, artillery pieces, machine guns, horses and mules, and vehicles will be abandoned and lost — a huge loss for Italy considering the shortage of these vital supplies before this setback had even occurred.

The potential reasons for this disaster, and later defeat, already caused political quarrels within 48 hours of the first assault. Blame was placed on all sides of the political spectrum, as well as other factors. General Cadorna, who was already unpopular before the battle, blamed the Austro-German breakthrough on: "The inadequate resistance of units of the Second Army, cowardly retreating without fighting or ignominiously surrendering to the enemy". However, this has been viewed as an unfair assumption by many, as the Foggia Brigade's experience of poor defensive positioning, inconsistent orders, and scarce supplies represented the entire situation. Several descriptions indicate that the Italians fought courageously, for as long as they had ammunition and officers. However, as soon as these crucial needs were no more, and their enemy gained more momentum, it was hard to maintain an overall positive attitude.

3

29.10.1917   This morning, my company again has one pig, ten geese, many chickens, and wine. Only bread is missing. We are living only on the food from the land because we don't receive food during our forced marches. This offensive is extremely interesting but also very exhausting — no rest and constant marching. Yesterday, I was able to wash myself for the first time since the 23rd of October. The houses in this area are built from blackish limestone and therefore have a gloomy appearance like ancient ruins. Our Commanding General, von Berrer, was shot dead in a car in Udine yesterday. An immense amount of loot has supposedly been captured there, with entire depots and trains full of provisions.

At half past 12 in the afternoon, we continue marching west through Nogaredo di Prato in nice weather, where the population welcomes us like their allies. Everyone shouts "Evviva Bravi Soldati!" *("Hooray Good Soldiers!")* and they let the bells ring, initially making us believe it to be a betrayal. They ask if we are hungry and bring us wine and bread. My company, which is in the lead, receives fire in the village of Plasencis. I immediately initiate an attack on the enemy, Bersaglieri Bicyclists, who retreat while leaving behind five prisoners and many bicycles. The latter are very welcome. Like everywhere else, a cheering population welcomes us with shouts of "Evviva!".

We continue ahead through Savalons, Nogaredo di Corno, and Flaibano towards San Odorico, where my company is the first troop to reach the Tagliamento River. In every village, we have captured Italian soldiers who were just waiting for it. Along the way, we also found one aircraft, one heavy artillery piece, and many trucks. I now have a bicycle. We were not able to bring horses with us over the mountains.

We go south from San Odorico to the village of Redenzicco, where we capture a car with an Italian captain who cluelessly drives towards us. I slept very well in a bed here. It was a very nice day. We had no casualties and have come a long way.

30.10.1917   Now comes a day like I have never experienced before and never thought possible — At 9 o'clock in the morning, we march south along the Tagliamento and through Rivis, towards the Della Delizia Bridge near Codroipo; the next to last bridge that the enemy still has to retreat. I stay with my company as flanking cover in a large stone house near the Di Campagna Mill, whilst two of our companies at the front support a Württembergian battalion in the attack on the bridgehead. It pours down with rain again. Then, there is suddenly a terrible bang — half the house collapses on top of us, and a gigantic smoke cloud rises. At first, nobody actually knows what is going on. Eight from my company are wounded, and even I am lightly wounded due to a stone hitting my left shin. It finally turns out that the mill 100 metres away blew up, and with it, Lieutenant von Forrell and three men from my company who were there as backup; and several artillery officers too. You can now only see a huge explosion crater instead of the mill. There was probably an explosives warehouse there. It is no longer possible to determine whether it was blown up by own carelessness or by the enemy.

We move forward. Our 1st and 4th Companies occupy the entrances to the three parallel bridges and thereby block the crossing. One single man from the 4th Company confronts the fleeing Italians, and entire battalions lay down their weapons in front of this one man. The loot is immense. The roads are covered for many kilometres with luggage, artillery pieces, cars, countless horses and mules; all packed together in an inextricable bundle. Unmistakable columns of captives withdraw, and new regiments keep arriving for hours. Entire battalions throw away their weapons, wave with white pieces of cloth, and march backwards into captivity. Small squads of jägers take battalions captive.

Captured motor vehicles on the Udine-Codroipo Road

Our 1st and 4th Companies initially tried to get to the other bank amid the fleeing Italians, and thereby secure the bridges. When the first people are over there, the bridges blow up and we are now cut off — in front of us the Tagliamento which has become a raging torrent, and behind us, countless thousands of Italians. All of a sudden, an enemy squadron of lancers rides towards my company, and from a distance of 150 metres, we fire into them with machine guns and rifles from our occupied trench in the meadow. They break away in a frantic gallop. It looks wonderful how the struck horses and riders tumble over. Only a few escape.

Austrian National Library: The detonated Tagliamento Bridge near Codroipo – 30.10.1917

Austrian National Library: The destroyed Tagliamento Bridge near Codroipo

The situation keeps getting more and more complicated — several 100 jägers in the middle of enemy regiments. I go ahead with a few people and my sergeant to fetch ourselves some riding horses. We then suddenly receive violent fire 30 metres away, from the motorcades on the road embankment which have long been in our possession. I don't know whether prisoners have re-armed themselves or whether they are new troops. We lie without cover on the open field and again shoot into the cars and carriages which light up in a flash. We have casualties. A civilian dressed fully in black waves soldiers closer and points over to us. I hereby take the rifle of a jäger next to me who has been shot in the foot, and as the person in black becomes visible again between the wagons, I gun him down. Help finally comes from the company once our desperate situation has been noticed. Hand-grenade troops advance along the rows of carriages, and when we few men also follow along while shouting "Hurrah!", the guys throw down their weapons and surrender. The man in black lies on the road by the last carriages, shot through the middle of his chest.

More new columns keep marching in and let us few men disarm them while they beam with joy. I don't know how many thousands there are. The loot is literally immeasurable. It is worth millions. At night, we secure the railway line towards the south. I spent the night outside and froze very much and slept little. We had many casualties because the Italians also fought back in some areas, and then also due to the explosions. We lost five officers alone.

Concrete Italian M.G position at the western end of the Tagliamento Bridge

31.10.1917   We are picking out the best from the countless masterless horses and mules, and are mounting them. I have a very pretty, good-going small horse that I am naming 'Delizia', in memory. In the morning, we march further southwest past Codroipo and towards the village of Intizzo. We are unsuccessfully pelted with bombs by a squadron of planes on the way there.

It is lovely weather. We are in the second line today and are staying the night in Intizzo. The residents are very friendly. I slept splendidly in a good bed.

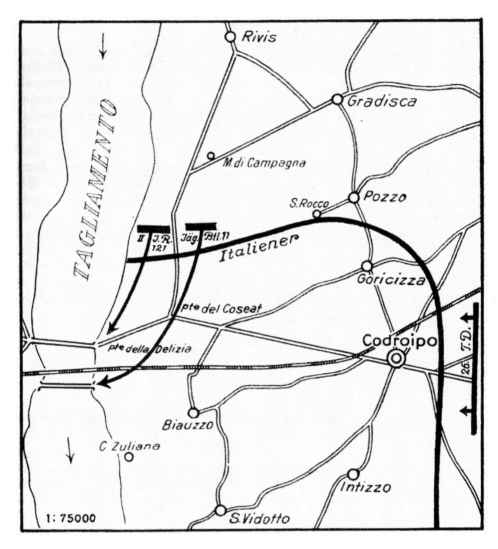

*The battalion's direction of attack from the north towards the bridges
– The thick black line is the starting position of the Italians.*

1.11.1917   We march towards San Vidotto at noon, and at 9 o'clock in the evening, towards Pieve di Rosa via Camino. Bridges are to be built over the Tagliamento, and four jäger battalions are to cross the river at night. However, the Tagliamento is so deep and torrential due to the downpours that bridge building is impossible. We therefore turn back to San Vidotto and into our quarters. Very good bed.

'San Vidotto – Italy'.

3.11.1917   We are directed back north, and at 9 o'clock in the morning in the loveliest weather, we march through Codroipo and Plasencis towards Ceresetto, where we arrive at 8 o'clock in the evening. I am living in a villa. I slept very well.

4.11.1917   It is the purest summer weather. It is wonderful here. The roses are still blooming, and there are lizards running around in the garden. The entire country is one big vineyard, and there are also a lot of mulberry trees. In the afternoon, the division commander expressed his highest appreciation to the assembled battalion.

6.11.1917   It is the loveliest warm weather again; so much so that you can sit out in the open all day. It is particularly nice that the greatest plague of the East — the flies — is almost completely absent here.

7.11.1917   Cloudy and cool. The weather seems to be changing. We don't know what it looks like on the Front, but it seems like we have crossed the Tagliamento now. Large pontoons are constantly passing by to build bridges. I have an Italian knapsack full of soap, and another full of chocolate, handkerchiefs, sewing silk and so forth. I loaded a mule along with my loot from the luggage wagons. If only I had everything at home. The Italian army was superbly equipped. Yesterday, we confiscated the masses of copper dishes found in every household. This caused a lot of complaining, of course. I got several quintals of copper from one liquor factory alone.

8.11.1917   We depart westwards in pouring rain at 8 o'clock in the morning, towards Coseano via Martignacco and San Vito. The quarters are miserable in Coseano, but they come with a very good bed covered with white sheets like everywhere else.

9.11.1917   We continue at 4 o'clock in the night during rain. At 7 o'clock in the morning, we cross the Tagliamento near Bonzicco on a long, restored wooden bridge. We then go across the several-kilometre-wide white scree bed of the Meduna, where there is currently not a single drop of water; and then through Cordenons towards the pretty small town of Pordenone. It looks unbelievable here. All the shops have been looted by the civilians.

11.11.1917   We march off at half past 7 in the morning via Fontanafredda and Sacile, a picturesque but somewhat shot-up and completely looted place; and go 25 kilometres west towards San Fior, where we arrive at 2 o'clock in the afternoon and move into very poor quarters. It is cloudy and cold, but at least it isn't raining.

12.11.1917   We continue marching at 7 o'clock in the morning, over the beautiful, picturesque town of Conegliano with its old castle. We then go through the magnificent mountainous landscape at the foot of the Alps via San Pietro, and towards the rich town of Solighetto; a few kilometres from the Piave, on the other bank of which the Italians sit. There is still plenty of food and wine here, whilst there is hardly anything left on the main streets. On the way, we found enough apples, grapes and dried figs in a house for the entire battalion. Even though the place is overcrowded with troops, I still find very good quarters with a good family.

17.11.1917   We march a few kilometres west to Posmone at 7 o'clock in the morning, where the living quarters are very poor. We are unable to cross the Piave, and we are probably waiting until the pressure of our troops pushing south in the mountains makes itself known.

19.11.1917   Enemy planes are to be seen again after a long time. I have applied for a holiday today with the permission of the battalion.

2.12.1917   It is foggy and rainy. At half past 5 in the evening, we march back to Soligo via Farra. We then go north into the mountains, through Farro and Cison di Valmarino towards Tovena, which is occupied by Austrians and why we have to sleep on straw. My company is spending the night in the church.

3.12.1917   We continue north over the mountains in the morning. We go through a deep gorge on endless serpentine roads, towards the heights of San Boldo from where you can see the ocean and Venice to the south, and the Dolomites to the north. It is very nice weather but cold.

Over Sant'Antonio and down into the Piave Valley, where we occupy quarters in scattered houses in Trichiana, between Belluno and Feltre. The area is barely touched by the war, and there is therefore a lot of food. A lovely view of the Dolomites.

5.12.1917   At half past 9 in the morning, we continue over Mel to the beautifully situated Feltre and the small village of Porcen, on the northwest slope of the 1600-metre-high Monte Tomatico. It is lovely sunny weather, but very cold. The rock-hard frozen roads do not thaw throughout the day. It is very dusty, which is twice as unpleasant given the heavy truck traffic.

7.12.1917   I found out yesterday that my holiday has been approved. At 9 o'clock in the morning, I first drive in a car and then with a truck to Primolano, which you can see lying several 100 metres, almost vertically deep below. The road leads down there in incredible serpentines. The pass is blocked by extensive fortifications whose huge walls are riddled with holes caused by Austrian shells.

I continue through Borgo via train, where many Italian prisoners are unloaded; and towards Trento where I arrive several hours late, which is usual in the country.

Further over the Brenner Pass in an overcrowded and heated train.

8.12.1917   Through Innsbruck and towards Kufstein in beautiful sunshine, where I have a very good lunch.

The evening in Munich — a delay of 1.5 hours.

Further with the German train to Nürnberg and Saalfeld, arriving at 4 o'clock in the morning.

Continuing to Weida at 5:30 in the morning — Arrival at 7:30.

HOLIDAY!

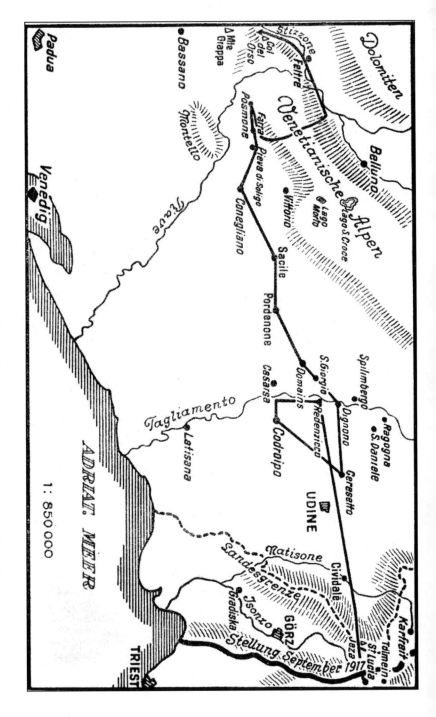

The direction of advance from the starting position in October (top right) and through North-East Italy.

4

11.1.1918 Departure from Weida at noon. I am staying in Treuchtlingen for several hours at night because the route has to be cleared by the military first.

12.1.1918 Arrival in Munich at 6 o'clock in the morning, 7.5 hours late. At 8 o'clock, I continue to Wörgl via Kufstein in lovely sunny weather — good lunch. Then, through Saalfelden (a view of the 'Ramseider Scharte' with the 'Riemann House') past the frozen Zeller Lake to Schwarzach St. Veit — dinner.

Delayed at 8 o'clock in the evening to Villach via Gastein — arrival at 12:30 in the night.

All the hotels are overcrowded, but I finally got a very nice heated room in the Park Hotel for 3.50 Krones. You can get unbranded food everywhere in Austria, only there is no bread. Since I heard on the way that the Alpine Corps was near Udine, I have decided to go there too.

13.1.1918 At half past 9 in the morning, I continue through the beautifully situated commune of Tarvisio, and towards the shot-up Pontafel-Pontebba border stations where the positions were. I met people from the battalion here, who tell me that we are now in Ragogna, northwest of Udine as of a few days ago. I therefore took the branch line through Gemona, and a few more stations further to Pinzano, where I then walked in the rain for 1.5 hours over the Tagliamento to Ragogna. Here, I arrived back at the battalion at 4 o'clock in the afternoon. Ragogna lies on the slope of a high mountain on which there is an Italian fort. From here, there is a wonderful view of the Tagliamento Valley, the plain, and the snow-capped mountains.

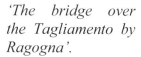

'The bridge over the Tagliamento by Ragogna'.

'The family I am living with in Ragogna – January 1918'.

'The view northeast into the Tagliamento Valley from Monte di Ragogna, overlooking Osoppo and Gemona – February 1918'.

Up until **7.2.1918**, the time in Ragogna is passed with drills and exercises. Confiscated fabric is being sold. I have taken various things, including a very large, new linen bed sheet for 4.50 Mark. There is otherwise nothing here anymore. There was a feast at the headquarters for the Kaiser's birthday — roasted rabbit and Tagliamento fish.

I recently visited Master-Tailor Seidel, from Weida, who is in Pinzano with his Landsturm company.

'The Italian landscape'.

'In Italy – The second from left (drinking red wine) is me'.

'View towards San Daniele (Italy) – January 1918'.

'Marketplace in San Daniele (Italy) – January 1918'.

8.2.1918   We march off through San Daniele, Fagagna, Cividale, San Pietro, Caporetto, Idrsko and Tolmin towards Sankt Luzia, our former starting point. The accommodation was very poor along the way, especially in Sankt Luzia, which is completely shot up, and where we could only find a small room for 10 officers in which we slept on empty ammunition boxes. We will be loaded here this evening.

'Caporetto – Isonzo'

'Idrsko – Isonzo'.

'Isonzo'

Back On The Western Front
(1918)

1

11.2.1918   We were loaded in Sankt Luzia today. The carriages delivered to us by the Austrians are in a disgraceful condition, without a toilet and some without windows. In beautiful weather, we are travelling over Assling and Villach, past the very beautiful Veldeser Lake, through the 8000-metre-long 'Karawanken Tunnel' for 20 minutes; and unfortunately, in the night, through the Tauern *(high mountain passes)* towards Salzburg via Gastein.

We continue further to Rosenheim where we are deloused for eight hours. After a very nice bath, we spent the time in bathrobes with food and in deckchairs. Our belongings were treated separately — our clothes with hot steam, and our uniforms, leather things and so forth, with sulphur. One of us mistakenly placed his leather gloves into the washing bag. When he got them back, they had shrunk to the size of children's gloves and had become rock-hard. We are receiving new and very nice carriages from hereon. Our people have been completely equipped with new clothes.

We continue via Munich, Augsburg, Ulm, Stuttgart, Bietigheim, Karlsruhe, Rastatt, Hagenau and Saargemünd to Benningen on the Metz-Saarbrücken route, where we are unloaded on the evening of *14.2.1918*.

15.2.1918   At night, we marched 1.5 hours to Spittel, a small town in Lorraine near Saarbrücken. We are living in the working colonies that belong to the coal mines, and we live very well throughout. Every man has his own bed. We were given a very friendly welcome because they are all Germans and not people from Lorraine. I am living very nicely with a short mining official. My transport is alone here for the time being. The other two are still missing. I haven't received any post for 14 days. From tomorrow onwards, I will send the things I brought from Italy in packages. You have to do this from the Prussian town of Lauterbach since closed shipments are not permitted here in Lorraine. I still have cornmeal, linen cloths, fabrics, knitting cotton, edible chestnuts, artificial honey, and condensed milk.

17.2.1918   The people here are much better off with food than at home, but nothing is allowed to be exported. All packages are inspected. We have very nice weather, but it is very cold. I took a trip to Saint-Avold on foot yesterday, which takes an hour to walk. We are going to the local cinema tonight. There is otherwise nothing going on here.

20.2.1918   Yesterday, I had a cornmeal pudding made using the following recipe — 1 cup of milk, 1 cup of water and 4 sugar pieces. This is cooked, and then enough cornmeal is stirred in until it becomes a thick mass. This is then filled into a cold mould. Plus, fruit juice. It tasted perfect, and the pudding looks so yellow that you think there are a lot of eggs in it. There is nothing new here. It looks like we are going to be here for a long time. The local population lives in constant fear of air raids. Some were reported yesterday, but they did not come here.

2.3.1918   It is rather boring here. As a result of the holiday ban, you are not even allowed to travel to Saarbrücken. The weather has been very bad in the last few days. There is snow today. The day before yesterday, there was a company inspection which went very well. We thereby stood in the rain from 8 o'clock in the morning to half past 1 in the afternoon. We have yet another inspection on the 4th of March, and then the larger exercises will begin. We will surely be staying here for some time.

'One of my light machine-gun squads with gasmasks – March 1918'.

8.3.1918   Both inspections went very well for me. My company was one of the best in the entire regiment. During a regimental dinner a couple of days ago, the regiment commander once again expressed his special appreciation to me. His orderly officer also told me that he constantly talks about the 3rd Company.

'Gas mask roll call of the 3rd Company'.

12.3.1918   We were abruptly alerted on Saturday and marched south for two days to the area of Duss (Dieuze). We are apparently expecting a French offensive. Everyone here speaks French, and the residents are extremely unfriendly; worse than in enemy territory. The living quarters are miserable. It was certainly different in Spittel, where we were viewed as family members and where there were a lot of tears when we said goodbye.

'Burgaltdorf, Lorraine – I lived in the corner house behind the fountain – March 1918'.

'Weisskirchen by Dieuze – March 1918'.

27.3.1918 We are still here. We go on large marches very openly behind the Front, and we light campfires in the night. These are apparently deception tactics for the enemy. But it seems as if we will be going somewhere else in the near future.

28.3.1918 We were loaded today and travelled over Metz, Luxembourg, Mons and Valenciennes towards Cambrai, where we stayed for one night. There I learned, to my greatest shock, that I have to give up the leadership of my company. It came like so — Due to a new regulation, which means an incredible reduction in reserve officers, active officers, who have their Abitur *(school leaving exams)*, will be fast-tracked by many months. In this way, Lieutenant Petersen, who was still a platoon leader under me and only became a lieutenant months after me, suddenly became longer-serving than me by almost half a year. I thus became the shortest-serving company commander. He thereby just has the emergency Abitur, whereas I have the proper Abitur and even served my year before the war and participated in exercises.

Then came the added misfortune that First-Lieutenant Cranz used this as a way to bring his brother to the battalion; a retired previously-active officer, even though he had never been with us before. Since he is now a captain, I had to step back as the shortest-serving and hand the battalion over to him. My anger was obviously immeasurable, and I did not put up with it easily. I put on my Stahlhelm, reported myself to Captain von Gräffendorff, and explained to him that if I am expected to act as a platoon leader again after two years of leading the company in countless battles, then I am to immediately request my transfer to the infantry. Gräffendorff then said that this was out of the question. Everything has already been considered, and another convenient post will be found for me.

29.3.1918 This morning, we started the advance into the Somme region towards Péronne and reached Nurlu, a completely destroyed village where we are spending the night in English Nissen huts *(a half-cylindrical steel structure designed to accommodate troops)*. The march was particularly strenuous because there was no water along the way, and the field kitchens also had to fetch water to here from afar. I met Mr Bruno Hoffmann from Weida here, who is a sergeant in an aircraft unit, and I spent a very inebriated evening with him.

2

30.3.1918   I was suddenly made leader of the regiment's trucks tonight. Since then, I have been transporting provisions for the division day and night. This is very tiring for the time being, but also very interesting because this way you get to know different people and learn about the communication-zone activity. I have always been very kindly invited to breakfast or lunch at the provision offices. These people have everything that doesn't exist on the Front. It is nice that I now always have my luggage with me. Driving on the shot-up roads is unpleasant. The entire Somme country is a complete 50-kilometre-wide wasteland. No house is whole anymore, all the wells are buried, and the trees are hacked over. I have seen a lot in the 3.5 years of war, but never such complete devastation.

Every day, I now drive through the area of our last offensive. There is a zone where not a square metre is without a shell impact. Large numbers of Englishmen are working everywhere to restore the roads. I am in Péronne for the time being, and I am living in an English Nissen hut. I drove to Cambrai with my vehicles on the first morning, where aeroplanes were just throwing bombs that exploded in the side street. We picked up oats and bread there, which we brought to Aizecourt between Nurlu and Péronne. I was attached to the division motor column the next day, and for several days, we brought the rations from Roisel and Bellicourt west of Péronne to Aizecourt. These trips were very interesting, as the English lines lay between Bellicourt and Hargicourt which had been stormed in the last great offensive. In the last two days, we drove from Péronne on the large, dead straight road south of the Somme, and through the area of the former Somme Battle via Estrées-Foucaucourt; then south through Rosières and to Warvillers, east of Moreuil. During this time, I lived near Péronne with Lieutenant Espey, the leader of the divisional motor column; at the former English tank repair yard, inside a small hut consisting of a slatted frame covered with oil paper. Instead of windowpanes, the English apply white canvas everywhere. Various English tanks stood there in need of repair.

Our trips are very tiring since we always depart at 4 o'clock in the morning and don't come back until late in the evening. It is again interesting though because you travel through a large part of the battle area. Péronne must have once been a very pretty old town. I searched in vain for the village of Estrées along the large Péronne-Amiens Road, and I then finally found a couple of earth mounds and tree stumps. There was nothing else left of the very large village. By the former village of Villers-Carbonnel, the English erected a signpost with the distinctive inscription: "This Was Villers-Carbonnel". I reached Warvillers, which lies east of Moreuil and northwest of Roye. The enemy artillery reaches all the way to here.

The Evidence of The Past

Before I visited France & Belgium, I heard many stories of how the former battlefields are still littered with military ordnances and relics from over 100 years ago. Just considering the mass devastation caused, as described by Alexander, it is hard to believe that this isn't the case. As I was paying attention while walking beside the fields and through the areas of former battle sites, I was shocked to realise that the evidence of what happened was clear everywhere and not difficult to spot — Unexploded shells and shrapnel, a live hand grenade, bullet cartridges, bullet tips, and much more. True witnesses of the horrors that occurred here.

6.4.1918 In Warvillers, I was assigned as a company commander to the reception station *(the recruitment training depot)* of the 200th Infantry Division, which is still in Lorraine. I went with the truck towards Péronne at noon and waited for the train until 5 o'clock. It was an empty train with 38 wounded in the freight carriage — departure at 11:30 in the night.

7.4.1918 Arrival in Cambrai at 8 o'clock in the morning. Bombs dropped while I was rolling in. I stayed the night in Cambrai. Everyone is living in cellars here, and the smoking stove pipes protrude everywhere from the cellar windows with stones and sandbags built around them.

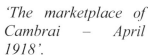

'The marketplace of Cambrai – April 1918'.

8.4.1918 I continued at 7:30 via Le Cateau, Charleville-Mézières, and Sedan.

9.4.1918 I arrived in Metz at 7 o'clock this morning, with a large delay until 1:15 in the afternoon. I arrived in Dieuze in the afternoon where the reception station was supposed to be, but where it never was. I finally discovered that it lies in Rackringen near Mörchingen. I spent the night in Dieuze.

10.4.1918 I went to Mörchingen with the train in the morning, and then to Rackringen on foot. I probably owe this new command to Gräffendorff who is now the division adjutant, whilst his predecessor, Captain von Detten, now leads our battalion. I of course didn't like leaving the battalion, but then again, I have been on the Front long enough; much longer than most of the other officers in the battalion, all of whom are younger than me. I now have my permanent accommodation here, live in peace and order, have my luggage with me at all times, and don't have to worry about constant alarms. I am receiving the same pay here, as well as the company-commander allowance of 60 Mark; so, 370 Mark in total. I still haven't received any post since the transport from Lorraine on the 28th of March.

'Rackringen – April 1918'.

14.4.1918   I have nothing to do here for now. A first lieutenant will be leaving here though in the next few days, and I will then get his company.

'Rackringen – April 1918'.

17.4.1918   Today, I finally received the first forwarded post. Since yesterday, I have moved to the neighbouring village of Bermeringen where the 2nd Company is located, of which I have taken over leadership. My command can take a very long time, possibly until the end of the war because they don't like to change the company commanders at the reception stations — So, I have now become a proper communication-zone pig — I live with a teacher, have a riding horse, and an Italian coach with two flawless, white Hungarian horses. You can endure it here but there is a lot of work, and the commander, an old active captain, compensates for his lack of war experience with constant nagging. Everyone complains about him. The man makes a very strange impression on me.

'My accommodation in Bermeringen – April 1918'.

22.4.1918   We constantly have bad weather — it has just been snowing again. You are very well off with food in Lorraine, just not in the places where the living quarters are. There are almost 400 men in my town, and there is of course not much to go around. There are only a few eggs, and they cost only 40 Pfennigs each. Butter is not available whatsoever. I would like to send something home, but I only have to rely on the field-kitchen food. Things seem to be bad on the Front. The battalion is apparently located near Moreuil, south of Amiens. According to a short message, our regimental commander, Major von Bünau, and Lieutenant Lingelbach are wounded. I am going to the cinema in Mörchingen with the company this afternoon, where the new assault method will be demonstrated. There is otherwise not much going on there. The post arrives here very quickly; only three days.

25.4.1918   My attendant, who I brought with me from the Front, Private Kurt Oberreich from Niedertrebra near Apolda, is going on holiday today for 4 weeks.

28.4.1918   Almost the entire reception station has been transported off to the Front as a replacement today, and we are now waiting for new people from the homeland. The weather is miserable — it almost always rains. Felix Niese is the cook and baker for Captain Cranz, who, like most active officers, is extremely demanding and has a lot of people constantly jumping around to serve him. My company was not used to that with me, because I always made do with just my attendant and did not ask for any food other than the troop provisions. Now that there is nothing to buy in the country, you can only get better food at the people's expense, and I have never done that. It was much different in the past. We often lived wonderfully and happily then since the country was not as drained as it is now, and there were still also vast amounts of loving gifts and parcels from home. My village is about 25 kilometres behind the Front, in a hilly landscape with huge ponds and large oak forests. We are currently on the language border here. Most of the residents speak German, and you don't hear the disgusting French language here as often as in the Dieuze area where everyone speaks French.

'Weisskirchen – April 1918'.

'Weisskirchen – From left to right: Lt. Eisenbach, Lt. Held, and me – April 1918.'

30.4.1918 Our transport strength was required today, which is always a sign of an impending evacuation. Of course, no one knows whether we will just be drawn closer to the division or whether it will take us somewhere else. Opinions vary between Italy and the Dutch border. This is fine with me, as I am so used to the gypsy life that I cannot stand being in one place for longer than 14 days. While on exercise a few days ago, I was visited by Prince Oskar of Prussia (a son of the Kaiser) who is the inspector of the reception stations.

3.5.1918 We are being loaded tomorrow morning, and I need to get up at 4 o'clock. We finally have nice weather since the 1st of May. Hopefully, it will stay like this throughout our journey. We are apparently going to the area of Valenciennes. Our division should now be at rest.

4.5.1918 At 11 o'clock in the morning, we went over Metz, Sedan, Mézières-Charleville and Aulnoye, and were unloaded in Landrecies on the 5th of May at 11 o'clock in the morning (by the Maubeuge-St. Quentin railroad). We are located 3.5 kilometres northwest in the village of Fontaine au Bois. All around are nothing but meadows with fruit trees surrounded by hedges. You only see a few fields, but there are large oak and beech forests nearby. The residents live mainly from livestock farming. The cows stay on the pasture day and night. There is nothing going on in Landrecies, which has 5000 to 6000 inhabitants. It is a completely unattractive city that is not worth visiting. Tomorrow, I want to drive to the big town of Le Cateau, eight kilometres away, because I have to buy a coffee pot, soup tureen and so on. I have very good quarters here — a living room and bedroom in a small villa. We will probably stay here for a long time.

The town hall of Le Cateau

9.5.1918 Since we don't have any recruits here again, my entire activity now consists of walking and riding. The day before yesterday, I was in Le Cateau with my car, a large but not very pretty factory town.

What the situation is like with the battalion on the Front is best shown in the letter below dated the 30th of April, from my former sergeant. The battalion is apparently at rest now, but I don't know where yet. My sergeant wrote to me:

"We are lying in position near Moreuil, a proper sinister area where we receive flanking fire from three sides. There isn't an emplacement here yet. Everyone lies in holes and cannot let themselves be seen during the day. The losses are of course in line with this. The company is currently in position with 70 men including oberjägers. The kitchen operator, Bergmoser; the stretcher bearer, Kleinschmidt; Private Günther; Jägers Kessler, Silchmüller and Altrichter; and Private Ficker, have fallen. Oberjägers Hundt, Örtel and Willikowski; Vice-Sergeants Langer and Seelig; Private Wolf; Oberjäger Dersch; Jägers Debus, Knorz, Wagner, Gerlach and so forth, are wounded. Besides this, at least 15 men are subject to disease and are absent due to the bad weather. Lieutenant Seemann is leading the company, and Captain Cranz leads the battalion. Captain von Detten is off sick in Germany. Lieutenants Petersen and Hitzeroth have received the Iron Cross 1st Class. During the large French attack on the 18th of April along the Morisel Road, the battalion particularly distinguished itself and captured, or rather knocked out 5 tanks. We certainly hope to get out of here soon."

*From the Battalion Diary – tent camp
near Moreuil-Morisel – April 1918.*

The German Spring Offensive

3.5 years of continuous service on three major Fronts of the Great War — This is something that not many soldiers during this time survived to be able to claim, or even had the opportunity to go through. Alexander has survived all of this, with his heart and loyalty still bound to his battalion despite him now becoming what he has always hated the most (a communication-zone pig). You may be thinking that this is probably a well-deserved rest, or on the other hand, that he should still be leading his old company into battle which he successfully did for a long time. However, you will soon come to realise that this recent command almost certainly saved his life.

By early 1918, the enemies of Germany on the Western Front were becoming exhausted from years of failed offensives and campaigns, having low morale, being overstrained, and running out of manpower. The German army was instead strengthened by the masses of men returning from Italy and the Eastern Front, and occupied with planning a series of large attacks today known as 'The Kaiserschlacht' or 'The German Spring Offensive', which began on the 21st of March 1918. With the United States having entered the war in April 1917, it was determined that the only way to defeat the enemy allied forces would be with one big blow before fresh soldiers and resources could arrive on the continent. As of this point in Alexander's diary, the German army has made the greatest advances either side has ever made on the Western Front, but issues with logistics have made it difficult for the fast-moving stormtroopers to maintain their momentum along the frontlines. Alexander now also notices how things have started to decline in this area compared to when he left it for the mountains almost two years ago. The land is completely drained, there is less food, and the overall standards are evidently lower.

Battle methods and inventions have also progressed while he was away from the Western Front. These include popular items we use today such as wristwatches and sanitary pads, but also improved weapons and the wide use of stormtrooper tactics. Furthermore, Alexander's battalion has now been confronted with a creation that offers another great challenge never overcome before — Tanks. The letter from Alexander's sergeant mentions this along with the hardships that followed. Here is further insight from the battalion diary:

"At 6:10 a.m., 5 tanks emerged from the thick fog and gun smoke, and they were quickly approaching the position. At the same time, enemy rifle and machine-gun fire swept the tops of the trenches. Waves of French infantry were advancing behind the tanks... From the new position, the machine gun placed the tank under piercing bullet fire and caused it to turn away immediately. When the machine gun had fired its only case of piercing ammunition and now had to turn to the charging infantry, the tank drove along the front German trench, firing continuously from the cannon and the machine gun".

3

19.5.1918   I am currently feeling better than I have ever felt during the war. Lessons on the light machine gun and shooting from 10 to 11 o'clock in the morning — this is our only duty because our replacement isn't here yet. The rest of the time, I spend hours strolling through the marvellous oak and beech forests on my horse. We have had the most beautiful weather for a week. Today is also the right holiday weather. Our division will be on holiday in the next few days, but I still have half a dozen men before my turn.

24.5.1918   I do not believe that I will ever be returning to the Front again, as they are glad at the reception stations when they have an older and war-experienced officer to provide training. Our commander has very suddenly been thrown out at the behest of his adjutant, who reported him to the division for irregularities. I had an instinctive dislike towards the man from the start. He didn't seem like an officer to me at all, but rather like an imposter. We don't have a successor yet.

   I have now become a gas-protection officer, meaning I have the supervision of the gas masks. This gives me a chance to be assigned to the 10-day course at the Army Gas School in Berlin.

27.5.1918   Eight days from today, I am going to Le Quesnoy for a meeting with the gas officers. I am sure I will meet someone from the battalion there and learn everything that has happened on the Front.

31.5.1918   The weather here has been lovely for two weeks. The replacement still hasn't arrived, so I have next to nothing to do all day — a one-hour machine-gun lesson in the morning, a communal meal at lunchtime, two hours of riding in the evening, and everyone for themselves at dinnertime. I had to clear my villa because many troops are now here — one Bavarian battalion, one convoy, and a horse hospital. But I have found a nice room again and live in a house with Captain Bindewald, the deputy station commander. At the reception station are also 4 lieutenants, 2 sergeant-lieutenants, a doctor, a couple of deputy officers, as well as a larger number of oberjägers. Of the lieutenants, two are from Silesia, one is from Baden, and one is from Bavaria. Most of the officers have hardly ever been on the Front and are terrified of being ordered back there. On the other hand, I always emphasise how nice it was on the Front, and that I would be very happy to return to the battalion. The others are not able to comprehend this.

7.6.1918   I always receive 38 grams of sugar here every day, which I collect and always send home once I have a pound. Our new commander, Major von Schütz, from the Guards, is arriving in the next few days. The division still lies in rest near Le Quesnoy. Several of us are currently on leave, and I now only have two men left before me.

13.6.1918   Today I sent home: 1 package of rock candy, 1 package of clear sugar, and 1 package of Dutch washing powder. Our division is on the march, but where to is unknown. Our new commander arrived yesterday, but he has a shot in his leg that hasn't healed yet, so he cannot walk or ride. There is still no replacement, so we have little to do. I will get a holiday in August and will of course try to get more than 14 days.

The fortification, gateway, and belltower of Le Quesnoy.

16.6.1918   The command to Berlin may take even longer, as the divisional gas officer just told me that men from the artillery would now be assigned first.

22.6.1918   I now have lots to do. I am training my oberjägers on the German light and heavy machine guns, as well as the English and French light machine guns. I am also taking part in a course for mortars. On Thursday, there is an inspection of the training staff by the inspector of the reception stations. The other two company commanders are already extremely agitated, as they are afraid that they will be moved to the Front if everything doesn't work out. This doesn't bother me at all because I would very much like to go to the Front again. I now sometimes really long for my battalion. We still don't have a replacement.

28.6.1918   I now have slightly more time again after our inspection yesterday. The weather here was very unfriendly for a week. In the next few days, the last man before me is going on holiday for four weeks.

3.7.1918 Everybody here is now affected by the mysterious Spanish illness that was brought over by holidaymakers. I have been spared from it so far. The weather is now too strange; a few oppressively hot days, and then it is immediately cold again for days. Our division is at rest, but we will probably go somewhere again in the next few days.

Note: The mysterious illness, now known as 'The Spanish Flu', will eventually spread throughout the world and kill around 50 million people.

6.7.1918 A few days ago, I received the wound badge for the light wound I received back then in Italy by the Tagliamento.

10.7.1918 My holiday request was sent to the division yesterday. The major initially didn't want to let me go at all, and it took me three-quarters of an hour to wheedle him. I requested three weeks not including the journey. However, it can take 14 days until I am informed since the division is not based here.

14.7.1918 The man before my turn went on holiday yesterday. He waited 13 days to be notified. I will be travelling through Metz because I won't have to change trains from Aulnoye to Eisenach.

23.7.1918 I fear that it will drag on a lot with my holiday, as the division was along the Marne *(river)* and is said to have had very heavy losses. Regular correspondence is of course out of the question under these circumstances. From the battalion, I only heard that Lieutenant Kramer had fallen.

28.7.1918 There must be an unbelievable amount of dawdling in our division. If it takes three weeks to do something as simple as approving a holiday request, then you shouldn't be surprised that the war has been going on for four years now.

26.8.1918 I was on holiday for three weeks, which I partly spent in Bad Salzungen. At half past 10 last night, I happily returned and encountered the reception station which is still here in Fontaine-au-Bois. A lot of space became available on my train at Frankfurt, and I could lie down in the night. Onwards from Charleville, on the other hand, it became less pleasant. Everything was terribly overcrowded and very slow. The journey was very hot. I am just glad that the station hasn't disappeared, because travelling into the unknown is no fun now. Nothing has changed here.

29.8.1918 One day after my arrival, my attendant, Oberreich, was unfortunately transferred back to the Front again. My new attendant, who also comes from my old 3rd Company, told me a lot about the Front. In addition to Kramer, two officers, who had just become so, were killed. Totzek has become the adjutant, and two very young lieutenants are company commanders. I now have 30 recruits, mostly Poles from Upper Silesia who have only been trained for six weeks and can still do very little.

1.9.1918 Nothing is going on here. It rains every few moments. I again received 25 recruits yesterday. Such a small bunch arrives every week. Our division is again to be deployed on the Front. If it doesn't rain this afternoon, I would like to go to the blackberries which are here in incredible quantities.

8.9.1918 Captain Bindewald was dismissed by the major with whom he didn't get along. He has applied to the division for him to be transferred.

12.9.1918 It is cold and uncomfortable here — not a day without rain, and you are thereby outside all day long. There is colossal artillery fire on the Front. You can hear it very clearly here. Our retreat has now apparently stopped, and we have reached the line where vigorous resistance is being carried out.

17.9.1918 We are going further back in the next few days, but where is still unknown. The Front has moved too close to us, and we have to make room. It was very restless here the night before last. One air raid followed another, and the bombs were crashing all around us. Only our village was spared. Quite a bit of damage has been caused to houses in Landrecies. Our division lies in Champagne. My attendant writes that my old company is now only 16 strong and is led by a very young officer.

21.9.1918 We are waiting for the transport. Perhaps we will go to Belgium. I am glad that we are going somewhere else again, as it is gradually becoming boring here now that you know every corner.

The Beginning of The End

"During the night, artillery fire from both sides continued to pour in on the rear positions and communication trenches. The pontoon and temporary bridges over the Marne in particular are under heavy fire, and supply traffic can hardly be maintained. At sunrise, the fire towards the battalion's position is increased again and continues without interruption throughout the day".

"At 6 o'clock in the afternoon, the order comes to clear the southern bank of the Marne... The bridge areas are under constant heavy fire, the pontoon bridge is badly damaged, and many pontoons have been shot away and filled with water. There are numerous corpses and horse carcasses to the right and left of the route of advance, but the eerie river valley is crossed without any casualties".

These two excerpts, from the battalion diary, detail the battalion's situation between the 17th and 19th of July 1918. At this point, the battalion was involved in 'The 2nd Battle of The Marne', the German attempt to draw the enemy allied troops away from Flanders in order to initiate an attack in this region. However, the offensive came to an end on the 18th of July when the enemy counteroffensive began, causing the Germans to retreat to their former Aisne-Vesle lines. With the German army becoming ever more exhausted and steadily outnumbered each week, owing to the growing number of casualties and the arriving American forces, the shift in the balance of power has begun. Further northwest in the Somme Region, 'The Battle of Amiens' commenced on the 8th of August lasting 3 to 4 days, initiated by the enemy allied forces who took advantage of this power shift. Germany's defeat in this battle led to the beginning of the 'Hundred Days Offensive', a complete turning point in the war. From this point onwards, the German army is steadily being pushed back, with this enemy-allied offensive threatening its complete collapse.

The German General, Erich Ludendorff, thus later describes the 8th of August 1918 as "The Black Day of The German Army". The battle is also notable for the large number of German surrendering forces and a blow to German morale. The war from now on is also starting to severely affect matters at home, with food shortages and a war-weary populace; and therefore, like with Russia, the rapid spread of socialist and communist ideas. At this point in Alexander's diary, the battalion is situated in the Champagne Region of France and has endured one month of positional warfare. Talks of the approaching great enemy offensive keep growing, but there seem to be no signs of it yet. They have just moved into positions near Sainte-Marie-à-Py. No shots are fired, and only a few aircraft have been seen. However, on the 25th of September, at 11 o'clock in the evening, this peace will finally be broken by violent enemy artillery fire followed by gas and smoke the next day.

4

27.9.1918   We marched out of Fontaine-au-Bois on the 24th of September. We went through the gigantic Mormal Forest, which has largely been cut down since large sawmills and wood wool factories were built in it for the army's needs. We then went through Berlaimont and towards Pont-sur-Sambre. On the 25th, we went through Maubeuge in extremely dreadful weather — rain, wind, and cold — up to the Belgian village of Grand-Reng which lies close behind the border. It is a shame that I wasn't able to photograph the beautiful fortress gates in Maubeuge. It rained too much. On the 26th, we reached our destination of Trivières-Saint-Vaast in lovely weather, north of Binche between Mons and Charleroi.

'St. Vaast (Belgium) – The house to the right of the tower with the white windows is my accommodation'.

'Road in St. Vaast (Belgium) – September 1918'.

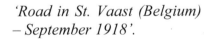

     We now lie in the middle of the coal region. You can see the high and pointed piles of rubble everywhere. All the villages are connected, and the entire population is still here. You see an awful lot of children. Electric railways come from all sides, which is very enjoyable because you can very cheaply and quickly go to the next towns of Binche, Mons and so forth. You can still buy everything here, just at incredible prices. One pair of shoes for a 10 to 12-year-old girl costs 60 Mark. My accommodation has improved compared to before. I live in a brewery and have a very good bed, a lovely washbasin, and electric lighting. There is very good beer here, a large bottle costing 25 Pfennigs. Soap costs 2 to 4 Mark a piece; and bonbons, 20 Mark per pound. I will go to Mons and Binche sometime in the next few days and see what's going on there. In general, the people here are very friendly. I will buy some washing powder here and send it home. This is available in every shop here, as well as pudding powder.

'The church of St. Vaast from the year 1400 – September 1918'.

'A street in St. Vaast'.

29.9.1918   There isn't much going on in Binche, but in La Louvière, 8 minutes from here on the electric train, there is great city-like life. We have now received a lot of recruits. My company is over 350 strong. I haven't received any more post since we left Fontaine. We prefer it here a lot more than in Fontaine, as there is somewhat life here after all. Only the major isn't satisfied here due to there being no opportunities to hunt. The division is once again in an area that is being heavily attacked. We don't have any further news yet.

10.10.1918   Yesterday, I finally received post again for the first time since we left. I will probably stay at the reception station for a long time. The major is glad that he has me, as I am the only older officer who has a considerable amount of frontline experience. You cannot use younger officers as company commanders here.

Our division seems to have had a hard time again. I haven't heard anything from the battalion yet. The commander, Captain Cranz, who took my company away from me, and the adjutant of the 5th Jäger Battalion, were killed; as were the commander and adjutant of the 6th Jäger Battalion. Everybody here is horrified by our latest begging for peace. We will of course be set terms that we cannot accept, and then it will just go on.

I went to a theatre night in La Louvière yesterday evening. It was very nice. Tonight, I will be eating a partridge that one of my sergeants poached for me.

11.10.1918   We will probably be leaving here in the next few days. The Belgian mines have a holiday today. There are rumours of a ceasefire and an evacuation of Belgium within 30 days — so we have given up after all — it is such a shame. The four years of fighting have now been for nothing, and we have to creep out of the occupied land as the defeated. It will now take weeks until I receive post from home.

16.10.1918   I just received a letter from home dated the 6th of October. This will probably be the last one for a long time because you will not receive any post with the current chaos. On the 12th of October, to arrange living quarters for the reception station in Lodelinsart, I rode the electric railway through La Louvière and Charleroi in advance. We didn't go there, however, but arrived in Gosselies, north of Charleroi. I have splendid accommodation at a lawyer's place with a servant, a water closet, a bath, and duvets. Everything is covered with carpets. There is also a garden, so you can endure it here for some time. The weather is unfortunately very bad. Children's shoes cost 100 Francs here. You can also buy soap here; the finest glycerine soap for 5 Mark in the canteen. We will probably go back to Germany in the next few days, constantly on foot.

9.11.1918   The revolution surprised us while in the village of Waremme, northwest of Liège. Since all the provision warehouses were instantly looted by the people in the communication zone, and our food supplies only lasted a few days, we decided to immediately leave for Germany in forced marches; especially since we also had to make room for the troops returning from the Front. Each company was to march separately. On the 10th of November, I therefore marched off with my more than 350 men (all 18-year-olds) and the entire baggage entourage, after we had destroyed everything unnecessary and loaded up with all the food that we could get hold of.

A group of the little scoundrels, who had been overcome by the revolution frenzy, wanted to be cheeky and had put on red cockades. I then told them that we would be marching through the Eifel, so through a proper rural region, and that they would certainly not get anything to eat from the farmers if they saw the red rags. The red colour soon disappeared again as a result. We even got so far that while in Euskirchen on the march back, my people bought themselves little black-white-red paper flags with the picture of Hindenburg, and marched decorated with them across the Rhine. My oberjägers, who remained sensible for the most part, also acted strictly. For example, one of the recruits, who threw his rifle into the Maas as we passed the bridge, therefore received a mighty slap in the face. The return march generally went quite well, except that small groups disappeared every day, probably thinking that they could smuggle themselves onto a train somewhere and thus avoid the marches.

So, we crossed the Maas west of Liège and spent the night in a village high up on the other bank. The next day, we continued to the Belgian spa town of Spa where we stayed in the beautiful villas there. We marched across the border on the third day, and we then marched several days over the High Fens *(an upland area)* and across Malmedy and Hellenthal to Euskirchen. The area was superb. If only it hadn't been for the dark thoughts, as we really had no idea what things were like at home. Along with this also came worries about food because 350 men consume a large amount, and we were only dependent on what we carried along with us on our wagons. Bread was particularly missing. We did have several quintals of flour with us, but you cannot eat it like that. I therefore always sent a reliable oberjäger a day's march ahead with a wagon full of flour to some village and had bread baked there with our flour. But with anxious concern, I saw the time approaching, not far off, when our flour would also run out. We would then starve since no one cared about us. We therefore continued in accelerated marches, and my sergeant and I were actually very pleased when it was discovered in the morning that another portion of recruits had run off, as we now no longer had to feed them.

'The Rhine Bridge – November 1918'.

We stayed the night in Euskirchen on the 21st of November. At noon on the 22nd, with a strength of 1 officer, 7 oberjägers, 210 jägers, 18 horses and 5 vehicles, we marched over the Rhine Bridge in Bonn, and then even further to Siegburg. We stayed here for a few days, during which I tried in vain to get a train to take us to Marburg. But all the telephone calls, even to the railway headquarters in Frankfurt, were for nothing. Under the leadership of an oberjäger who received an identification card from me, I thus had no choice but to gradually accommodate the rest of my men in small squads on the trains heading east, with instructions to report in Marburg. This also worked quite well.

In return for a receipt, I gave the wagons and horses to the mayors of a few villages behind Siegburg; so, behind the line probably occupied by the enemy. In the end, my attendant and I were the only ones remaining, and when we saw that we had done everything to the best of our knowledge, we too got on the train on the 24th of November and went to Marburg. Here, I was immediately given leave to go home until the 10th of December, which was just a matter of formality, and I arrived back in Weida on the 28th of November. On the 10th of January 1919, I then received a notice from the registration office in Neustadt that my mobilisation order had been lifted on the 30th of November 1918. I was therefore a civilian again, and the war had come to an end for me. Unfortunately, the end was not how I had imagined during my departure on the 4th of August 1914.

—.—.—.—.—.—.—.—

"The battalion, which came back to its garrison following 51 months of war, had undergone significant changes compared to its state in 1914 when it bravely marched into the battlefield with unwavering determination and readiness to make sacrifices. More officers along with more oberjägers and jägers, than those part of the outgoing battalion at the time, had demonstrated their unyielding devotion to Germany with their deaths. They now lie in both identified and unidentified graves on the battlefields in Belgium and France, the Carpathian Forests, Bukovina, and Italy. The active battalion had to sacrifice more than three times its initial strength in total casualties. However, the ethos of the Jägers from 1914, the ethos of wholeheartedly carrying out their duties, of constantly demonstrating unwavering commitment to the highest degree, and of being prepared to make sacrifices even unto death, had not forsaken the battalion despite the horrors of war, the enduring hardships, and the often superhuman efforts. Even amidst death-defying and hard-hitting assaults, amidst nerve-wracking barrages of artillery and almost hopeless and desperate circumstances, the jägers' discipline and comradeship remained unaltered. With their heads proudly held high, the home-returning officers and enlisted men of the 11th Kurhessian Jäger Battalion could lay down their weapons, in memory of their fallen comrades — Throughout eternity, a shining example of unwavering male valour, impeccable battle integrity, and the immeasurable love for the Fatherland".

- *The War Diary of The 11th Kurhessian Jäger Battalion*

LIST OF THE FALLEN

In date order, this list is dedicated to all 37 men known personally or simply mentioned in Alexander's diary to have died, no matter what side. May they forever live on in memory:

Lt. Georg von Boxberger – B. 28.06.86 (Marburg) – D. 28.9.14 (Variscourt) – *Remembered at the Sissonne German Cemetery* (Block 3, plot 468)

Lt. Prince Heinrich XLVI zu Reuß – B. 28.04.96 (Kauschen, Silesia) – D. 20.10.14 (Richebourg l'Avoué) – His brother, Heinrich XLI, fell on 26.11.16 in Romania.

Lt. Hans Müller – B. Unknown (Halle, Saale) – D. Christmas, 1914 (Richebourg l'Avoué)

Lt. Lutz von Seebach – B. 28.09.94 (Altenburg) – D. Christmas, 1914 (Richebourg l'Avoué)

Pte. Percy Walsh – B. 1892 – D. 22.12.1914 (Richebourg l'Avoué) – *Remembered at the Le Touret Memorial, Richebourg* (Panel 27 and 28)

Lt. Karl von Baumbach – B. 27.08.93 (Strasbourg, Elsaß) – D. 10.03.15 (Neuve Chapelle)

Cpt. Walter Beutin – B. Unknown (Sülze, Mecklenburg) – D. 16.05.15 (Richebourg l'Avoué) – *Remembered at the Billy-Berclau German Cemetery* (Block 3, Plot 187)

Lt. Friedrich Brauch – B. Unknown – D. 16.05.15 (near La Bassée) – *Remembered at the Lens-Sallaumines German Cemetery* (Block 7, Plot 103)

Lt. William Middleton Wallace – B. 23.9.1893 – D. 22.8.1915 – *Remembered at the Cabaret-Rouge British Cemetery* (Plot XII. D. 11)

Lt. Charles Gallie – B. 4.2.1892 – D. 22.8.1915 – *Remembered at the Cabaret-Rouge British Cemetery* (Plot XII. D. 11)

1st-Lt. Erich Swart – B. Unknown (Rumbeck, Cassel) – D. 24.09.15 (Field-hospital. 9 of the 7th Army Corps) – *Remembered at the Billy-Berclau German Cemetery* (Block 6, Plot 21)

Lt. Ernst von Baumbach – B. 03.11.93 (Mürschnitz, Sonneberg) – D. 25.09.15 (Auchy, near La Bassée) – *Remembered at the Billy-Berclau German Cemetery* (Block 6, plot 20)

Lt. Hans Erich von Baumbach – B. 14.01.94 (Ropperhausen, Ziegenhain) – D. 25.09.15 (Auchy near La Bassée) – *Remembered at the Billy-Berclau German Cemetery* (Block 6, Plot 22)

OC. Alfred Karl von Bothmer – B. 07.12.94 (Frankfurt am Main) – D. 25.09.15 (Auchy, near La Bassée) – *Remembered at the Billy-Berclau German Cemetery* (Block 6, Plot 23)

OC. Hubert Brieden – B. Unknown (Olpe, Westphalia) – D. 25.09.15 (Auchy, near La Bassée) – *Remembered at the Billy-Berclau German Cemetery* (Block 6, plot 19)

Pte. Joseph Andrew Langford – B. Unknown (Oldham, Lancashire) – D. 25.09.15 (Auchy, near La Bassée) – *Remembered at the Cabaret-Rouge British Cemetery, Souchez* (Plot VIII. J. 16)

Maj-Gen. George Handcock Thesiger – B. 06.10.68 – D. 27.09.15 (Auchy, near La Bassée) – His body was never recovered, and he is among the missing.

Jg. Fuchs – B. Unknown – D. 27.07.16 (Visovölgy, Romania)

Lt. Ernst Filler – B. Unknown (Thüringen) – D. 1916 (Verdun) – Ernst was the brother of Alexander's wife, Johanna. He was a talented pianist.

Cpt. Karl Thielmann – B. Unknown (Pfirt, Altkirch) – D. 11.08.16 (Skupova, Ukraine)

Lt. Martin Kellermann – B. Unknown (Witten, Westphalia) – D. 11.08.16 (Skupova, Ukraine)

V.Sgt. Hermann Wels – B. Unknown (Stettin, Pomerania) – D. 21.08.16 (Mt. Stepanski, Ukraine)

Lt. Hermann Stachelhausen – B. Unknown (Zerbst, Anhalt) – D. 11.10.16 (Stajki, Ukraine)

Lt. Otto le Roi – B. Unknown (Zweibrücken, Rhenish Palatinate) – D. 11.10.16 (Stajki, Ukraine)

Lt. Kurt Bode – B. Unknown (Goslar, Lower Saxony) – D. 11.10.16 (Stajki, Ukraine)

Lt. Helmuth Weber – B. Unknown (Schweidnitz, Silesia) – D. 02.09.17 (Waschkoutz, Ukraine)

Lt. Rudolf Ernst – B. Unknown (Marienmünster, Westphalia) – D. 02.09.17 (Waschkoutz, Ukraine)

Lt-Gen. Albert von Berrer – B. 08.09.57 (Unterkochen, Aalen) – D. 28.10.17 (San Gottardo, Udine)

Lt. Leo von Forell – B. 11.11.97 – D. 30.10.17 (Codroipo, Italy) – His brother, Karl, fell on 19.12.14 near Koslow-Slajecki – *Remembered at the Pordoi Military Cemetery* (under the unknown)

KO. Bergmoser – D. 1918 (Moreuil, Somme)

SB. Kleinschmidt – D. 1918 (Moreuil, Somme)

Jg. Kessler – D. 1918 (Moreuil, Somme)

Jg. Silchmüller – D. 1918 (Moreuil, Somme)

Jg. Altrichter – D. 1918 (Moreuil, Somme)

Pte. Ficker – D. 1918 (Moreuil, Somme)

Lt. Kurt Kramer – B. Unknown – D. 17.07.18 (La Chapelle) – *Remembered at Soupir German Cemetery* (Block 2, Plot 1124)

Cpt. Helmut Cranz – B. 08.05.84 (Cüstrin, Königsberg) – D. 03.10.18 (St.Marie- á-Py)

AFTER THE WAR

As we have now come to the end of Alexander's 4-year journey, you are probably wondering what happened to him after all this — What kind of life did he live? What was he like? How long did he live? — When I was young, I heard many stories from my grandfather and great-grandmother, who knew him on a very personal level; and also, from others who met him, or were told stories about him. But it wasn't until my early twenties that I wanted to gain further understanding, and began to show true interest in his life. As I soon discovered, you could quite literally say that the only reason I exist is because of all the events written about in his diary that led to his safe return home. While he was serving in the war, the country he departed in 1914 had developed significant negative changes and eventually plummeted into turmoil. Many friends, families, and people in his community that he always knew, did not exist anymore, and attached to those people were numerous grieving individuals and families. Like many others, he was left with many haunting memories that would be impossible to overcome. Those memories included the horrific battles around La Bassée, seeing his men become obliterated to nothing from artillery fire, and the time when he saw the lifeless, bloody body of Captain Beutin. The number of awful details seems immense, but even then you have to remember that everything he told us is only what he was willing to admit.

Today, while sitting in the comfort of our homes and going through our day-to-day lives, we simply couldn't possibly imagine what Alexander and all others on all sides had to go through during the war. This also applies to the time after, when they had to relive the memories over and over again, developed feelings of shame and regret, and in many cases, suffered long-lasting depression. But as was the case with Alexander, they all had no other choice but to adapt to civilian life again as though nothing had happened. He eventually recommenced his duties in the family-run textile company, and almost exactly 9 months after his return to Weida once the war had ended, my great-grandmother Ingrid Pfeifer was born.

Left: My great-grandmother Ingrid with her mother and older sister – Bottom: a few years later.

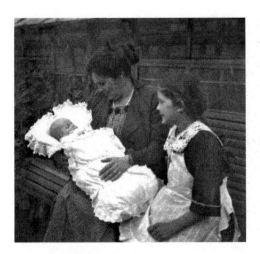

Just like Alexander, my great-grandmother always told of having a nice childhood which was mostly spent in the large family home in Weida. Despite Germany then experiencing an economic crisis, the family was able to spend time on holiday, go on trips, and do activities that most other Germans at the time weren't able to. Alexander also seemingly lived a relatively normal life of a typical father, who showed little sign of being a battle-hardened company commander of three major Fronts of the Great War.

Even with having what would seem to most like a pleasant life of a family man, I do know that his time at war occupied him a lot more than anyone could imagine. How else do you explain his dedication to creating the diary, consistently documenting and organising so many photographs, and collecting newspaper articles, maps, and journals relating to his service? After the war, several veterans' associations were founded, with the most popular being 'Der Stahlhelm' *(The Steel Helmet),* which he was a member of until its association with the Nazi Party. Amongst other things, this was a way to meet like-minded people in his community and beyond, who had experienced similar to what he had. This likely served as a form of therapy too, and a way to share stories and make new friends.

Alexander in around 1930 in his Great War uniform.

He carries the following awards in order:

Prussian Landwehr Service Award II Class
Iron Cross II Class
Order of the White Falcon
Iron Cross I Class
Wilhelm-Ernst War Cross
The Carpathian Insignia
The Wound Badge

In the 1930s, life continued as normal for the family, including that of my great-grandmother. However, with the start of another world war, these events would further mould the future of the family, especially that of Ingrid. In 1938, she trained as a field nurse and would soon put her training to use following the outbreak of the war in 1939.

This was again a hard time for the family, with many of its extended members being directly involved and losing their lives as a result. Ingrid spent a lot of time at the soldiers' hospital in Weida for the wounded from the Front, and she also spent time in Paris amongst other areas away from the frontlines. It was during her service that she met her future husband, Werner, who was wounded on the Eastern Front and ended up in her care. It was not long until she developed a relationship with him, later becoming his wife and giving birth to my grandfather, Gunter. Gunter was born in

312

October 1944 and was raised in the big family home that he would remember and speak of for the rest of his life. Nevertheless, you could say that the events that unfolded shortly after the war didn't favour Gunter very much. The country was split apart, with Weida becoming part of Communist East Germany. His father was from Cologne in the West, which resulted in his parent's marriage coming to an end and a life destined without his father. This was the case with many young children at the time, who lost one or both parents due to the war or the partitioning of the country. Considering Gunter's situation, he would naturally look up to the one person in his life who offered true guidance and was the closest he had to a father figure — Alexander.

Alexander developed a very close bond with Gunter, teaching and showing him things that a father would usually do. He introduced him to many of his own interests such as history, science, nature, geography — and of course, his war stories, items, and diary. As you can imagine, Gunter greatly admired and looked up to him. He also had a very close relationship with his grandmother, Johanna.

But life at this point wasn't the same for the family compared to the past. East Germany was a communist state, and many of the family's assets had been seized by the government as a result, meaning the dissolution of the family textile company. They then also didn't have as many freedoms as before, which allowed them to travel and go on regular trips that would have broadened their minds. Any critique aimed towards the government would also lead to harsh punishment. All this meant that Gunter had nowhere near the same privileges that his mother and Alexander once had at the same age. Nevertheless, the family had to adapt like everyone else, and Gunter lived his life under these conditions. In 1959, Johanna died at the age of 74, and Alexander died in 1966, aged 86.

After both his grandparents had passed away, Gunter, due to unforeseen circumstances, managed to relocate to West Germany where he married my grandmother. She soon after gave birth to his daughter, Katrin (my mother). It wouldn't be long until my great-grandmother Ingrid would also follow suit, living nearby in the same small village. Even though he now lived in a different country away from his hometown, he always had a deep connection to Weida and would regularly visit with his family when he could. However, the authoritarian nature of East Germany meant that there were many restrictions, and he couldn't go as much as he would have liked to. Despite this, he made the most of the time by visiting the old family home and garden, and also his good friends and family. My mother also remembers the time spent in Weida very well, and she formed a close bond with her godparents and the town in general.

As an adult, Gunter spoke of his grandparents only with high regard and with utmost respect. If either of them were mentioned in the slightest, he would instantly praise them and discuss their kind and respectful nature. As my grandmother and mother tell me, he always seemed to be extremely knowledgeable about almost everything, including very niche topics. These entailed the interests that Alexander introduced to him, which he too would pass on to other people given the opportunity. He also treasured Alexander's items from the war, the diary in particular, which he kept in a special cabinet with many things on display. These items included Alexander's medals, uniform parts, pictures, certificates, and of course the items from various fallen soldiers which were kept safe in a metal box.

When my mother married my English father and soon gave birth to me, I moved from Germany to England. My brother was born 3 years later too. My grandparents would come to visit as much as possible, just like we would visit them. It was something I looked forward to very much, but the long distance and time before the next visit made saying goodbye difficult on each occasion. This was

always the biggest disadvantage of my background. Shortly before we would go to Germany to visit, Gunter always announced to people: "My Englishmen are coming!". He truly enjoyed spending time with me and my brother; taking us on walks, visiting Weida with us, and introducing us to new things. In 2007, when I was 11 years old, he died suddenly, and with him his personal memories of Alexander and everything else he learned from the man. However, this cannot be said about the many things he left behind.

Alexander Pfeifer
(1880 – 1966)

FINAL WORDS

At the time of writing this, it has been over 4 years since I started the preface for this book while sitting on Alexander's furniture, surrounded by the many other things my family inherited. With the death of my great-grandmother Ingrid (aged 98) when I was 21, almost all who knew Alexander on a personal level have gone. I spent many hundreds if not thousands of hours putting this book together entirely on my own, which in time has of course given me the feeling as if I too had known him personally despite never meeting him. It is a strange feeling. Perhaps you also feel the same way after reading this book. I have even got to know the many different individual people connected to Alexander's diary, such as his fellows who fought and died by his side, his enemy counterparts, and so many others he found interesting enough to tell us about. His experiences at the time also enabled me to embark on my own journey, meeting people and seeing places that I otherwise never would have come across. They also led me to some of the places where he spent a lot of his time in the war and developed good and terrible memories. I also visited the graves of the many persons who fell victim to the battles that raged there. The things I have learned have given me a good overall understanding of what the people on all sides had to go through during the Great War, in addition to deepening my insight into my family's history and roots. The entire process of working on this book has been a truly unforgettable experience.

The more I think about it, I believe there are several reasons why Alexander worked on his diary so extensively and preserved everything else that goes along with it. We will never know if he always intended to keep it in the family, or if he did have hopes of it reaching a greater audience someday. After his death, everything he owned could easily have been forgotten about or given to people who showed no real interest. Luckily, this wasn't the case. The only reason why we now know so much about him and the things he went through, is because he documented it — every battle, the many people and the interactions he had with them, the photographs; and every little or big event, no matter how significant or trivial. Irrespective of his wider intentions, this was all done to help the reader comprehend what was genuinely witnessed firsthand during this time. Regardless of whether you are well-educated or new to the topic of the Great War, you will no doubt have learned something new or perhaps have a different outlook compared to before. I personally have realised that everything we do has a lasting impact, no matter how significant or unimportant these actions may seem. In this book, I have delved into how much Alexander's actions influenced the course of the future. However, he was just one man out of the many million during the war who manipulated this.

When reading about Alexander's story and the family history I share with him, most will certainly think that this is all unique, but I can assure you that I am just a regular person who you come across in your day-to-day life. That being said, I would like you to think about the many tales which have led to where you are today, and ask yourself — What is your story? If you are unsure, then I highly recommend that you explore further and piece together an answer to this question, because you will be amazed at what you may find.

REFERENCES

Alice Keating (1911) Census Return For 7 Marple Street, Oldham. Oldham Sub-District. *Public Record Office:* 237.

Beckett, I. F.W (2007) The Great War (2nd ed.) *Longman.*

Bihl, W. (1980) Die Ruthenen, in: Wandruszka, A; Urbanitsch, P (Hrsg.): Die Habsburgermonarchie 1848–1918, Band III: Die Völker des Reiches. *Wien 1980, Teilband 1.*

Busche, H. (1998) Formationsgeschichte der deutschen Infanterie im Ersten Weltkrieg 1914–1918 (in German). *Owschlag: Institut für Preußische Historiographie.*

Cadet, A (2015) L'Explosion des Dix-huit Ponts. Un "AZF" lillois en janvier 1916. Préface d'Yves Le Maner. *Les Lumières de Lille Éditions.*

Cadorna, L (1915) Attacco frontale e ammaestramento tattico. *Rome.*

CWGC Archive, INDEX No. Fr. 924 CABARET-ROUGE Brit. Cem. PART I (A-L).

CWGC Archive, INDEX No. Fr. 924 CABARET-ROUGE Brit. Cem. PART II (M-Z).

CWGC Archive, Index No. M.R.19 LOOS MEMORIAL PART 12.

Dabrowski, P.M. (2018) Poles, Hutsuls, and Identity Politics in the Eastern Carpathians after World War I. *Zeitschrift für Genozidforschung 16 (1): 19-34.*

Davies, F; Maddocks, G (2014) Bloody Red Tabs: General Officer Casualties of the Great War 1914-1918. *Pen and Sword Books.*

Edmonds, J. E. (1922). Military Operations France and Belgium, 1914 Mons, the Retreat to the Seine, the Marne and the Aisne August-October 1914. Vol. I (1st ed.) *London: Macmillan.*

Edmonds, J.E. (1928). Military Operations France and Belgium, 1915: Battles of Aubers Ridge, Festubert, and Loos. History of the Great War Based on Official Documents By Direction of the Historical Section of the Committee of Imperial Defence. Vol. II (1st ed.) *London: Macmillan.*

Edmonds, J. E. (1993) [1932] Military Operations France and Belgium, 1916: Sir Douglas Haig's Command to the 1st July: Battle of the Somme. History of the Great War Based on Official Documents by Direction of the Historical Section of the Committee of Imperial Defence. Vol. I *(Imperial War Museum & Battery Press ed.). London: Macmillan.*

Edmonds, J. E; Wynne, G.C. (1995) [1927] Military Operations France and Belgium, 1915: Winter 1914 – 15: Battle of Neuve Chapelle: Battles of Ypres. History of the Great War Based on Official Documents by Direction of the Historical Section of the Committee of Imperial Defence. Vol.I *London: Macmillan.*

Edmonds, J. E.; Davies, H. R.; Maxwell-Hyslop, R. G. B. (1995) [1937] Military Operations France and Belgium: 1918 March-April: Continuation of the German Offensives. History of the Great War Based on Official Documents by Direction of the Historical Section of the Committee of Imperial Defence. Vol. II *(Imperial War Museum & Battery Press ed.). London: Macmillan.*

Fitzpatrick, S (2008) The Russian Revolution. *Oxford University Press US.*

Gellner, E. (2006) Nations and Nationalism. *Wiley-Blackwell, Oxford.*

Gibelli, A. (2002) La Grande Guerra degli italiani. *Milan.*

Halpern, P.G (2004) The Battle of the Otranto Straits: Controlling the Gateway to the Adriatic in World War I. *Bloomington.*

Heenan, L E (1987) Russian Democracy's Fatal Blunder: The Summer Offensive of 1917. *New York: Praeger.*

Hofschröer, P. (1984) Prussian Light Infantry, 1792-1815. *London: Osprey*

Jany, C. (1967) Geschichte der Preußischen Armee vom 15. Jahrhundert bis 1914. *Osnabruck: Biblio Verlag.*

Jones, S. (2010) Underground Warfare 1914–1918. *Pen & Sword Military.*

Kerensky, A.F (1927) Chapter 9: The Catastrophe, *Periodicals Service Co.*

Kitchen, M. (2001) The German Offensives of 1918. *Stroud: Tempus.*

Lloyd, I. (2015) The Queen's Uncle and the Bravest Last Stand: Choking on gas, blown up, riddled with bullets... heroics of the Queen Mum's brother revealed 100 years after his death. *Daily Mail 26 Sep 2015.*

McCrery, N (2014) Into Touch: Rugby Internationals Killed in the Great War. *Pen and Sword.*

Mockler-Ferryman, A.F (1916) The Oxfordshire and Buckinghamshire Light Infantry Chronicle, 1915-1916: An Annual Record of the First and Second Battalions, Formerly the 43rd and 52nd Light Infantry. Vol XXV. *London: Eyre & Spottiswoode.*

National Army Museum Archive, UK, Army Registers of Soldiers' Effects (1914-1915), Hamilton. Record No. 222684.

Otto, A. (1931) Kriegstagebuch des Kurhessischen Jäger-Bataillons Nr.11. *Schmalkalden.*

Patterson, A. (2018) 'First World War: From the History Today Archive: Armistice Centenary Special. 100 Years On'. The Catastrophe at Caporetto. *History Today, November, pp. 38-41.*

Pietsch, P (1963) Die Formations- und Uniformierungs-Geschichte des preußischen Heeres 1808-1914. *Hamburg: Verlag Helmut Gerhard Schulz.*

Pipes, R. (2008) A Concise History of the Russian Revolution. *Paw Prints.*

Saunders, N (2011) Trench Art: A Brief History and Guide, 1914–1939. *Pen and Sword Military, Barnsley, 2nd revised edition.*

Schindler, J.R (2001) Isonzo: The Forgotten Sacrifice of the Great War. *Praeger.*

Sewell, E.H.D (1919) The Rugby Football Internationals Roll of Honour. *London, Edinburgh: T. C. & E. C. Jack.*

Spignesi, S.J. (2004). Catastrophe! The 100 Greatest Disasters Of All Time. *Kensington Publishing Corporation.*

Stevenson, D. (2017) 1917: War, Peace, and Revolution. *Oxford: Oxford University Press.*

The National Archives (TNA) WO 95/1270/1 – War Office: First World War & Army of Occupation War Diaries - 2 Infantry Brigade: 1 Battalion Loyal North Lancashire Regiment 1914 Aug 1 – 1914 Dec 12.

The National Archives (TNA) WO 95/1730/1 – War Office: First World War & Army of Occupation War Diaries - 2 Battalion Lincolnshire Regiment 1914 Nov - 1918 Jan.

The Times (1938) Thursday, 23 June; p.16; col. D *London.*

Verlustlisten Erster Weltkrieg/Projekt. (2. November 2023). *GenWiki, Retrieved on 8. July 2024 from https://wiki.genealogy.net/index.php?title=Verlusten_Erster_Weltkrieg/Projekt&oldid=2446455.*

Vickers, H (2006) Elizabeth: The Queen Mother. *Arrow Books/Random House.*

Wegner, L (2016) Rear Area on the Western Front, in: 1914-1918-online. International Encyclopaedia of the First World War. *Freie Universität Berlin.*

Wilcox, V (2016) Morale and the Italian Army during the First World War. *Cambridge University Press.*

Photos & Maps

Ancestry.com. Great Britain, Royal Aero Club Aviators' Certificates, 1910-1950: Charles Gallie; *559*

Bailey, Chris – Private Photo Collection – depicted in Chapter 8: *'A view towards the enemy position';* *'Another view towards the English lines before the explosion – The long stack of bricks is to the right'.*

Drakegoodman (Flickr) – Private photo collection – depicted in Chapter 11*: 'English aeroplane shot down on 22.8.1915 by Field-Artillery Regiment 58'.*

ONB - Gesprengte Tagliamentobrücke bei Codroipo 30.10.17. *(n.d.) https://data.onb.ac.at/rep/BAG_15612291*

ONB - Zerstörte Tagliamento Brücke bei Codroipo 6.11.17. *(n.d.) https://data.onb.ac.at/rep/BAG_15609650*

Otto, A. (1931) Kriegstagebuch des Kurhessischen Jäger-Bataillons Nr.11. *Schmalkalden: pp. 41, 48, 57, 70, 97, 117, 151, 160, 161, 213, 215.*

Sewell, E.H.D (1919) The Rugby Football Internationals Roll of Honour. *London, Edinburgh: T. C. & E. C. Jack.*

If you enjoyed this book, please don't forget to leave a review

Made in United States
Troutdale, OR
01/19/2025

28108383R00193